NUTCASES

CONSTITUTIONAL ADMINISTRATIVE LAW

AUSTRALIA
Law Book Co
Sydney

CANADA and USA
Carswell
Toronto

HONG KONG
Sweet & Maxwell Asia

NEW ZEALAND
Brookers
Wellington

SINGAPORE and MALAYSIA
Sweet & Maxwell Asia
Singapore and Kuala Lumpur

NUTCASES

CONSTITUTIONAL AND ADMINISTRATIVE LAW

MAUREEN SPENCER,
MA (Oxon), MA (Open) LLM Ph.D
Principal Lecturer in Law
Middlesex University

JOHN SPENCER,
MA (Oxon), M Math LLM
Barrister
Honorary Visiting Lecturer
Middlesex University

London • Sweet & Maxwell • 2006

Published in 2003 by Sweet & Maxwell Limited of
100 Avenue Road, London NW3 3PF
www.sweetandmaxwell.co.uk
Typeset by LBJ Typesetting of Kingsclere
Printed in Great Britain by Ashford Colour Press,
Gosport, Hants
Reprinted 2006

No natural forests were destroyed to make this product:
only farmed timber was used and replanted

A CIP catalogue record for this book is available
from the British Library.

ISBN 0 421 928 00X

CONTENTS

CONTENTS

TABLE OF CASES

TABLE OF STATUTES

1. GENERAL PRINCIPLES OF THE CONSTITUTION

Role of Conventions

Key Principle: Conventions may be recognised by the courts but are not enforced by them.

Madzimbamuto v Lardner-Burke
A state of emergency was proclaimed in the Crown colony of Southern Rhodesia on November 5, 1965 and the following day the Justice and Law and Order Minister ordered the detention of a number of people including the claimant's husband. On November 11, the Southern Rhodesian Prime Minister unilaterally declared independence. The colony's governor issued a proclamation on behalf of the Queen that the Government ceased to hold office and called on all citizens to refrain from acts which would further the objectives of the illegal authorities. On November 16, Parliament passed the Southern Rhodesia Act which provided that no laws could be made or business transacted by the Rhodesian legislative assembly. In February 1966 the state of emergency was illegally renewed and the Justice and Law and Order Minister made an order under it renewing the detention of the claimant's husband. She challenged in the courts the legality of her husband's detention.

Held: (PC) The emergency powers regulations made after November 11, 1965 had no legal validity, force or effect and the detention order made under them was invalid. While the legitimate government was trying to regain control it was impossible to hold that the usurping government was for any purpose a lawful government. Even if there was a principle which recognised the need to preserve law and order in territory controlled by a usurper, such a principle could not override the legal right of the UK Parliament to legislate for a territory under the sovereignty of the Queen in the UK Parliament. The appeal was allowed. [1969] 1 A.C. 645.

Commentary
In passing the Southern Rhodesia Act 1965 Parliament was ignoring the previous constitutional convention that it would not

exercise its sovereignty in Commonwealth affairs without the consent of the Rhodesian Government.

Key Principle: **The conventional doctrine of Cabinet secrecy can give rise to a duty of confidentiality enforceable in equity.**

Attorney-General v Jonathan Cape

Richard Crossman, a Cabinet minister, kept a political diary and after his death the diary was sent to the Cabinet Secretary for approval before publication. The Cabinet Secretary refused to authorise publication, and the literary executors undertook not to publish without prior notice to the Treasury Solicitor. When extracts began to be published in the *Sunday Times*, the Attorney-General sought an injunction against further publication.

Held: (QB) The court had power to restrain publication of information in breach of confidence. Cabinet discussions were confidential until such time as their disclosure would not undermine the doctrine of joint Cabinet responsibility. But given the lapse of time since the discussions from 1964–66 the contents of the diary would not undermine the doctrine, so there were no grounds for granting an injunction. [1976] Q.B. 752.

Commentary

The court came close here to enforcing a convention. In an appropriate case the court would, it appears, intervene to uphold by injunction the maintenance of the doctrine of Cabinet confidentiality since this was in the public interest.

Key Principle: **Conventions can only become laws by statutory intervention.**

Reference Re Amendment of the Constitution of Canada

The Government of Quebec referred certain questions to the provincial Court of Appeal including the following: "Does the Canadian constitution empower, whether by statute, convention or otherwise, the Senate and the House of Commons of Canada to cause the constitution to be amended without the consent of the provinces and in spite of the objection of several of them, in such a manner as to affect (i) the legislative competence of the provincial legislatures in virtue of the Canadian constitution? (ii) the status or role of the provincial legislatures or governments within the Canadian federation?" The matter went on appeal to the Supreme Court of Canada.

Held: (Supreme Court) A majority of the court held that as a matter of convention the constitution did not so empower the Senate and House of Commons of Canada, but that as a matter of law it did. The majority held also that the nature of a convention was inconsistent with its legal enforcement. (1982) 125 D.L.R. (3d) 1.

Commentary
The judgment gives a very succinct summary of the differences between laws and conventions.

> "The main purpose of constitutional conventions is to ensure that the legal framework of the constitution will be operated in accordance with the prevailing constitutional values or principles of the period. . . . Perhaps the main reason why conventional rules cannot be enforced by the Courts is that they are generally in conflict with the legal rules which they postulate and the Courts are bound to enforce the legal rules. The conflict is not of a type which would entail the commission of any illegality. It results from the fact that legal rules create wide powers, discretions and rights which conventions prescribe should be exercised only in a certain limited manner, if at all."

Key principle: **There was no constitutional convention that an Act of parliament which altered the UK constitution in a fundamental way could not be proposed if it did not have prior approval of the electorate.**

R. v Secretary of State for Foreign and Commonwealth Affairs Ex p. Southall

The applicant sought permission to appeal from refusal of permission to apply for judicial review of the ratification of a proposed new European constitutional treaty. He maintained that since it changed the constitution its adoption should be preceded by a referendum.

Held: (CA) There was no seriously arguable case that a court would determine that an Act of Parliament was unenforceable because it had not been the subject of a referendum. Nor was there any convention that it was not open to Parliament to change the constitution in a fundamental way in the absence of a referendum or a general election. [2003] EWCA Civ 1002 July 14, 2003.

Commentary

The court observed: "The fact is that so far no court in the last century and more had set aside any provision of an Act of Parliament as being unlawful save in the circumstances set out in the European Communities Act." The court also stated that it was not for the courts to declare the existence of a constitutional convention.

Rule of Law

Key Principle: **The executive cannot lawfully assume powers which are not known to the courts.**

Entick v Carrington

Two King's messengers, acting under a warrant issued by the Secretary of State, broke into the claimant's house and carried off his papers. The action was part of an investigation into certain seditious articles. The plaintiff sued the messengers for trespass. They claimed to have acted lawfully under the Secretary of State's warrant.

Held: The warrant was illegal and without effect. The Secretary of State could invade the rights of a subject only if his action was authorised by law. No statute or common law right authorised the invasion of the claimant's house. The argument of the Secretary of State that the power to issue such a warrant was essential to government had no validity. (1765) 19 St. Tr. 1029.

Key Principle: **The court's duty to ensure that the executive does not abuse its power includes that of staying a prosecution as an abuse of process.**

R. v Horseferry Road Magistrates' Court Ex p. Bennett

A New Zealander, wanted in England, claimed to have been kidnapped in the Republic of South Africa as a result of collusion between the South African and British police and returned to England, where he was arrested and brought before magistrates. He was refused an adjournment so that he could challenge the court's jurisdiction. He sought judicial review of the magistrates' decision. The Divisional Court held that the English court had no power to inquire how a person appearing before it had been brought within the jurisdiction. The defendant appealed.

Held: (HL) Where a defendant had been brought back to the United Kingdom in disregard of available extradition process and in breach of international law and the laws of the state where he had been found, the UK courts would refuse to try the defendant. The High Court had power to inquire into the circumstances by which a person had been brought within the jurisdiction and could stay the prosecution as an abuse of process. [1994] A.C. 42, HL.

Commentary

The House of Lords considered that even if the conduct of the actual trial were fair the legitimacy of the judicial process was at issue since the executive had procured the defendant by means which were in deliberate violation of international law and correct extradition procedures. The concept of a right to a fair trial thus includes the pre-trial process, an approach taken by the Strasbourg Court in applying Art.6 of the European Convention.

Key Principle: **The state does not need express authority for its actions if they do not breach common law or statute.**

Malone v Metropolitan Police Commissioner (No.2)

The plaintiff was charged with handling stolen goods. At his trial, the prosecution admitted that his telephone had been tapped under a warrant from the Home Secretary and his conversations recorded. He brought proceedings against the Home Secretary for a declaration that the phone tapping was unlawful.

Held: (Ch D) The tapping of a telephone could lawfully be done because there was nothing to make it unlawful. No statute authorised phone tapping with or without a warrant. But that did not mean tapping was unlawful. A search of premises which was not authorised by law was illegal because it involved the tort of trespass. But no act of trespass was involved in telephone tapping. [1979] Ch.344.

Commentary
The case may be contrasted with *Entick v Carrington*. In that case the state needed express authority which it did not have because the search warrant was expressed in general terms. Without express authority it was committing the tort of trespass. There is no tort of invasion of privacy and so the Post Office did not need express authority for the tapping of telephones at the request of the police.

Key Principle: **The common law is the guardian of rights of the individual.**

Derbyshire CC v Times Newspapers Ltd
A local authority brought a libel action against a newspaper which had questioned the propriety of its handling of a super-annuation fund. On a preliminary point, the judge held that the council could sue for libel in respect of its governmental and administrative functions. That decision was reversed in the Court of Appeal and the council appealed.

Held: (HL) Uninhibited public criticism of an elected body was vital in a democracy. The threat of libel actions would inhibit legitimate criticism. It was contrary to the public interest for central or local government institutions to have any common law right to sue for libel. The action would be struck out. [1993] A.C. 534.

Commentary
The Court of Appeal applied Art.10 of the European Convention on Human Rights in finding that a local authority cannot sue for libel. The House of Lords however held that in this case the common law could determine the issue in favour of protecting free speech. The case is an important instance of a robust use of the

common law to protect individual rights. The House acknowledged however the guidance of the Court of Appeal judgment in
cases where the common law was uncertain.

Key Principle: **The executive is not above the law.**

M v Home Office

A citizen of Zaire sought political asylum, which was refused, as
was his application for leave to bring judicial review proceedings. A date was set for his removal and on that day, shortly
before he was due to be removed, he made a renewed application in the Court of Appeal for leave to move. The judge
understood counsel for the Home Secretary to have given an
undertaking that the removal would not go ahead while the
application was being considered. However his removal went
ahead. When the judge heard that he had been removed, he
ordered the Secretary of State to organise his return to the
jurisdiction. Home Office officials took steps to comply with the
judge's order, but they were over-ruled by the Secretary of State
in reliance on legal advice that the order had been made without
jurisdiction, being a mandatory interim injunction against an
officer of the Crown. The judge dismissed a motion for committal, but it was allowed in part by the Court of Appeal. Both
parties appealed.

Held: (HL) The Secretary of State had not been entitled to
claim Crown immunity, since an action could be brought
against him personally for a tort committed or authorised by
him in his official capacity, and an injunction could be granted
against him in that capacity. The Crown itself could not be
found in contempt, but a government department or a minister
could. The injunction had been granted against the Secretary of
State in his official capacity, and the department for which he
was responsible was in contempt. Accordingly, the appropriate
finding was that the Secretary of State for the Home Department
was in contempt. [1994] 1 A.C. 377.

Commentary

Lord Templeman put the decision in a historical context. ". . . the
argument that there is no power to enforce the law by injunction
or contempt proceedings against a minister in his official capacity

would, if upheld, establish the proposition that the executive obey the law as a matter of grace and not as a matter of necessity, a proposition which would reverse the result of the Civil War."

It was held however that since the Home Secretary had acted on advice it would not be proper to find him personally in contempt of court.

Key Principle: **There is a body of customary international law which is part of the common law**

R. v Bow Street Metropolitan Stipendiary Magistrate Ex p. Pinochet Ugarte (No.3)

The former Chilean dictator was arrested in London on a Spanish warrant. The warrant alleged that he had ordered torture and hostage-taking while he was in power. The Divisional Court held that the applicant as a former head of state was entitled to immunity from civil and criminal process in the English courts in respect of acts committed in the exercise of sovereign power. The House of Lords allowed an appeal by the prosecutor, but this decision was set aside because one of the judges, Lord Hoffman, was an office-holder in a charity controlled by Amnesty International. The case was reheard before a differently constituted court.

Held: (HL): Though a former head of state had immunity from the criminal jurisdiction of the United Kingdom for acts done in his official capacity as head of state, torture was an international crime against humanity and there was a universal jurisdiction to extradite or punish a public official for torture. That principle extended to heads of state because the state parties who had created the international jurisdiction by the International Convention against Torture, Inhuman or Degrading Treatment could not have intended to create an immunity for a head of state who was a torturer. Per Lords Millett and Phillips the systematic use of torture was an international crime against humanity for which there could be no immunity even before the International Convention came into effect. There was therefore no immunity against customary international law for the offences relating to torture alleged against the applicant. [1999] 2 W.L.R. 827.

Commentary
This decision shows that English courts are prepared to apply customary international human rights law. Pinochet subsequently avoided extradition to Spain by pleading ill health. (See also p.141).

Doctrine of Separation of Powers

Key Principle: **The judiciary's task is to apply legislation and not interpret it in such a way as to provide their own view of what the law should be.**

Duport Steels Ltd v Sirs
The Government used its statutory powers to stop public investment in the British Steel Corporation, obliging it to meet operating costs out of earnings. As a consequence pay negotiations broke down and the Iron and Steel Trades Confederation called a strike in the Corporation, which was a nationalised industry. Two weeks into the strike, the union called out its members in the private steel companies as a way of putting pressure on the government. Sixteen private steel companies sought an injunction against the ISTC. The judge refused, but the Court of Appeal granted the injunction on the basis that the ISTC was really in dispute with the Government, not the employers, and the economic consequences were so disastrous that the extension of the strike should be prevented. The union appealed.

Held: (HL) Provided a person honestly believed he was acting in the course or furtherance of an industrial dispute, he was entitled to immunity in tort. The court was not entitled to look at the remoteness of the act from the immediate source of the dispute, or the extent to which it had reasonable prospects of furthering the dispute, save in assessing the genuineness of the defendants' professed purpose. Parliament might not have expected when it granted the relevant immunities that they would be used so as to produce consequences so injurious to the nation. But the legal limit on those immunities was set by the construction of the statute, not by judges making their own preferred amendments where they felt necessary in the public interest. [1980] 1 W.L.R. 142.

Commentary
Here the relationship between the courts and Parliament is set out. The judges have a great deal of discretionary power, as Lord

Scarman said "to do justice so wide that they may be regarded as law makers". Lord Diplock said in the course of his judgment "at a time when more and more cases involve the application of legislation which gives effect to policies that are the subject of bitter public and parliamentary controversy, it cannot be too strongly emphasised that the British constitution, though largely unwritten, is firmly based upon the separation of powers: Parliament makes the laws, the judiciary interpret them".

There has been considerable scrutiny over the question whether judges should be constitutionally permitted to be part of the executive or the legislature. In *McGonnell v United Kingdom* (2000) 30 E.H.R.R. 289 the Strasbourg court held that there had been a breach of Art.6(1) when the Bailiff of Guernsey, who presided over the legislature, had set on an appeal tribunal. Any direct involvement in the passage of legislation, or of executive rules, was likely to be sufficient to cast doubt on the judicial impartiality of a person later called upon to determine a consequential dispute. Subsequently, the Constitutional Reform Act 2005 modifies the office of Lord Chancellor and makes changes to the way in which some of the functions vested in that office are to be exercised. The Act also creates the Supreme Court of the United Kingdom and abolishes the appellate jurisdiction of the House of Lords. It creates the Judicial Appointments Commission to select people for judicial appointments in England and Wales, and provides for judicial discipline in England and Wales. The Act modifies the jurisdiction of the Judicial Committee of the Privy Council and removes the right of the Lord President of the Council to sit judicially. Before the Act the Lord Chancellor's office was both ministerial and judicial, and he acted as head of the judiciary while sitting in the Cabinet. The Act implements a policy of separation of powers, depriving the Lord Chancellor of his power to sit as a judge. The new head of the judiciary in England and Wales is the Lord Chief Justice. The Act implements an agreement known as the Concordat reached in January 2004 between the Lord Chief Justice and the Chancellor. It provides that persons appointed by the Prime Minister to the office of Lord Chancellor shall be qualified by "relevant experience" and shall take a special oath, different from that required of other ministers, to "respect the rule of law, defend the independence of the judiciary and discharge my duty to ensure the provision of resources for the efficient and effective support of the courts". Relevant experience could be experience as a minister, MP or peer or as a legal practitioner or academic. As the most senior judge in England and Wales, the Lord Chief Justice will henceforth be able to make representations to parliament on justice related matters. Similar provisions are made for Scotland and Northern Ireland. The government and those involved in the administration of justice, including the appointment of judges, are given a statutory obligation to respect and maintain judicial independence. Ministers are required not to seek to influence particular judicial decisions through any access to the judiciary over and above that which might be exercised by a member of the general public. In future rules of court will be subject to a veto by the Lord Chief Justice, though the Lord Chancellor can direct the Lord Chief Justice to make rules for a particular purpose. Similarly, the powers to issue directions which were exercised by the Lord Chancellor are, in future, to be exercised by the Lord Chief Justice or his delegate. This means in practice that the rules will be drawn up by the heads of the Criminal, Civil and Family Divisions of the High Court under the supervision of the Lord Chief Justice. The Lord Chancellor also loses his powers to appoint judges. These will now be exercised by the Queen on the advice of the Lord Chancellor, after candidates have been selected by the Judicial Appointments Commission, composed of lay members appointed by the Lord Chancellor and judicial members appointed by the Lord Chief Justice. The Lord Chief Justice will also be responsible for the posting and roles of individual judges. The Lord Chancellor retains responsibility for setting the framework for the organisation of the court system, providing the resources for the administration of justice, including pay, pensions and terms and conditions of the judiciary and their staff, and the determination of the overall number of judges. The Lord Chancellor's historic office as Speaker of the House of Lords is done away with, so that the House of Lords can make its own arrangements for appointment of a speaker. Part 3 of the Act creates a Supreme Court of the United Kingdom which will take over the appellate jurisdiction of the House of Lords and the devolution jurisdiction of the Privy Council. The new Supreme Court, its members chosen by a newly created selection commission, will be separate from parliament. There are restrictions on the right of peers to sit and vote in the House of Lords while they are holding full-time judicial office. This implements a rigorous separation of judiciary and legislative constitutional roles. Other innovations include the creation of a Judicial Appointments and Conduct Ombudsman to field complaints about judicial misconduct, who will report annually to parliament.

Key Principle: **The United Kingdom has Treaty obligations to change the law so as to comply with human rights obligations under the European Convention on Human Rights.**

The Sunday Times v United Kingdom

The *Sunday Times* brought an action before the European Commission on Human Rights claiming that the injunction upheld by the House of Lords [1974] A.C. 273 infringed their right to freedom of expression guaranteed by Art.10 of the European Convention on Human Rights. The Commission referred the case to the Court of Human Rights.

Held: (ECHR) The interference with the applicants' freedom of expression was not justified under Art.10(2) which permitted such restrictions "as are prescribed by law and are necessary in a democratic society . . . for maintaining the authority and impartiality of the judiciary". There was no "pressing social need" for the injunction. [1979] 2 E.H.R.R. 245.

Commentary

This is one example where the United Kingdom introduced legislation to implement the Court of Human Rights' decisions. The judgment led to the Contempt of Court Act 1981.

Key Principle: **International treaty obligations may provide guidance when a court is called upon to interpret an ambiguous statute.**

R. v Secretary of State for Home Department Ex p. Brind

The Secretary of State made orders under the Broadcasting Act 1981 banning television and radio stations from broadcasting the words spoken by spokesmen of organisations proscribed under anti-terrorism legislation. Broadcasters sought judicial review of the orders as being outside the Secretary of State's powers because the ban was disproportionate to its ostensible object of preventing intimidation by the organisations concerned and also because he should have regard to the European Convention on Human Rights. The application was dismissed by the Divisional Court and by the Court of Appeal. The broadcasters appealed.

Held: (HL) The presumption that Parliament had intended to legislate in conformity with the European Convention might be resorted to in order to resolve ambiguity in a statute, but in the present case there was no ambiguity and no presumption that the Secretary of State had to exercise his discretion under the Act in accordance with the Convention. [1991] 1 A.C. 696.

Commentary

Lord Ackner said that since there was no ambiguity in the relevant section of the statute there was here no need to have recourse to the Convention. He said that the limits placed upon discretion were that the power should be used for the purpose for which it was granted and that it must be exercised reasonably in the *Wednesbury* sense. He also referred to Lord Denning's judgment in *R. v Chief Immigration Officer Ex p. Salamat Bibi* [1976] 1 W.L.R. 979 where he said:

> "The position as I understand it is that if there is any ambiguity in our statutes, or uncertainty in our law, then these courts can look to the Convention as an aid to clear up the ambiguity and uncertainty."

The status of the European Convention in UK law has been changed as a result of the Human Rights Act 1998. (See Ch.3.) From October 2000 the courts must "take into account" the judgments of the Court of Human Rights and the Opinions of the former European Commission on Human Rights. This on its wording has a stronger meaning than calling on the Convention as an aid to interpretation in cases of ambiguity. The status of other treaty obligations is unchanged by the HRA but in practice they are far less often at issue. In *Brind v United Kingdom* (1994) 77 D.R. 4 the Commission rejected the journalists' contention that there was a violation of Art.10. The ban was proportionate in view of the need to combat terrorism. This decision illustrates that in some instances the incorporation of the Convention will be unlikely to have any effect.

Key Principle: **An order for derogation from international treaty obligations must be consistent with the principles of affording equality before the law and protecting the human rights of all individuals with the UK.**

A v Secretary of State for the Home Department

Under the Anti-Terrorism, Crime and Security Act 2001 foreign nationals suspected of terrorism could be imprisoned indefinitely without trial if they could not lawfully be deported to their country of origin. Implementation of s.23 of this measure required the government to derogate from its obligations under Art.5(1) of the European Convention on Human Rights (right to liberty and security of person). Accordingly the government declared that there existed a public emergency threatening the life of the nation. The claimants were nationals of a variety of states which were known to practice torture. The Special Immigration Appeals Commission held that although the terrorist acts on September 11, 2001 in the United States had created a public emergency threatening the life of the nation, the effect of the provisions of the 2001 Act was discriminatory in that the government had no power to detain British subjects without trial. The discrimination constituted a violation of Art.14 of the Convention. The Court of Appeal overturned the decision of the SIAC and the claimants appealed to the House of Lords.

Held: (HL) SIAC was within its discretion in finding that there was a public emergency such as to threaten the life of the nation. But the courts were required to give close scrutiny to inroads into the right to personal liberty, one of the most fundamental human rights. The discriminatory nature of s.23 and the fact that it could be applied to persons who did not pose a terrorist threat meant that it did not pass scrutiny and did not rationally address the threat to security. It was not consistent with the UK's obligation under international treaty to afford equality before the law and protect the human rights of all individuals within its territory. The derogation order was quashed. The House of Lords made a declaration that s.23 was incompatible with Arts 5 and 14 of the European Convention. [2005] 2 A.C. 68.

Commentary
This was a dramatic clash between a government using authoritarian methods to combat terrorism and a judiciary determined to ensure adherence to human rights and the rule of law.

Key Principle: **Evidence obtained by torture wherever it takes place is not admissible against a party to proceedings in a British court.**

A v Secretary of State for the Home Department (No.2)
In the course of *A v Secretary of State for the Home Department* (for facts see above) the issue arose whether the Special Immigration

Appeals Commission could receive evidence which had been or might have been obtained abroad by torture. The Court of Appeal by a majority of two to one (Neuberger L.J. dissenting) held that evidence obtained by torture inflicted by officials of a foreign state without the complicity of the British authorities could be admitted. The claimants appealed to the House of Lords.

Held: (HL) From its earliest days the English common law had set its face firmly against torture because of the cruelty of the practice, the unreliable nature of evidence so obtained and the belief that it degraded all who lent themselves to it. Lord Bingham delivered a magisterial rebuke to the Court of Appeal majority, saying he was startled, even a little dismayed at their acceptance that that deeply rooted tradition could be overridden by a statute (the 2001 Act) which made no mention of torture at all. The principles of the common law, standing alone, compelled the exclusion of third party torture evidence as unreliable, unfair, offensive to ordinary standards of humanity and decency and incompatible with the principles which should animate a tribunal seeking to administer justice. They were reinforced by the European Convention on Human Rights and by the UN Torture Convention which made it mandatory to exclude statements made as a result of torture as evidence in any proceedings. Where it was established on the balance of probabilities that evidence had been obtained by torture it was inadmissible. (*The Times*, December 9, 2005).

Commentary
The House of Lords was divided over the burden and standard of proof applicable where it was alleged that evidence had been extracted by torture. The majority favoured the test given above. Lords Bingham, Nicholls and Hoffmann thought this was not enough. In their view evidence ought to be excluded if the tribunal was unable to conclude that there was not a real risk torture had been used to obtain the evidence.

2. PARLIAMENTARY SUPREMACY

Key Principle: **An Act of Parliament takes precedence over international law.**

Mortensen v Peters
The captain of a Norwegian trawler was convicted of fishing with an otter trawl net in the Moray Firth contrary to the Herring Fishery (Scotland) Act 1889. He appealed on the grounds that he was not a British subject and had not been fishing in territorial waters.

Held: (Court of Session) If the captain's conduct fell within the Act, the court was bound to give effect to its terms. There was a presumption that Parliament would not seek to exceed what an international tribunal might hold to be its proper sphere of legislative competence. However, that presumption had been overtaken by the plain words of the statute. (1906) 8 F.(J.) 93.

Commentary
The courts have here and in other cases acknowledged a presumption that Parliament would not seek to exceed what an international tribunal might hold to be its proper sphere of legislative competence but the presumption would fall in the face of express statutory words or clear implication. The standing of international treaties is important in assessing the status of the European Convention on Human Rights (see p.36).

Key Principle: **The monarch cannot add to or amend legislation or the common law by means of a proclamation.**

Case of Proclamations

James I was short of money and issued a proclamation declaring it to be against the law to build new houses in London or to make wheat starch. His aim was to levy fines from offenders.

Held: (Court of Common Pleas) The King could not by proclamation change the common law or create any new offences. The King had no prerogative powers other than those allowed by the law. However, if he proclaimed an existing offence that offence would in future be aggravated. (1611) 12 Co. Rep.74.

Commentary
The Bill of Rights 1688 confirmed that it would be illegal for the monarch to attempt without the approval of Parliament to impose taxes, suspend the operation of laws, or dispense with penalties. Earlier, in *Dr Bonham's Case* (1610) 8 Co. Rep.114, the court had referred to a higher natural or fundamental law which not even an Act of Parliament could override but this doctrine has not been of practical importance since the English Revolution.

Key Principle: **Courts have no power to challenge the validity of an Act of Parliament.**

R. v Jordan
The leader of a right-wing party was imprisoned for 18 months for offences against the Race Relations Act 1965. He sought legal aid to bring an action for habeas corpus on the ground that his rights of free speech had been unlawfully curtailed by the Act, which was consequently invalid.

Held: (DC) The courts had no power to question the validity of an Act of Parliament, which was supreme. [1967] Crim. L.R. 483.

Commentary
One often debated issue is whether the common law could strike out an Act of Parliament as repugnant to natural justice. In *Dr Bonham's Case* the president and censors of the College of Physicians ordered the claimant to be committed to prison because he had continued to practice medicine when ordered not to do so and refused to pay fines levied for having done so. The claimant claimed to practise under a degree awarded by Cambridge University. He brought an action against the president and censors of the college for false imprisonment. It was held that the censors had no power to commit the claimant to prison, since their power was limited to the control of bad practice and not of good practice of medicine. The order for the claimant's imprisonment had been wrongly made by the president and censors of the college, though only the censors had jurisdiction even in cases of bad practice. The

college should have given written rather than oral reasons for their decision. Lord Coke C.J. said:

> "And it appears in our books, that in many cases, the common law will control Acts of Parliament and sometimes adjudge them to be utterly void: for when an Act of Parliament is against common right and reason or repugnant or impossible to be performed, the common law will control it and adjudge such an Act to be void."

The matter has not been a live issue since then.

Key Principle: **It is for Parliament not the courts to investigate whether an Act has been obtained in breach of parliamentary procedure.**

British Railways Board v Pickin

A railway line was constructed under an Act of 1836 by which the lands on which it was built should, if abandoned, revert to the owner of the adjoining lands. The lands were subsequently vested in the British Railways Board. In 1968 the Board obtained a private Act of Parliament, the British Railways Act, which nullified the effect of the 1836 Act and vested abandoned lands in the Board. The claimant owned land beside the track and claimed to own the track to its centre-line. He said the Board had misled Parliament by a false preamble to the 1968 Act, and in obtaining the unopposed passage of the Bill. The judge struck out those sections of the claimant's claim, but they were reinstated in the Court of Appeal. The Board appealed.

Held: (HL) The court's function was to consider and apply Acts of Parliament. It was not open to a litigant to impugn the validity of statute by seeking to establish that Parliament had been misled. Nor, if Parliament had been misled, would that enable a litigant to establish a claim in equity against the other party. The court would not look into the manner in which Parliament had exercised its function. [1974] A.C. 765.

Commentary

This principle is known as the enrolled act rule. The courts cannot question the procedure by which an Act of Parliament is passed any more than its content. The following case appeared to suggest that this principle may not always apply.

Manuel v Attorney-General
The Queen gave Royal Assent to the Canada Act 1982 which authorised a new procedure for amending the Canadian constitution, in which the UK Parliament would no longer have any part. The legislation recognised and affirmed the existing aboriginal and treaty rights of the Indian peoples of Canada. A number of Indian chiefs, representing their peoples, issued writs against the Attorney-General seeking declarations that the UK Parliament had no power to amend the Canadian constitution so as to prejudice the Indian nations without their consent and that the Canada Act 1982 was ultra vires because it was inconsistent with the constitutional safeguards provided for the Indian peoples in the Statute of Westminster 1931. The Attorney-General moved to have the chiefs' applications struck out as showing no cause of action. The judge held that the Canada Act 1982 was not ultra vires and that he had a duty to apply it, and that the Attorney-General was the wrong defendant, since the obligations the chiefs sought to enforce were those of the Queen in right of Canada, and not the Crown in right of the United Kingdom. The chiefs appealed.

Held: (CA) The only requirement imposed by the Statute of Westminster (a certificate that Canada had requested the procedure change) had been complied with, so that even if the Canada Act 1982 had to comply with the Statute of Westminster, it had done so. The applications had been correctly struck out. [1983] 1 Ch. 77.

Commentary
Megarry V.C. in the Chancery Division had held that the case was covered by *British Railways Board v Pickin*. The Court of Appeal however accepted that prior consent of the Dominion of Canada might have been required to make a valid Act but that in this case the preamble to the statute declared on its face that it had such consent.

———

Key Principle: **There is no constitutional principle preventing Parliament from altering its own constitution. The Parliament Act 1949, passed using the Parliament Act 1911 so as to exclude the House of Lords, was good law as was the Hunting Act 2004, passed by the procedure laid down in the 1949 Act.**

R. (on the application of Jackson and others) v Attorney General

After a great deal of debate, the Hunting Act 2004, banning hunting with dogs, was passed by the Commons under the procedure laid down in the Parliament Act 1949. This allowed the Commons to send a Bill for Royal Assent if it had been delayed in the Lords in two successive sessions and more than a year had elapsed since its introduction. Supporters of hunting brought an action for judicial review claiming that the 1949 Act was delegated legislation, since it had been passed in accordance with the truncated procedure laid down in the 1911 Act and so could not be considered as a primary Act of Parliament. They claimed that it was a principle of statutory construction that powers conferred on a body by an enabling Act might not be enlarged or modified by that body in the absence of express words authorising enlargement or modification.

Held: (HL) Since the 1911 Act provided that legislation passed according to the procedure laid down in it was an Act of Parliament, such legislation was primary and not delegated legislation. On the authority of *Pickin v British Railways Board* [1974] A.C. 765 the courts had no power to declare enacted law to be invalid. [2005] UKHL 56.

Commentary

The litigation was, arguably, a challenge to the course Parliament has taken over the last 100 or so years, a process generally regarded as democratisation in which the power of hereditary legislators has been diminished to the benefit of elected members. The conventional view is that provided Parliament's own procedures have been followed, the courts will treat the legislation as valid. The militant wing of the hunting lobby had organised an intrusion into the Commons chamber to demonstrate against the Act. The decisive rejection of the challenge can be regarded as asserting the supremacy of the elected chamber.

Doctrine of Implied Repeal

Key Principle: **The provisions of a later Act in so far as they are inconsistent with those of an earlier Act must prevail. Parliament cannot bind itself as to the substance or the form of subsequent legislation.**

Ellen Street Estates Ltd v Minister of Health
Section 7 of the Acquisition of Land (Assessment of Compensation) Act 1919 enacted that the provisions of the Act or order by
which land was authorised to be acquired, or of any Act
incorporated therewith "Shall in relation to the matters dealt
with in this Act, have effect subject to this Act, and in so far as
inconsistent with this Act those provisions shall cease to have or
shall not have effect". An improvement scheme was made in
1922 over an area of the East End of London, part of which was
owned by the plaintiff. The scheme lapsed without being acted
on, but was subsequently revived by the London CC under the
Housing Act 1925. The claimant claimed that the 1925 Act was
inconsistent with s.7 of the 1919 Act. The judge upheld the
revived scheme and the claimant appealed.

Held: (CA) Parliament could not bind itself as to the form of
subsequent legislation. It was impossible for Parliament to enact
that in a subsequent statute dealing with the same subject-
matter there could be no implied repeal. Where a subsequent
Act of Parliament indicated that the earlier statute was being to
some extent repealed, the court must give effect to that intention. [1934] 1 K.B. 590.

Commentary
In *Manuel v Attorney-General* (see above at p.19) the Court
accepted that its proposition that the Statute of Westminster could
restrict the form of subsequent legislation in requiring Dominion
consent to constitutional change was in conflict with *Ellen Street
Estates Ltd v Minister of Health*. But it said it was not pronouncing
on the matter. The orthodox doctrine of implied repeal has
however been modified by the European Communities Act (see
below) and by authorities from subordinate legislatures.

Key Principle: **Ordinary statutes can be repealed by implication. So-called constitutional statutes, like the European Communities Act 1972, can only be repealed explicitly.**

Hunt v Hackney London Borough Council
A number of market traders were prosecuted for selling pro-
duce by the pound, in violation of the Units of Measurement
Regulations 1994 and the Weights and Measures Act 1985

(Metrication) (Amendment) Order 1994, even though the Weights and Measures Act 1985 provided for the use of both metric and imperial weights. They contended on appeal that the 1985 Act impliedly repealed the European Communities Act 1972 under which the regulations and the order had been made, pursuant to European directives.

Held: (DC) All specific rights and obligations under EU law were incorporated into English law by the 1972 Act and ranked supreme, so anything in English law inconsistent with EU law had to give way. The 1972 Act belonged to a category recognised by English common law as constitutional statutes which could not be impliedly repealed. The fundamental legal basis of the United Kingdom's relationship with the EU rested with the domestic, not the European, legal powers. The appeals were dismissed. [2002] EWHC Admin 195.

Commentary
Laws L.J. defined a constitutional statute as one which (a) conditions the legal relationship between citizen and state in some general, overarching manner, or (b) enlarges or diminishes the scope of what we would now regard as fundamental constitutional rights. He also instanced Magna Carta 1297, the Bill of Rights 1689, the Union with Scotland Act 1706 the Reform Acts of 1832, 1867 and 1884 the Human Rights Act 1998, the Scotland Act 1998 and the Government of Wales Act 1998. Constitutional statutes were not affected by the doctrine of implied repeal and could only be repealed or amended by unambiguous words on the face of the later statute.

Key Principle: **A Bill from a subordinate legislature cannot become law in violation of a constitutional requirement.**

Attorney-General for New South Wales v Trethowan
The New South Wales legislature in 1929 amended the Constitution Act 1902 to provide by s.7A that no Bill for abolishing the legislative council should be presented for Royal Assent until it had been approved by a referendum of electors. The same was to apply to a Bill for repealing s.7A. The following year both Houses of the legislature passed Bills abolishing the legislative council and repealing s.7A. Two members of the legislative

council sued the state Attorney-General for a declaration that the Bills could not lawfully be presented for Royal Assent until approved by the electors in accordance with s.7A. The matter came by way of appeal to the Privy Council.

Held: (PC) The provision that Bills must be approved by the electors before being presented was a provision as to "manner and form" under s.5 of the Colonial Laws Validity Act 1865 which empowered the state legislature to make laws respecting the constitution, powers and procedure of the legislature. Section 5 provided that legislation comply with such provisions as to manner and form as might from time to time be required by Act of Parliament, letters patent, Order in Council or colonial law. Accordingly, the Bills could not lawfully be presented until they had been approved by a majority of the electors voting. [1932] A.C. 526.

Bribery Commissioner v Ranasinghe
The respondent had been tried before a Bribery Commission on a charge of bribery and challenged orders made against him on the grounds that the persons composing the tribunal were not validly appointed, since they had been appointed under the Bribery Amendment Act 1958. That Act provided that the tribunal members be appointed by the Governor-General on the advice of the Justice Minister. It conflicted with the Ceylon (Constitution) Order in Council 1946 which provided by s.55 that "the appointment . . . of judicial officers is hereby vested in the Judicial Service Commission".

Held: (PC) The Ceylon legislature had no power to ignore conditions of law-making imposed by the instrument which itself regulated the power to make law. This was so even where the legislature was sovereign, as was the Ceylon legislature. The constitution could be amended or altered by the legislature if the regulating instrument so provided and if its terms were complied with, but the mere fact of the establishment of a legislature did not give it some inherent power to overrule the provisions of the instrument by which it was established. The court accepted that an alternative, narrower, view was taken in regard to English law. However, it pointed out there was never a need for UK courts to look into the process of a Bill becoming law because there was no governing instrument which prescribed law-making powers. [1965] A.C. 172.

Commentary
It appears that these cases contradict *British Railways Board v Pickin* (see above at p.18). But since they are concerned with proceedings in subordinate legislatures they are not authority for the practice of the Westminster Parliament which is the supreme legislature in England and Wales.

Key Principle: **The Act of Union 1707 did not limit the power of the Westminster Parliament to legislate on public rights.**

MacCormick v Lord Advocate
The petitioners objected to the Queen's being styled in Scotland as "Queen Elizabeth II". In the Outer House the petition was dismissed because the adoption of the numeral had been expressly authorised by the Royal Titles Act 1953, and an Act of Parliament could not be challenged in any court for breach of the Treaty of Union or any other cause. Further, the Treaty of Union did not expressly or by implication prohibit the use of the numeral, and in any event the petitioners had no legal title or interests to sue. The petitioners appealed to the First Division.

Held: The Royal Titles Act 1953 had no real bearing on the matter. The numeral "II" had been adopted on the Queen's accession in consequence of a practice of numbering sovereigns from the Norman conquest of England which the court would not criticise. However, the principle of unlimited parliamentary sovereignty had no counterpart in Scots law. The Scottish king and Parliament never acquired unlimited powers and so such powers could not have been transferred to the new Parliament of Great Britain in 1707. There was no provision in the union legislation that the Parliament of Great Britain should be absolutely sovereign. But the Court of Session was not competent to declare legislation as regards public law ultra vires. (1953) 69 L.Q.R. 512.

Gibson v Lord Advocate
The Act of Union 1707 allowed Parliament to change Scots law save that "no alteration be made in laws which concern private right except for evident utility of the subjects within Scotland". Relying on the Act, a Scottish fisherman challenged EEC regulations which opened Scottish waters to fishermen from other Member States.

Held: (Court of Session) The court could not rule on whether a particular Act of the UK Parliament altering a particular aspect of Scots private law was or was not "for the evident utility" of the subjects within Scotland. It might be a different matter if Parliament proposed to abolish the Court of Session or the Church of Scotland or to substitute English law for the whole body of Scots private law. (1975) S.L.T. 134.

Commentary
When the Scottish and English Parliaments passed the Acts of Union they in effect declared their own abolition as separate organs and created a new sovereign entity, the British Parliament. Thus, in theory, Parliament could again limit its sovereignty by giving its sovereignty to another Parliament. This has led some to argue that Parliament has the ability to limit its legislative power. Some of the dicta in the above cases have appeared to indicate that the courts might in certain circumstances be prepared to question legislation which might be in violation of the Act of Union, specifically in relation to private rights. It is important to stress however that the attitude of the courts towards parliamentary supremacy has always been essentially realistic and practical.

Impact of the European Union

The EC's view—new legal order

Key Principle: **Member States permanently limited their sovereign rights by transferring powers from their domestic legal systems to the EC. Community law prevails over domestic legal provisions.**

Costa v ENEL
Italy nationalised electricity production and distribution and transferred the assets of private electricity companies to a new state body, ENEL. Costa, a shareholder in one of the private companies, claimed in an Italian court that the nationalisation infringed the Treaty of Rome. The magistrate requested a preliminary ruling under Art.177 (now Art.234) of the Treaty.

Held: (ECJ) Community law prevailed over incompatible national law, even where the national law had been enacted after the relevant Community law. The Member States had in certain spheres restricted their sovereign rights and created a body of law applicable both to their nationals and to themselves. (6/64) [1964] E.C.R. 585, C.M.L.R. 425.

Commentary
The "new legal order" is both recognised in international law and also impacts on the domestic legal systems of Member States. Some rights and duties flowing from Community law have direct effect in the Member States meaning that they are directly enforceable in the national courts.

Key Principle: **European Communities Act, s.2(1):**

> "All such rights, powers, liabilities, obligations and restrictions from time to time created or arising by or under the Treaties, and all such remedies and procedures from time to time provided for, by or under the Treaties, as in accordance with the Treaties are without further enactment to be given legal effect or used in the United Kingdom shall be recognised and available in law, and be enforced, allowed and followed accordingly, and the expression 'enforceable community right' and similar expressions shall be read as referring to one to which this subsection refers."

Key Principle: **Enforceable community rights including Art.119 of the EEC Treaty should be given effect in UK law.**

McCarthy's v Smith
A woman warehouse manager employed by a pharmaceutical firm was paid £50 a week whereas the man who did the job previously had been paid £60. She brought industrial tribunal proceedings claiming that by virtue of s.1(1) and (2)(a) of the Equal Pay Act 1970, her contract of employment should be treated as if she were entitled to the same salary as her predecessor. The claim was upheld by the industrial tribunal and on appeal by the Employment Appeal Tribunal. The Court of Appeal on the interpretation of Art.119 asked for a preliminary ruling from the European Court of Justice.

Held: (ECJ) Art.119 (now Art.141) of the EEC Treaty applied directly to all forms of direct and overt discrimination as regards equal work and equal pay. The decisive test was whether there was a difference in treatment between a man and a woman performing equal work within the meaning of Art.119. The Article's scope was not limited to situations where men and women were doing the same work simultaneously. [1980] E.C.R. 1275.

Commentary

Lord Denning in a dissenting judgment in the original Court of Appeal hearing had argued that the Equal Pay Act should be given a purposive interpretation to give effect to the objects of Art.119 and thus a reference to the ECJ was not required. This approach is also that of the European Court of Justice which has now held in *Marleasing S.A. v La Commercial Internacional de Alimentación S.A.* (C-106/89) [1990] E.C.R. I–4135 that a purposive construction should be applied to national law whether the provisions in question were applied before or after the relevant Directive. See *Webb v EMO Cargo (UK) Ltd (No.2)* [1995] 1 W.L.R. 1454. The Treaties of Maastricht (1992), Amsterdam (1999) and Nice (2001) amend the original Treaty of Rome.

Key Principle: **European Communities Act 1972, s.2(4)**

"The provision that may be made under subsection (2) above (which provides for implementation of Community obligations by secondary legislation) includes subject to Schedule 2 of this Act, any such provision (of any such extent) as might be made by Act of Parliament, and any enactment passed or to be passed, other than one contained in this part of this Act, shall be construed and have effect subject to the foregoing provisions of this section."

Key Principle: **This section is a principle of construction to be used wherever possible to construe UK legislation consistently with Community law.**

Garland v British Rail Engineering Ltd

British Rail provided all employees with travel concessions while they were in its employment. They also gave concessions to former employees. Wives and dependent children of male former employees were also allowed concessions, but no concessions were made to partners of female former employees. A

female employee complained that this arrangement discriminated against her. An industrial tribunal rejected her claim, but
it was upheld on appeal by the Employment Appeal Tribunal.
The tribunal decision was reversed by the Court of Appeal on
the basis that British Rail was not contractually obliged to
provide travel concessions. On her appeal to the House of
Lords, the European Court was asked as a preliminary to
determine whether the alleged discrimination infringed Art.119
of the EEC Treaty.

Held: (HL) On its correct interpretation the national legislation
gave entitlement to the benefits. [1983] 2 A.C. 751.

Commentary

The House of Lords had referred the matter to the European
Court of Justice after the Court of Appeal had ruled that the
woman was not the victim of unlawful discrimination under
English law. The European Court of Justice ruled that her
treatment was a violation of an enforceable Community right.
When the case returned to the House of Lords it ruled that there
was in fact no conflict between the relevant UK statute and
Community law.

Litster v Forth Dry Dock & Engineering Co (in receivership)

Forth Dry Dock, a Leith ship-repair business, appointed a
receiver. Two of its managers formed a new company, Forth
Estuary, which bought Forth Dry Dock from the receiver for
£35,000. One and a half hours before the transfer, the receiver
dismissed the 25 employees of Forth Dry Dock. After the
transfer Forth Estuary took on new workers at lower pay.
Twelve former employees succeeded in an industrial tribunal
claim for unfair dismissal contrary to the Transfer of Undertakings (Protection of Employment) Regulations 1981. The Employment Appeal Tribunal affirmed the industrial tribunal decision,
but it was reversed by the Court of Session. The employees
appealed.

Held: (HL) The regulations were enacted to comply with the
Directive on transfer of undertakings so that the benefits and
burdens of a contract of employment passed from the transferor
to the transferee on the transfer of an undertaking. The Directive
provided that the transfer of an undertaking should not constitute grounds for dismissing an employee. To construe the
regulations on the basis that the employees had been dismissed

before the transfer would mean that Parliament had failed to comply with the obligations imposed on it by the Directive. The court was entitled to apply a purposive construction to the Regulations in order to give effect to the United Kingdom's Treaty obligations and, where necessary, imply words appropriate to comply with those obligations. A transferee could not avoid his liability to employees of an undertaking by requesting the transferor to dismiss the employees before the transfer thus leaving the employees with a worthless remedy against an insolvent transferor. [1990] 1 A.C. 546.

Commentary

Lord Oliver referred to the fact that the "greater flexibility available to the court in applying a purposive construction to legislation designed to give effect to the United Kingdom's Treaty obligations enables the court 'where necessary' to supply by implication words appropriate to comply with those obligations". This went beyond the ordinary rules of construction applicable to a purely domestic stature and without reference to Treaty obligations.

This purposive approach to interpretation has been adopted by the House of Lords on a number of occasions; see also *Pickstone v Freemans plc* [1989] A.C. 66. In *Hunt v Hackney London Borough Council* (see p.21) Laws L.J. referred to *Pickstone* as "a case which illustrates the lengths our courts will go in construing Acts of Parliament to uphold the supremacy of substantive Community rights". This approach followed that set out by the European Court of Justice in *Van Colson and Kamann v Land Nordrhein-Westfalen* [1984] E.C.R. 1891.

It is important to stress in relation to Art.234 referrals that the national courts retain jurisdiction on findings of fact, see *Arsenal Football Club v Reed* [2003] 3 All E.R. 865.

Key Principle: **Purposive statutory construction should not be applied to legislation which was not introduced to comply with obligations under the EEC Treaty.**

Duke v Reliance Systems Ltd

The applicant was obliged by her employer to retire in line with a policy that female employees retired at 60 and men at 65. She claimed discrimination under s.6(4) of the Sex Discrimination

Act 1975. She also said that even if s.6(4) made it lawful to discriminate on grounds of sex in relation to retirement age, it should be construed so as to give effect to the Equal Treatment Directive.

Held: (HL) The 1975 Act was not passed to give effect to the Equal Treatment Directive. It had been intended to preserve discrimination in retirement ages. Nothing in the European Communities Act 1972 required or allowed an English court to distort the meaning of a statute in order to conform with EEC law which was not directly applicable. [1988] A.C. 618.

Commentary
The applicant's employer was a private employer therefore she could not rely on the direct effect of the Equal Treatment Directive (see *Marshall v Southampton and South West Hampshire Health Authority (No.1)* (152/84) [1986] E.C.R. 723). The House of Lords could not accept that s.2(4) of the European Communities Act required it to distort the meaning of a British statute so as to achieve an equivalent effect against a private employer. The House did not make a reference under Art.177 (now Art.234) and its very narrow and much criticised interpretation should be contrasted with that of the European Court of Justice in *Marleasing S.A. v La Commercial Internacional de Alimentación S.A.* and its own judgment in *Webb v EMO Air Cargo (UK) Ltd (No.2)* (see p.33).

Key Principle: **The rule that an injunction cannot be granted against the Crown should be set aside if it prevents the granting of interim relief in a dispute governed by EC law.**

R. v Secretary of State for Transport Ex p. Factortame (C-213/89)
A Spanish-owned company owned fishing vessels which were registered in the British merchant fleet. The Merchant Shipping Act 1988 established a new register open only to British-owned vessels. The Spanish-owned company failed to qualify for the register and challenged the provisions of the Act by way of judicial review. The Divisional Court referred to the European Court of Justice the question whether EC law affected the registration conditions which a Member State might impose on

merchant shipping. The court granted the applicants an interim injunction disapplying the operation of the register and restraining the Secretary of State from enforcing the Act pending the European Court of Justice decision. The injunction was discharged on appeal by the Court of Appeal and the applicants appealed to the House of Lords, which held that under English law the courts had no jurisdiction to grant interim relief in terms that would involve either overturning a statute or granting an injunction against the Crown. The House referred to the European Court of Justice the issue whether Community law either obliged the national court to take interim steps to protect rights claimed or empowered the court to do so.

Held: (HL) Where an application was made for interim relief in a case concerning Community law, a rule of national law must be set aside if the national court considered that rule to be the only obstacle to the grant of interim relief. [1991] 1 A.C. 603.

Commentary
The House of Lords decided in the light of the European Court of Justice decision to uphold the injunction originally granted by the Divisional Court.

The *Factortame* series of cases is of great importance in establishing that an Act of Parliament should not be implemented in part if it denies enforceable rights under Community law. To achieve this the rule that injunctions should not lie against the Crown was abrogated. The House of Lords in effect is acknowledging the primacy of EC law over national legislation. However, two qualifications should be borne in mind. First, the whole statute was not repealed; only those sections which applied to EU nationals were not applied. Secondly, the case does not deal with a situation where Parliament was expressly and intentionally flouting a provision in EC law. Thirdly, Lord Bridge in giving judgment stated that "whatever limitation of its sovereignty Parliament accepted when it enacted the European Communities Act 1972 was entirely voluntary."

Secretary of State for Employment Ex p. Equal Opportunities Commission
The right not to be unfairly dismissed and to redundancy pay were limited by the Employment Protection (Consolidation) Act 1978 to employees working continuously for more than two years and more than eight hours a week. The Commission believed this to discriminate indirectly against women workers,

more of whom worked part-time than men, and argued that this
was a breach of the United Kingdom's obligations under the EC
Treaty. The Commission asked the Secretary of State to do away
with the discrimination and when he refused on the grounds
that it was objectively justified sought judicial review of his
refusal. The Divisional Court would not direct the Secretary of
State to introduce legislation or declare that the United Kingdom was in breach of its treaty obligations. The statutory
provisions were discriminatory but had been objectively justified. The Court of Appeal by a majority upheld the Divisional
Court decision. The Commission appealed.

Held: (HL) The Divisional Court had jurisdiction to declare
that the 1978 Act was incompatible with EC law. The onus of
showing that the discrimination was objectively justified was on
the Secretary of State. That it brought about an increase in part-
time work, as the Secretary of State claimed the measure had
done, could be an objective justification of the statute. However,
the evidence before the Divisional Court did not establish that
the policy had resulted in any greater availability of part-time
work. The 1978 provisions would be declared incompatible with
the EC Treaty and directives made under it by the European
Community. [1995] 1 A.C. 1.

Commentary
The House of Lords was here applying the principle derived from
Factortame.

Key Principle: **An act in breach of EC law gives rise to
liability in damages.**

**R. v Secretary of State for Transport Ex p. Factortame Ltd
(No.5)**
(For facts see above.)

Held: (HL) The adoption of legislation which was discriminatory on the ground of nationality in respect of the registration of
British fishing vessels in breach of clear and unambiguous rules
of European Community law was sufficiently serious to give
rise to liability in damages to individuals who suffered loss as a
consequence. [1999] 3 W.L.R. 1062.

Commentary
This case turned on whether the respondents were entitled to compensation for financial loss suffered as a result of the United Kingdom's breach. The ECJ had earlier ruled that individuals suffering loss or injury were entitled to reparation if there was a breach of a rule of EC law which was intended to confer rights upon them, the breach was sufficiently serious and there was a direct causal link between the breach and the damage sustained by the individual: see *Brasseries du Pecheur S.A. v Federal Republic of Germany; R. v Secretary of State for Transport Ex p. Factortame Ltd (No.4) [1996]* Q.B. 404. It was then for the domestic courts to decide if the breaches were sufficiently serious to give entitlement to compensation. The House of Lords, while acknowledging that the UK Government had acted in good faith, considered that if damages were not held to be recoverable in this case it would be hard to envisage any case short of one involving bad faith where damages would be recoverable.

Key Principle: **Courts must interpret legislation so far as possible to conform with any relevant EC directive but they must not distort the meaning of the domestic legislation.**

Webb v EMO Air Cargo (UK) Ltd (No.2)
The applicant was employed to cover for another worker during the latter's maternity leave. Shortly after she was engaged, she discovered she herself was pregnant. She was dismissed and claimed that her dismissal constituted discrimination against her on the ground of her sex. The application was dismissed by an industrial tribunal and before both the Employment Appeal Tribunal and the Court of Appeal. The House of Lords sought a ruling from the European Court of Justice as to whether her treatment was discrimination on grounds of sex contrary to the Equal Treatment Directive (76/207/EEC). The European court ruled that it was and sent the case back to the Lords.

Held: (HL) The domestic legislation must be read to mean that where a woman had been engaged for an indefinite period, the fact that pregnancy was the reason for her temporary unavailability at a time when to her knowledge her services would be particularly required was a circumstance relevant to her case that could not be present in the case of the hypothetical man. [1995] 1 W.L.R. 1454.

Commentary
This case is an illustration of the application of the principle
known as "indirect effect", set out by the ECJ in *Marleasing S.A. v
La Comercial Internacional de Alimentación S.A. (C-106/89)*
[1990] E.C.R. I-4135, ECJ. The relevant terms of the Sex
Discrimination Act could be construed in the light of the Directive.

Key Principle: **Community Law is a relevant factor when a
national judge is considering whether to grant an injunction
against the implementation into national law of a European
Directive that was subject to challenge.**

R. v Secretary of State for Health Ex p. Imperial Tobacco
Tobacco manufacturers won an injunction at first instance in the
High Court restraining the government from implementing
European Parliament and Council Dir.98/43/EC to ban tobacco
advertising. The injunction was granted pending a ruling by the
European Court of Justice on the legal basis of the advertising
directive. The judge held that for the purposes of deciding
whether to grant an interim injunction he did not need to
concern himself with the jurisprudence of the ECJ, which would
have required the tobacco companies to show that they would
suffer irreparable damage from the implementation of the
disputed measure. The Court of Appeal allowed an appeal by
the government. The tobacco companies appealed to the House
of Lords.

Held: (HL) Unless all the national courts followed the same
conditions for the grant of interim relief, it would be undesirable
for national courts within the EU individually to restrain their
governments from giving effect to a Community Directive
whose validity was under challenge. If such a matter needed to
be determined it ought to be decided by the European Court of
Justice as it concerned the implementation of Community law.
[2001] 1 W.L.R. 127.

Commentary
The House stated that the difference between the conditions for
injunctions set out in *American Cyanamid* [1975] A.C. 396 and in
the Community jurisprudence was a matter of debate.

Key Principle: **The United Kingdom as a member of the European Union and a party to the ECHR may be liable for a violation of the ECHR as a result of a decision of one of the EU institutions.**

Matthews v United Kingdom

Ms Matthews, a resident of Gibraltar, did not have the opportunity of voting in the elections for the European Parliament due to the limited scope of Annex 2 of the EC Act on Direct Elections 1976. She claimed that the right to free election under Art.3 of Protocol 1 of the ECHR had been infringed.

Held: (ECHR) There was a breach of the Protocol. [1999] E.H.R.R. 361.

Commentary

Prior to this decision the Court of Human Rights had considered all cases concerning EC law to be inadmissible. This decision paves the way for the intervention of the Court of Human Rights into areas previously thought to be within the jurisdiction of the ECJ. The Court of Human Rights accepted that the European Community could not be challenged because it was not one of the High Contracting Parties to the ECHR (see *Re Accession of the Community to the European Human Rights Convention* (1996), Opinion 2/94). However the United Kingdom, since it had participated in making the Council Decision, had violated the ECHR. If the Court had not acted the applicant would have lacked a remedy for a serious violation of a fundamental human right. The EU Charter of Fundamental Rights was proclaimed at the Nice Conference in 2000 but was not made part of the subsequent Treaty.

3. THE HUMAN RIGHTS ACT

Key Principle: **S.3 of the HRA.**

Interpretation of legislation:

1) So far as it is possible to do so, primary legislation and subordinate legislation must be read and given effect in a way which is compatible with the Convention rights.

2) This section—

a) applies to primary legislation and subordinate legislation whenever enacted

b) does not affect the validity, continuing operation or enforcement of any incompatible subordinate legislation if (disregarding any possibility of revocation) primary legislation prevents removal of the incompatibility.

Key Principle: **In applying a statutory provision in the light of the ECHR it may sometimes be necessary to adopt an interpretation which may appear to be linguistically strained.**

R. v A (No.2)
The defendant had been charged with rape. He had claimed that sexual intercourse with the complainant had been by consent and that they had had a prior sexual relationship for about three weeks. At a pre-trial hearing the judge relying on s.41 of the Youth Justice and Criminal Evidence Act 1999 had ruled that the complainant could not be cross-examined and that evidence could not be led about her alleged sexual relationship with the defendant. The defendant appealed against the decision. The Court of Appeal allowed the appeal and conveyed the following question to the House of Lords: "May a sexual relationship between a defendant and complainant be relevant to the issue of consent so as to render its exclusion under section 41 Youth Justice and Criminal Evidence Act 1999 a contravention of the defendant's right to a fair trial?".

Held: (HL) Section 41 of the 1999 Act should be read in accordance with s.3 of the HRA 1998 and given effect in a way that was compatible with the fair trial guaranteed under Art.6 of the ECHR. An implied provision should be read into the section that evidence or questioning which is required to secure a fair trial under Art.6 of the ECHR should not be treated as inadmissible. [2001] 2 W.L.R. 1546.

Commentary

This case illustrates the new interpretative technique introduced by the Human Rights Act and is an example of a bold use of the court's powers. The House of Lords (in a majority decision, Lord Hope dissenting) considered that the defendant's prior relations with the complainant, although they might be relevant, could not be admitted under normal canons of statutory interpretation under s.41 of the Youth Justice and Criminal Evidence Act. The House avoided making a declaration of incompatibility by interpreting the section in a manner compatible with the demands of Art.6 of the Convention. Lord Steyn (at para.44) made it clear that the courts should not imply the word "reasonable" into s.3. In other words they should find a possible, not necessarily a reasonable, interpretation according to the wording. It is arguable however that the kind of creative juridical reasoning adopted here flouts the will of Parliament. Lord Hope deferred to the original intention of Parliament and stated that compatibility was not "possible" if the legislation contained provisions that expressly or impliedly contradicted the meaning which the legislation would have to be given to make it compatible. In *R. v A* Lord Steyn's more liberal interpretation of s.3(1) of the Human Rights Act was in part based on the desirability of avoiding making a declaration of incompatibility. He said that such a declaration would only be made if "a clear limitation on Convention rights is stated in terms . . .". The position Lord Steyn is putting forward suggests that he would only make a declaration of incompatibility if the statute stated expressly that it was limiting Convention rights. Such an occurrence would be very rare. The courts are developing their approach to demarcate between the s.3 interpretive technique and incompatibility under s.4. In subsequent cases (e.g. *R. v Lambert*, see below) moved closer to Lord Hope's position in *R. v A*. In *Re S & Ors: Re W & Ors sub nom Re W & B (Children): W (Child: Care Plan)* [2002] 2 W.L.R. 720, the House of Lords held that the Court of Appeal had exceeded its role in making innovations in the construction and application of a provision of the Children Act 1989. It held that a meaning that departed substantially from a fundamental feature of an Act of Parliament was likely to cross the boundary between interpretation and amendment. When the HRA was introduced in parliament, the government gave assurances that the fact that Art.13 was not being incorporated into English law was not intended to be restrictive. Article 13 gives a right to a remedy for a breach of any Convention right. However, in *Re W* Lord Nichols stated (at para.60) that ". . . Art.13 is not a Convention right as defined in s.1(1) of the Human Rights Act. So legislation which fails to provide an effective remedy for infringement of Art.8 is not, for that reason, incompatible with the Human Rights Act". In *R. (Wooder) v Fegetter & Mental Health Act Commission.* Sedley L.J. stated that the "section 3 imperative is not anything like as revolutionary as strict constructionists have suggested" (see p.157). In *Donoghue v Poplar Housing and Regeneration Association* [2001] 3 W.L.R. 183 (see p.51) Lord Woolf argued that "Section 3 does not enable the courts to legislate; its task is still one of interpretation but interpretation in conjunction with the direction contained in Section 3".

Key Principle: **In interpreting legislation the court must ensure that permissible restrictions of Convention rights are proportionate.**

R. v Lambert

The appellant was convicted of the offence of possessing a controlled drug of class A with intent to supply, contrary to s.5(3) of the Misuse of Drugs Act 1971. His trial had taken place before the Human Rights Act came into force. In his defence he had relied on s.28(3)(b)(1) of that Act asserting that he did not believe or have reason to suspect that the bag which he carried contained a controlled drug. The judge had directed the jury to the effect that the prosecutors had to prove only that he had and knew that he had the bag in his possession and that the bag contained a controlled drug. To establish a defence under the section the defendant had to prove on the balance of probabilities that he did not know the bag contained a controlled drug. Such was the accepted law at the time. The appeal was on the grounds that the requirement to prove the defence on the balance of probabilities was contrary to the presumption of innocence guaranteed under Art.6 of the European Convention on Human Rights. The Court of Appeal dismissed the appeal. There was an appeal to the House of Lords. The Court also certified as a point of law whether a defendant whose trial took place before ss.6 and 7(1)(b) of the Human Rights Act were in force was entitled once they were in force to rely on an alleged breach of his Convention rights by the trial court or prosecuting authority. The appellant contended that he was so entitled and also that s.6 of the Human Rights Act meant that the House of Lords as a public authority sitting in judgment once the Act was in force could not affirm convictions obtained in breach of such rights before October 2, 2000.

Held: (HL) It was not justifiable or a proportionate response to the problem of illegal drugs to transfer the legal burden on the accused and require him to prove on the balance of probabilities that he did not know the bag contained a controlled drug. It was however possible using s.3 of the HRA to interpret s.28 as imposing an evidential burden only. Such a requirement was not a violation of the Convention. If the trial judge had given the direction to the jury that the accused had only the evidential burden the jury would have reached the same conclusion. The conviction should therefore stand. Furthermore the HRA was not available to the applicant since his conviction predated its coming into force. [2001] 3 W.L.R. 2006.

Commentary
This case indicates a move towards Lord Hope's minority view in *R. v A* since the majority stated that judges do not have the power to "overrule decisions which the language of the statute shows to have been taken on the very point at issue by the legislator". The differing decisions of the Court of Appeal and the House of Lords in *Lambert* illustrate contradictory views on the extent to which the State should be allowed to undermine the rights of defendants in the interests of protecting society against the dangers of drug dealing. More recently the House of Lords has held that the UK courts must adopt a purposive approach to interpretation of legislation to ensure that fundamental rights are upheld.

In *Ghaidan v Godin-Mendoza* [2004] 2 A.C. 557 the House held that the word "spouse" in the schedule to the Rent Act 1977 should be interpreted to include homosexual partners so as not to infringe Arts 8 and 14 of the European Convention on Human Rights.

The word proportionate does not appear in the text of the Convention. It relates to the application of the requirements for restrictions in rights to be "necessary in a democratic society", implying the existence of a "pressing social need" (see *Handyside v United Kingdom* (1976) 1 E.H.R.R. 737. The text is most often applied in considering the restrictions of rights under Arts 8–11 but also applies to Art.6, as here, and Arts 5, 12 and Art.1 of the First Protocol.

———————

Key Principle: **S.2 of the Human Rights Act**
Interpretation of Convention rights:

1) A court or tribunal determining a question which has arisen in connection with a Convention right must take into account any—

   a) judgment, decision, declaration or advisory opinion of the European Court of Human Rights;
   b) opinion of the Commission given in a report adopted under Art.31 of the Convention;
   c) decision of the Commission in connection with Art.26 or 27(2) of the Convention; or
   d) decision of the Committee of Ministers taken under Art.46 of the Convention

   whenever made or given, so far as, in the opinion of the court or tribunal, it is relevant to the proceedings in which that question has arisen.

2) Evidence of any judgment, decision, declaration or opinion of which account may have to be taken under this section is to be given in proceedings before any court or tribunal in such a manner as may be provided by the rules.

3) In this section "rules" means rules of court or, in the case of proceedings before a tribunal, rules made for the purposes of this section—

   a) by the Lord Chancellor or the Secretary of State, in relation to any proceedings outside Scotland;
   b) by the Secretary of State, in relation to proceedings in Scotland; or
   c) by a Northern Ireland department, in relation to proceedings before a tribunal in Northern Ireland—

      i) which deals with transferred matters; and

      ii) for which no rules made under paragraph (a) are in force.

———————

Key Principle: **The Strasbourg jurisprudence must be taken into account but not necessarily followed.**

Boyd v The Army Prosecuting Authority
Three noncommissioned officers who had been convicted of offences by a district court martial contended that their rights under Art.6(1) had been violated since the court martial did not constitute an independent and impartial tribunal. They argued *Morris v United Kingdom* [2002] 34 E.H.R.R. 221 should be followed. There the Strasbourg court had held that there were insufficient safeguards in place to exclude the risk of outside pressure being brought to bear on the junior officers who sat on the applicant's court martial.

Held: (HL) The decision in *Morris* is not binding but should be taken into account. The Strasbourg court was given less information than the House of Lords relating to the officers serving on the courts martial. The safeguards in place meant that Art.6 was not violated.

Commentary
In this case the House of Lords was clearly signalling its independence from Strasbourg. This independence was also illustrated in the House of Lords' attitude to *Osman v United Kingdom*. In *Barrett v Enfield LBC* [1999] 3 W.L.R. 79 Lord Browne-Wilkinson criticised *Osman* arguing that the ECHR had misunderstood the relevant case law.

Key Principle: **The Strasbourg jurisprudence may invoke proportionality as a new ground of judicial review.**

R. (Daly) v Secretary of State for the Home Department
The applicant, a prisoner, had stored in his cell correspondence with his solicitor. He was, like all prisoners in a closed prison, subject to standard cell searching without his being present. The applicant sought leave for judicial review of the decision to require examination of prisoners' legally privileged correspondence in his absence.

Held: (HL) A person sentenced to imprisonment retained the right to communicate confidentially with a legal adviser under the seal of legal professional privilege. The current policy amounted to an interference with the applicant's rights under Art.8(1) to a greater extent than was necessary for the prevention of disorder and crime. The courts should adopt a test of proportionality in reviewing executive decisions. [2001] 2 A.C. 532.

Commentary

The Strasbourg Court in *Smith and Grady v United Kingdom* (1999) 29 E.H.R.R. 493 stated that the threshold at which the Court of Appeal could find the MoD policy irrational was "placed so high that it effectively excluded any consideration by the domestic courts of the question of whether the interference with the applicants' rights answered a pressing social need or was proportionate to the national security and public order aims pursued, principles which lie at the heart of the Court's analysis of complaints under Art.8 of the Convention". This test was applied in *Daly*, signalling in effect that proportionality is a new ground of review. Lord Steyn denied that this meant a shift to review on merits. The House of Lords declared in this case that it was following *Campbell v United Kingdom* (1992) 15 E.H.R.R. 137 as well as a number of English authorities including *R. v Secretary of State for the Home Department Ex p. Leech* [1994] Q.B. 198. See Ch.10 for further examples of the impact of the Human Rights Act on judicial review. The effect of ss.2 and 3 of the HRA will be that the Strasbourg method of judicial reasoning will have increasing impact in English courts. However, it should be noted that the duty is to take account of the Strasbourg case law, not necessarily to follow it. See also *R. (Association of British Civilian Internees: Far East Region) v Secretary of State for Defence* [2003] Q.B. 1397. The differing approaches of the UK and Strasbourg courts on the question of proportionality are illustrated by the decisions on prisoners' voting rights. In *R. (Pearson) v Secretary of State for the Home Department* (2001) *The Times*, 17 April, the Divisional Court held that Parliament had taken the view that convicted prisoners in custody had forfeited their right to have a say in the way the country was governed. The issue was decided differently in Strasbourg. The Grand Chamber upholding the decision of the court in *Hirst v United Kingdom* (No.2) October 2005 held that the blanket exclusion from voting imposed on convicted prisoners in detention was disproportionate. There was no evidence that the legislature in the UK had ever sought to weigh the competing interests or to assess the proportionality of the ban as it affects convicted prisoners. See also *R. (On the application of CD and AD) v Secretary of State for the Home Department* [2003] EWHC 155 (Admin).

Declarations of Incompatibility

Key Principle: **S.4 of the HRA. Declaration of incompatibility.**

(1) Subs.(2) applies in any proceedings in which a court determines whether a provision of primary legislation is compatible with a convention right.

(2) If the court is satisfied that the provision is incompatible with a convention right, it may make a declaration of that incompatibility.

(3) Subs.(4) applies in any proceedings in which a court determines whether a provision of subordinate legislation, made in the exercise of a power conferred by primary legislation, is compatible with a convention right.

(4) If the court is satisfied—

(a) that the provision is incompatible with a convention right, and

(b) that (disregarding any possibility of revocation) the primary legislation concerned prevents removal of the incompatibility, it may make a declaration of that incompatibility.

(5) In this section "court" means—

(a) the House of Lords;

(b) the Judicial Committee of the Privy Council;

(c) the Courts-Martial Appeal Court;

(d) in Scotland, the High Court of Justiciary sitting otherwise than as a trial court or the Court of Session;

(e) in England and Wales or Northern Island, the High Court or the Court of Appeal.

(6) A declaration under this section ("a declaration of incompatibility")—

(a) does not affect the validity, continuing operation or enforcement of the provision in respect of which it is given; and

(b) is not binding on the parties to the proceedings in which it is made.

Key Principle: **Declarations of incompatibility are an indication that consideration should be given by the executive to changing the law.**

R. (H) v Mental Health Tribunal North and East London Region (2001)

Section 73 of the Mental Health Act 1983 states that a restricted patient should be discharged if the tribunal is satisfied that certain conditions apply and it is not appropriate to continue with treatment. The conditions include that he is not suffering from mental illness and it is not necessary for him to receive treatment either for his benefit or for the safety of others. The question was on whom was the burden of proof that the conditions were satisfied. If the patient was not to be discharged unless the tribunal was satisfied as to the conditions this arguably would reverse the burden of proof and be a breach of Art.5 whereby a person could only be detained in accordance with the law.

Held: (CA) Section 73 of the 1983 Act was incompatible with the HRA. The Convention required that the discharge should be ordered unless the criteria were made out. S.73 did not provide this. [2001] 3 W.L.R. 42.

Commentary

In response to the decision, the Mental Health Act (Remedial) Order was made, changing the onus of proof in such cases. Those who had suffered under the former regime were granted the possibility of getting compensation. In *International Transport Roth GmbH v Secretary of State for the Home Department* [2002] 3 W.L.R. 344 the Court of Appeal considered the relationship between legal and political powers or what has been called "judicial deference". The majority decision was that the scheme adopted under Pt II of the Immigration and Asylum Act 1999, which imposed penalties on those responsible for bringing clandestine entrants to the United Kingdom, was incompatible with Art.6. It imposed strict liability on the carriers and also reversed the burden of proof. Laws L.J. in a minority decision set out guidelines for assessing where the boundaries should lie between the judiciary and the executive or what has been referred to as the scope of judicial deference. He stated that it was essential to determine whether the objective of the statute was the imposing of criminal sanctions or securing the state's borders. He said "the constitutional responsibility of the democratic powers particularly included the security of the State's borders, thus including immigration control, and that of the court particularly includes the doing of criminal justice". If the scheme of the 1999 Act is essentially to be treated as an administrative scheme for the betterment of immigration control, the courts should accord a much greater deference to parliament in deciding whether there is any violation of Convention rights than if it is to be regarded as a criminal statute. The concept of judicial deference to Parliament is related to that of margin of appreciation in the Strasbourg jurisprudence. As a result of the decision in *International Transport* new provisions were included in the Immigration, Asylum and Nationality Bill. Declarations of incompatibility have been made by the House of Lords on a number of occasions. In *Bellinger v Bellinger* [2003] 2 A.C. 467 the House of Lords held that a person born with one sex, even after undergoing reassignment surgery, could not lawfully marry as a person of the opposite sex within the meaning of s.11(c) of the Matrimonial Causes Act 1973. It followed that this section interfered with the claimant's right to respect for private life under Art.8 of the European Convention on Human Rights and with her right to marry under Art.12. A declaration of incompatibility was granted. Similarly, in *R. (Anderson) v Secretary of State for the Home Department* [2003] 1 A.C. 837 the House held that there was no way of reading s.29 of the Crime (Sentences) Act 1997 so as to make it convention-compatible and issued a declaration of incompatibility. Such cases illustrate an increasingly robust approach to issuing declarations in contrast to the interpretative approach in *R. v A*. On the other hand the House of Lords have on occasion overturned decisions by the lower courts where declarations have been issued, see for example *Wilson v First County Trust* [2003] 3 W.L.R. 568, *R. (Alconbury Developments Ltd) v Secretary of State for the Environment* [2001] 2 W.L.R. 1389, *Matthews v Ministry of Defence* [2003] UKHL 4 and *R. (Uttley) v Secretary of State for the Home Department* [2004] 1 W.L.R. 2278.

Key Principle: **Positive obligations on the state under unqualified rights are not absolute.**

R. (On the Application of Q) v Secretary of State for the Home Department

Six applicants challenged the decision of the Secretary of State for the Home Department to refuse support under s.85(1) of the Immigration and Asylum Act 1999 to asylum seekers who did not make a claim for asylum immediately on arrival in the United Kingdom. Section 55 of the Nationality, Immigration and Asylum Act 2002 required the Secretary of State to refuse support unless he was satisfied that the claim was made as soon as reasonably practicable after the claimant's arrival in the United Kingdom. The burden was on the applicant to satisfy the Secretary of State on that point. Under s.55(10) of the 2002 Act the refusal could not be challenged by appeal. The applicants claimed that there had been a failure to reach a lawful decision that the asylum claim was not made as soon as reasonably practicable and that there had been a breach of their rights under Arts 3, 6 and 8. Collins J. held that the Secretary of State did not follow a fair procedure and that Art.6 was breached. He also held that there was a "real risk" that an asylum seeker would be subjected to inhuman or degrading treatment under Art.3 of the ECHR. He allowed the applications for judicial review.

Held: (CA) There were procedural deficiencies in the process by which the Secretary of State for the Home Department decided to refuse claims for support for asylum seekers. However once these deficiencies in procedure had been remedied there was no reason why s.55 of the 2002 Act should not operate effectively. The fact that there was a "real risk" that an asylum seeker would be reduced to a state of degradation did not of itself engage Art.3 of the ECHR. [2004] QB 36.

Commentary

The court relied on *Pretty v United Kingdom* (2002) 35 E.H.R.R. 1 for the proposition that the burden of proving that support was necessary to avoid subjecting the applicant to inhuman or degrading treatment was on the asylum seeker and that the threshold was a high one. The judge was wrong therefore to hold that the fact that there was "a real risk" that an asylum seeker would be reduced to this state of degradation of itself engaged Art.3. It was not unlawful for the Secretary of State to decline to provide support unless and until it was clear that charitable support had not been provided and that the individual was incapable of fending for himself such that his condition verged on the degree of severity described in *Pretty v DPP* [2002] 1 A.C. Article 8 was capable of being engaged but added little to Art.3. In *Pretty* the court had also held that the positive obligations under Art.3 were not absolute.

Key Principle: **Human Rights Act 1998, s.5.**

"(1) Where a court is considering whether to make a declaration of incompatibility, the Crown is entitled to notice in accordance with rules of court.

(2) In any case to which subsection (1) applies—(a) a Minister of the Crown (or a person nominated by him), (b) a member of the Scottish Executive, (c) a Northern Ireland Minister, (d) a Northern Ireland department, is entitled, on giving notice in accordance with rules of court, to be joined as a party to the proceedings.

(3) Notice under subsection (2) may be given at any time during the proceedings.

(4) The person who has been made a party to criminal proceedings (other than in Scotland) as the result of a notice under subsection (2) may, with leave, appeal to the House of Lords against any declaration of incompatibility made in the proceedings.

(5) In subsection (4)—'criminal proceedings' includes all proceedings before the Courts-Martial Appeal Court; and 'leave' means leave granted by the Court making the declaration of incompatibility or by the House of Lords."

Key Principle: **The purpose of s.5 in conferring on a minister the right to be heard was to ensure that the relevant minister had the opportunity to participate in the hearing.**

R. v A (No.1)
For background facts see above.

There was no proposal by the parties that during the course of the appeal the House should be asked to consider making a declaration of incompatibility. Accordingly the circumstances had not arisen for applying the proceedings prescribed by Dirs 30.2 and 30.4 of the House of Lords practice directions and standing orders applicable to Criminal Appeals on the hearing of such an issue. The Home Secretary nevertheless petitioned for leave to intervene.

Held: (HL) Although as a general rule the effect on the fairness of a trial of the admission or exclusion of evidence was to be judged after its completion in the context of the proceedings as a whole, it was undesirable that the vulnerable witness, the complainant, should be exposed to the risk of having to give evidence again if the trial was found to be unfair. The issue of incompatibility was one of general public importance and it was in the best interests of all the parties that the issue should be determined in advance of the trial and without delay. The Secretary of State who had borne responsibility for the promotion of the 1999 Act should be joined as a party to the proceedings. [2001] 1 W.L.R. 789.

Commentary
The House considered that although the Crown was an appellant and represented by the Director, his role as prosecutor was different from that of a minister with executive responsibilities.

Key Principle: **Human Rights Act 1998, s.19.**

"Statements of compatibility

  1) A Minister of the Crown in charge of a Bill in either House of Parliament must, before a Second Reading of the Bill—

    a) make a statement to the effect that in his view the provisions of the Bill are compatible with the Convention rights ('a statement of compatibility'); or
    b) make a statement to the effect that although he is unable to make a statement of compatibility the government nevertheless wishes the House to proceed with the Bill.

  2) The statement must be in writing and be published in such manner as the Minister making it considers appropriate."

Key Principle: **Statements of compatibility are not binding on the courts.**

R. v A
For facts and holding see p.36.

Commentary
Statements of compatibility are, according to Lord Hope, no more than expressions of opinion by the minister. Counsel for the

Secretary of State did not rely on the statement in the course of argument. The court may make a declaration of incompatibility even where the minister in charge of the Bill has issued a statement of compatibility—see *R. (International Transport Roth GmbH) v Secretary of State for the Home Department* (2001) in relation to the Immigration and Asylum Act 1999.

Retrospectivity

Key Principle: **A defendant whose trial took place before the coming into force of the Human Rights Act 1998 was not entitled to rely in an appeal on an alleged breach of his Convention rights under s.22(4) of the HRA.**

R. v Lambert
For facts see p.38.

Held: (HL) Since the relevant provisions of the Human Rights Act 1998 were not in force at the date of the trial, the decision of the Court could not be challenged on the ground that it had acted in a manner contrary to the European Convention on Human Rights. The House should still however consider whether the transfer of the burden of proof under s.28 of the Misuse of Drugs Act 1971 was contrary to the Convention. [2001] 3 W.L.R. 206.

R. v Kansal (No.2)
At his trial in 1992 for obtaining property by deception, the prosecution adduced against the defendant answers he had given under compulsion when he was examined under oath in bankruptcy proceedings. The trial judge admitted the answers despite a defence submission that it was unfair to do so. His appeal was dismissed on the basis that the Insolvency Act 1986 had abrogated his privilege against self-incrimination and made his answers admissible in any proceedings. In 2000 he appealed to the Court of Appeal which quashed his conviction on the basis that the 1998 Act had made the right to a fair trial retrospective. The Crown appealed.

Held: (HL) The House was bound by the considered decision of a majority in *R. v Lambert* [2001] 3 W.L.R. 206, that appeals were excluded from the retrospectivity provisions of the 1998 Act. *Lambert* had been decided after the Court of Appeal decision in the appellant's case and the House would not depart from it without a compelling reason to do so. In tendering the disputed evidence, the prosecutor had been acting in accordance with primary legislation which could not at the time have been read differently in accordance with s.6 of the 1998 Act. Accordingly there had been no ground for the Court of Appeal to declare the conviction unsafe and the conviction would be reinstated. [2001] 3 W.L.R. 1562.

Commentary
The Court of Appeal in *Lambert* had commented that judicial authorities were divided as to the retrospective nature of s.22(4) of the HRA. This states that the right to rely on Convention rights in s.7(1)(5) of the Act "applies to proceedings brought by or at the instigation of a public authority whenever the act in question took place". In the House of Lords, the majority (Lord Steyn dissenting) held that an appeal brought by an unsuccessful defendant was not to be treated as proceedings brought by a public authority. (Despite this finding the Court did consider the substantive issue of the reverse onus of proof.) Lord Steyn considered that if there has been a breach of the Convention, whenever it occurred, it must be wrong to uphold the conviction, due to the requirements in s.6 of the HRA. The issue of retrospectivity under the Human Rights Act 1998 has thus been a matter of some controversy. It was considered in a number of cases, see *Wainwright v Home office* [2003] 3 W.L.R. 1137, *Aston Cantlow and Wilmcote with Billesley Parochial Church Council v Wallbank* [2004] 1 A.C. 546 and *Re McKerr* [2004] 1 W.L.R. 807, para.16. In the latter case, Lord Nicholls stated, "It is now settled, as a general proposition, that the [Human Rights Act 1998] is not retrospective. The Act itself treats s.22(4) as an exception."

Public Authorities

Key Principle: Human Rights Act 1998, s.6:

"Acts of public authorities

(1) It is unlawful for a public authority to act in a way which is incompatible with a Convention right.

(2) Subsection (1) does not apply to an act if—

(a) as the result of one or more provisions of primary legislation, the authority could not have acted differently; or

(b) in the case of one or more provisions of, or made under, primary legislation which cannot be read or given effect in a way which is compatible with the Convention rights, the authority was acting so as to give effect to or enforce those provisions.

(3) In this section 'public authority' includes—

(a) a court or tribunal, and

(b) any person certain of whose functions are functions of a public nature, but does not include either House of Parliament or a person exercising functions in connection with proceedings in Parliament.

(4) In subsection (3) 'Parliament' does not include the House of Lords in its judicial capacity.

(5) In relation to a particular act, a person is not a public authority by virtue only of subsection (3) (b) if the nature of the Act is private.

(6) 'An act' includes a failure to act but does not include a failure to—

(a) introduce in, or lay before, Parliament a proposal for legislation; or

(b) make any primary legislation or remedial order."

Key Principle: **The definition of a public authority under the HRA is not necessarily determined by the approach of the courts in identifying bodies and activities subject to judicial review.**

Donoghue v Poplar Housing and Regeneration Community Association Ltd

The appellant had been originally granted a tenancy by the local authority which later transferred it to Poplar Housing and Regeneration Community Association Ltd (Poplar). Poplar was a non-profit organisation created by the local authority to manage the housing stock. An order was made by the local authority for the possession of the appellant's property which was held under an assured shorthold tenancy according to s.21 of the Housing Act 1988. The authority had determined that the appellant was intentionally homeless. The appellant appealed against the order for possession on the grounds that Poplar, being a public authority in terms of s.6 of the HRA, was making a disproportionate interference under Art.8, the right to respect for private life. A subsidiary issue was the procedure to be followed when the Crown was notified that the court might be considering a declaration of incompatibility under s.4 of the HRA.

Held: (CA) Poplar was a public body but there was no breach of Art.8 in its application of s.21(4) of the Housing Act 1988. The transfer by the local authority to Poplar of their housing stock did not also transfer their public duties but only the means by which to enact them. Providing houses for rent was not, without more, a public duty. The court should defer to the will of Parliament which had given the courts limited intervention powers in the area of possession against people with low housing priority. (2001) U.K.H.R.R. 693 CA.

Commentary
The court gave extensive consideration to the factors which should be taken into account in deciding whether a body is a public authority under the HRA. Many of these were derived from the pre-existing administrative law jurisprudence but some controversial new issues were raised. In *Costello-Roberts v United Kingdom* (1993) 19 E.H.R.R. 112, the Strasbourg Court stated that "the state cannot absolve itself from responsibility by delegating its obligations to private bodies or individuals". Lord Woolf in *Donoghue* held however that the decision in that case meant that the Convention was not intended to make non-governmental bodies, acting in accordance with domestic law, directly liable for a breach. It could on the other hand be argued that *Costello-Roberts* implies that governments have responsibilities to ensure that Convention rights are observed in all areas of activity including those where its emanations such as local authorities devolve responsibility. The Court of Appeal in *Donoghue* expressed the view that a local authority in privatising some functions would not automatically make the actions of the private company public in nature. More controversially it stated that providing houses for rent was not in itself a public duty, no matter which section of society the houses were for. (See also the Court of Appeal decision in *St Brice v Southwark LBC, The Times*, August 6, 2001). In addition the fact that Poplar was a charity meant that the motivation of the organisation was more likely to be in the public good but that was not an indicator that it was a public body in terms of s.4 of the HRA. In the instant case however Poplar was functioning as a public authority. In *Heather v The Leonard Cheshire Foundation* [2002] All E.R. 936 the Administrative Court found that the charity was not to be amenable to judicial review despite the fact that many local authorities used it to provide care and support services for the disabled. It held that the HRA was not intended to make non-governmental bodies directly liable for breaches of the ECHR and that private bodies running services

under contractual relationships with local authorities were not likely by reason only of that relationship to be "public authorities" for the purposes of s.6 of the HRA. Lord Woolf observed that the residents had contractual rights against the charity and it would be open to a local authority and a provider to protect Art.8 rights through contract. In the light of increased reliance by local authorities on private contractors to carry out statutory duties it is arguable that this narrow decision means that individuals will have limited redress for breach of Convention rights. For some commentators the definition by the courts of a public authority under the HRA is too narrow. Others have pointed out however that there are advantages in excluding a body from the designation of "public authority" since as a result it has potential standing as a victim to make a claim under the Act in appropriate circumstances. The courts have also distinguished between pure public authorities and hybrid authorities. "Core" public bodies have special powers, democratic accountability, public funding, an obligation to act only in the public interest and establishment under statute. Other bodies, like the parochial church council in the leading case of *Aston Cantlow and Wilmcote with Billesley Parochial Church Council v Wallbank* [2003] UKHL 37 are classed as "hybrid" bodies. The House of Lords held that the requirement imposed on the owners of glebe land to pay for chancel repairs was a private right and its exercise did not contravene the owners' human rights. The test of whether a body was amenable to judicial review was not necessarily determinative for the purposes of the HRA.

Key Principle: **A limited company is susceptible to judicial review if it carries out acts of a public nature.**

R. (A) v Partnerships in Care Ltd

The applicant had a severe personality disorder and was detained under the Mental Health Act in a private psychiatric hospital registered as a mental nursing home. The managers changed her treatment. She sought judicial review of the change.

Held: (QBD) The decision of the managers was an act of a public nature. They were carrying out statutory duties and there was a public interest in the care and treatment of patients detained under the Mental Health Act 1983. The claim for judicial review should proceed to a hearing on the merits. [2002] 1 W.L.R. 2610.

Commentary

This case illustrates a different outcome in the application of the test than that in *Leonard Cheshire Foundation*. The test was that of the nature of the function not the source of the power. The application of the HRA depends on how readily the courts are to hold the actions of a private institution as public functions. Similarly in *R. v Hampshire Farmers Market Ex p. Beer* [2003] EWCA Civ 1056 the Court of Appeal held that a decision by a limited company to exclude a claimant from holding a stall at farmers' markets involved a public element making it amenable to judicial review. The company had taken over the functions of the local council in this regards. The Joint Committee on Human Rights has expressed concern about the approach of the courts in cases such as *Leonard Cheshire Foundation* since as a result "many oganisations that stand in the shoes of the State will not have responsibilities under the Human Rights Act". See also p.110.

Key Principle: **In judicial review proceedings witnesses may now be required to attend court and be available for cross-examination.**

R. (Wilkinson) v Broadmoor Special Hospital Authority

A secure patient at Broadmoor Special Hospital sought judicial review to quash decisions of his doctors to administer anti-psychotic medication. He also sought a declaration that the treatment was incompatible with his rights under the European Convention, because there was no avenue of appeal for him against the doctors' decisions. In interlocutory proceedings, the judge refused an application that the defendant doctors and the patient's own medical expert should attend the substantive hearing to be cross-examined on their witness statements.

Held: (CA) Where a decision to administer medical treatment to a mental patient without his consent under s.58(3)(b) of the 1983 Act was challenged by way of judicial review, the court was entitled to reach its own view as to whether the treatment infringed the patient's human rights. In such a case the patient was entitled to require the attendance of medical witnesses to give evidence and be cross-examined. [2001] EWCA Civ 1545; [2002] 1 W.L.R. 419.

Commentary

The case is of interest not because of the substantive law but because of the impact of the Human Rights Act on procedure. It was a claim for judicial review which is the most frequently used procedure under the HRA. The court seems to be minded that the claimant should have proceeded by originating summons. S.7 of the HRA does not state whether proceedings against public authorities should be in the administrative or ordinary courts. Here the applicant was seeking to invoke in judicial review proceedings a procedure that would have been open to him in a tort case, namely the right to cross-examine witnesses. The response of the court was to order the attendance of three doctors for cross-examination, not a judicial review practice. Note that in R. (Pretty) v DPP (see also p.46) the Divisional Court suggested that the applicant should have sought declaratory relief rather than seeking judicial review.

4. THE EXECUTIVE (1)

Royal Prerogative

The prerogative is a discretionary power exercisable by the government in certain spheres where Parliament has made no provision.

Key Principle: **The courts may determine the extent of prerogative powers.**

Burmah Oil v Lord Advocate

During the Japanese invasion of Burma the army command ordered that oil installations around Rangoon be destroyed so they could not be used by the enemy. It was not disputed that the destruction was lawful; it was assumed that it was carried out in the exercise of the royal prerogative, and it was admitted that the military situation at the time rendered the destruction expedient for the defence of His Majesty's other territories. The owners of the oil installations brought actions in Scotland claiming to be entitled to compensation from public funds to make good the damage sustained by them as result of the destruction. On appeal from an order sustaining pleas against relevancy, and dismissing the actions before trial, the Crown cross-appealed that the actions were incompetent and should be dismissed by virtue of the Public Authorities Protection Act 1893.

Held: (HL) There was a legal right to some compensation because if a subject was deprived of property through the exercise of the royal prerogative for the benefit of the state, he would generally be entitled to compensation at the public expense. Battle damages was an exception to the general rule, but the exception did not extend to destruction which was a part of a deliberate long-term strategy (such as economic warfare) and would not have been done in any event for battle operations. The Public Authorities Protection Act 1893 did not invalidate the claim. [1965] A.C. 75.

Commentary

This case is an example of the use of the prerogative as an emergency power when inevitably in the face of unpredictable conditions its precise extent cannot always be stated in advance. Lord Reid said "the prerogative certainly covers doing all those things in an emergency which are necessary for the conduct of war". However, since the practice in modern years was to pass emergency statutory powers, there were difficulties in applying the prerogative to modern conditions and "the prerogative is really a relic of a past age, not lost by disuse but only available for a case not covered by statute".

In the event the War Damage Act 1965 retrospectively provided that no person should be entitled to receive compensation for acts of the Crown in destroying property during or in contemplation of war. Thus the judgment was effectively overruled by statute.

Key Principle: **Where power was conferred on the Crown by statue, the Crown would have to take action under those powers not under equivalent pre-existing prerogative powers.**

Attorney-General v de Keyser's Royal Hotel Ltd

During the First World War the Crown took possession of a hotel to be used as a Royal Flying Corps' headquarters. The owners gave up possession under protest and asked the court by a petition of right for a declaration that they were entitled to rent for the use and occupation of the premises, or to compensation.

Held: (HL) The Crown was not entitled as of right, either under the prerogative or by statute, to take possession of a subject's land or buildings for administrative purposes in connection with the defence of the realm without paying compensation for their use and occupation. The hotel owner was not entitled to rent as there was no consensus on which to found a contract. [1920] A.C. 508.

Commentary

Per Lord Sumner in this case ". . . if there is adequate power to do all that is required under the statute, where is the emergency and public necessity which is the foundation for resort to the prerogative?" However, a somewhat different approach was taken in *R. v Secretary of State for the Home Department Ex p. Northumbria Police Authority* (p.162) where the prerogative power to keep the peace supplemented powers available under the Police Act 1964.

Laker Airways Ltd v Department of Trade

In 1972 the applicant company was granted a 10-year licence to operate an air service between London and New York. The start of the service was delayed by the need to obtain an American permit to run the service. This was done by designating the company as a carrier on that route and asking for a presidential permit. In February 1975 the state-owned airline applied unsuccessfully for the designation to be revoked. In July 1975 the Secretary of State for Trade announced a change of policy: only one United Kingdom airline would be allowed to operate on any long-haul route and accordingly the applicant's designation was withdrawn and the service would not be allowed to start. As a result the United States authorities withdrew its recommendation before the president had signed the permit. The applicant sought a declaration that the Department of Trade was not entitled to cancel the scheme. The judge granted the declaration and the Department appealed.

Held: (CA) The Secretary of State was entitled to reverse the previous policy and could have done so by legislation. However, he had exceeded his authority by introducing the new policy as "guidance" since such guidance should be consistent with the general objectives laid down in the relevant statute. [1977] 1 Q.B. 643.

Commentary

Here the court for the first time went some way to acknowledging that the exercise as opposed to the extent of the prerogative might be reviewable. It held that even where a statute does not entirely cover a prerogative power that residual power must be exercised in a way that expresses the will of Parliament and the purpose of the statute (see also *R. v Secretary of State for the Home Department Ex p. Fire Brigades Union*, p.64). Lord Denning was prepared to see an even more robust role for the courts and argued that a prerogative should not be used "unreasonably or" mistakenly whether a statute covered it or not.

Key Principle: **Inferior courts and tribunals created under the royal prerogative are subject to judicial review.**

R. v Criminal Injuries Compensation Board Ex p. Lain

The widow of a police officer who had been shot dead on duty applied for compensation from the board. The single board member who reviewed her case initially awarded her £300. She appealed, and three members of the board then decided that she was not entitled to any payment, because she had already received money from the police fund. She sought judicial review of the decision. The board claimed that it was effectively dispensing the bounty of the Crown and thus was not amenable to judicial review.

Held: (DC) The board was a body of persons of a public, rather than a domestic, character. It had power to determine matters affecting subjects and a duty to act judicially. The fact that it was constituted under the prerogative and not by statute did not bar the court's jurisdiction. However, the board had not erred in off-setting the payments from the police fund against the applicant's entitlement. [1967] 2 Q.B. 864.

Commentary
The reasoning in this case was applied in the landmark *GCHQ* decision (*Council of Civil Service Unions v Minister for the Civil Service*, p.61) which more clearly articulated the power of the courts to review the manner of the exercise as well as the existence of certain prerogative powers.

––––––––––

Key Principle: **Some actions under the prerogative in matters of defence may be judicially reviewable.**

R. (On the application of Bancoult) v Secretary of State for the Foreign and Commonwealth Office
The inhabitants of the British Indian Ocean Territory (BIOT) were forcibly removed from their homeland by the British government in the early 1970s to make way for an American military base. The inhabitants, known as the Ilois, were deported to Mauritius. Their removal was ordered by the islands' Commissioner purportedly exercising powers conferred by an Order in Council made in 1965 authorising him to "make laws for the peace, order and good government of the territory". The islanders challenged the legality of their removal on the grounds that (i) the ordinance affronted their rights and liberties under Magna Carta; (ii) the ordinance was made for an improper purpose under the terms of the Order in Council; (iii) that since the territory was a settled colony, the only legislative

powers of the Commissioner were those of a delegate. The government responded that (i) the appropriate venue for the hearing of the islanders' application was the Supreme Court of the British Indian Ocean Territory, from which appeals would go to the Privy Council; (ii) Magna Carta did not apply to colonies; (iii) the Commissioner in introducing legislation was entitled to give the widest interpretation to the terms of the Order in Council.

Held: (HL) Allowing the application, an order of certiorari, like any other prerogative writ, could reach every land in the Crown's dominion, and the existence of local courts did not oust the High Court's jurisdiction. Magna Carta was no more than the first statement of the rule of law and in that respect it followed the English flag. The power to legislate for BIOT derived from the Royal Prerogative. Discretionary public power had to be exercised in accordance with *Wednesbury* principles. The words "peace, order and good government" referred to the Ilois, who were to be governed, not removed. There was no principled basis on which s.4 of the ordinance could be justified as having been empowered by the Order and it had no other conceivable source of lawful authority. [2001] 2 W.L.R. 1219.

Commentary
In *R. v Ministry of Defence Ex p. Smith* [1996] Q.B. 517 the court had held that the refusal to admit gay people into the armed forces was judicially reviewable.

In *R. v Secretary of State for Foreign and Commonwealth Affairs Ex p. Rees-Mogg* [1994] 2 W.L.R. 115 Lloyd L.J. dismissed the application for a declaration that by ratifying the Treaty on European Union the Government transferred certain prerogative powers without statutory authority. However he accepted obiter that the principle of non-justiciability of certain aspects of the prerogative was not absolute and that s.6 of the European Parliamentary Election Act 1978 could require a court to consider whether any treaty the Government proposed to ratify involved an increase in the powers of the European Parliament.

Key Principle: **The courts have power to determine whether a prerogative power exists. No new prerogative powers will be recognised.**

BBC v Johns

The BBC appealed against a tax assessment, claiming Crown immunity from taxation. It claimed to be exercising, within the sphere of government, functions required or created for the purposes of government.

Held: (CA) The Crown had never claimed broadcasting as part of the sphere of government. The BBC was independent and free from government control. The court would not create a new prerogative power. [1965] Ch. 32.

Commentary

Diplock L.J.: "It is 350 years and a Civil War too late for the Queen's courts to broaden the prerogative." However since prerogative powers are so wide it is difficult for the courts to determine if and how ancient powers apply under new circumstances (see *R. v Home Secretary Ex p. Northumbria Police Authority*, p.162).

Key Principle: **The courts may review the manner in which certain prerogatives are exercised.**

Council for Civil Service Unions v Minister for the Civil Service (GCHQ case)

Mrs Thatcher as Minister for the Civil Service issued an order in council withdrawing from employees at the Government Communications Headquarters (GCHQ) the right to belong to a trade union. There had been no prior consultation with the unions or the employees. The Civil Service unions and six employees sought judicial review on the ground that the minister was under a duty to act fairly by consulting those affected. The single judge granted a declaration that the order was invalid. The Court of Appeal found for the Minister and the applicants appealed.

Held: (HL) Merely because the Minister was exercising a prerogative power she was not immune from judicial review or freed from the duty to act fairly. Apart from considerations of national security, the applicants would have had a legitimate expectation of being consulted and the procedure adopted would have been unfair. However, it was for the executive to decide whether the requirements of national security out-weighed fairness. The Government had shown that the decision was based on considerations of national security which did outweigh fairness. [1985] 1 A.C. 374.

Commentary

The House attempted to set out guidelines for determining which powers of the prerogative were non-justiciable. In the view of Lords Fraser and Brightman, delegated powers emanating from prerogative power were not necessarily immune, since the scope of such delegated powers would either expressly or impliedly be defined for example by reference to their object or the procedure by which they were to be exercised, with the result that such powers were subject to judicial control. In the view of Lords Scarman, Diplock and Roskill, the controlling factor in determining whether the exercise of the power was the justiciability of its subject-matter rather than whether its source was the prerogative. Lord Roskill concluded that the following prerogatives would not be justiciable: the making of treaties, the defence of the realm, the grant of honours, the prerogative of mercy, the dissolution of Parliament and the appointment of ministers. This list is itself however subject to change since the courts are increasingly called upon to review public powers whatever the source of their authority. Thus the justiciable prerogatives were essentially legal in character, involving either a legal right or legitimate expectation. Subsequently the European Commission of Human Rights decided that the ban on trade union membership was justifiable under the national security exception to Art.11 of the Convention. See *Council of Civil Service Unions v United Kingdom* [1988] 10 E.H.R.R. 269.

Key Principle: **The exercise of the prerogative of mercy is reviewable.**

R. v Secretary of State for the Home Department Ex p. Bentley

The sister of a man hanged for murder in 1953 sought judicial review of the Home Secretary's decision to refuse him a posthumous pardon. In the course of argument it emerged that the substance of her case was that the Home Secretary had failed to recognise the fact that the prerogative of mercy was capable of being exercised in many different ways.

Held: (DC) Such a failure to recognise the scope of the prerogative was reviewable. The court's powers could not be ousted simply by invoking the word "prerogative". The question was simply whether the nature and subject-matter of the decision was amenable to the judicial process. The prerogative was a flexible power which was now a safeguard against mistakes. The grant of a conditional pardon would be an acknowledgment by the State that a mistake had been made. The court would invite the Home Secretary to look again at the case. [1994] Q.B. 349.

Commentary

It now appears that the fairness of sentencing that falls under the exercise of the powers of remission of sentencing under the prerogative may be reviewed.

In *R. v Secretary of State for the Home Department Ex p. Quinn* [2001] A.C.D. 258 a long-term prisoner had put out fires during a riot in the prison and had calmed prisoners locked in their cells. A jury acquitted him of involvement in the riot. His solicitors urged the Prison Service to reward this meritorious conduct. But the Prison Service said the applicant's conduct was not such as to merit reward by way of early release. The applicant sought to quash the decision on the grounds that it was unreasonable to say the applicant's conduct had not been sufficiently meritorious, it was wrong in principle to take account of conflicting reports of the applicant's involvement, given his acquittal, and that his subsequent behaviour was irrelevant. The Administrative Court held that courts would be slow to interfere because applicants in such cases were seeking concessions and the policy conferred no substantive rights. The applicant had no legitimate expectation of reward, which was entirely discretionary. The applicant was not entitled to have his meritorious conduct looked at in isolation from his other conduct. The Secretary of State was not obliged to make rewards where he took the view that an applicant's general conduct made this inappropriate.

Key Principle: **The prerogative power of the issuing of passports is reviewable.**

R. v Secretary of State for Foreign and Commonwealth Affairs Ex p. Everett

A British citizen living in Spain applied to the embassy for a new passport. He was told no passport would be issued, though

the applicant could have a travel document to return to
England. He was told that a warrant had been issued in
England for his arrest and in these circumstances the Government would not issue a new passport. It was only after he had
begun judicial review proceedings against the Secretary of State
that the applicant was given details of the warrant which had
been issued. The judge held that the Secretary of State should
have inquired whether there was any reason why the policy
should not be applied in the applicant's case, and made an order
of certiorari to quash the refusal of passport. The Secretary of
State appealed.

Held: (CA) A decision whether or not to issue a passport was
an administrative decision which affected the individual's rights
and was unlikely to have foreign policy implications. It was thus
reviewable, even though taken under the royal prerogative, so
the court had jurisdiction. However, the Secretary of State was
entitled to refuse to issue a passport where there was an
outstanding warrant. The Secretary of State should have told the
applicant the details of the warrant and informed him that he
would consider any representation as to circumstances which
might justify making an exception to the usual rule. (1989) 1
Q.B. 811.

Key Principle: **The prerogative must not be exercised in a
way which defeats the will of Parliament.**

R. v Secretary of State for the Home Department Ex p. Fire Brigades Union

In 1964 the Crown under the prerogative introduced a Criminal
Injuries Compensation Scheme. The Criminal Justice Act 1988
enacted the scheme, and provided that the Act would come into
force on a day appointed by the Home Secretary. No appointment was made and the non-statutory scheme continued. In
1993 the Home Secretary announced the replacement of the
existing scheme by a non-statutory tariff scheme. The union
challenged the new scheme and sought declarations that the
minister had acted unlawfully by failing to introduce the
statutory scheme and that the tariff scheme was an abuse of his
prerogative powers. The Court of Appeal refused the first
direction but granted the second. The Secretary of State
appealed and the union cross-appealed.

Held: (HL) The Home Secretary was bound to consider whether to exercise his discretion under the 1988 Act to introduce the statutory scheme. The tariff scheme was inconsistent with the statutory scheme, and in introducing it the Home Secretary had acted unlawfully. But he had no legally enforceable duty to introduce the statutory scheme. [1995] 2 A.C. 513.

Commentary

The decision in this case underlines the continuing legislative role of Parliament. The prerogative should not be used to bring in a scheme other than one which conforms to the scheme originally envisaged. The argument of the dissenting minority was that Parliament could always change the scheme in future since the Minister had not put an end to it. This was not accepted since the Minister was contravening the will of Parliament at the time, albeit such contravention could later be reversed by statute.

Key Principle: **The court in reviewing a measure taken under the prerogative may question the Crown's claim that national security precludes entertaining the action.**

R. v Secretary of State for the Home Department Ex p. Ruddock

A member of the Campaign for Nuclear Disarmament learned that his telephone had been tapped under a warrant from the Home Secretary. He sought judicial review of the Home Secretary's decision to sign the warrant on the basis that the phone had been tapped for party political purposes and the tapping had not followed published criteria. He claimed to have a legitimate expectation that the published criteria would be followed. The Secretary of State declined to confirm or deny the existence of any warrant. He contended the court should decline jurisdiction on grounds of national security and that the doctrine of legitimate expectation did not apply since the applicant was not supposed to know his phone was being tapped.

Held: (DC) The duty of the court was to examine the evidence and consider whether the application was properly brought. Jurisdiction would not be declined just because the minister said national security was involved. The fact that the applicant was not supposed to know of the tapping made it more important that the minister should follow the criteria he had promised to apply. But there was no evidence that the information had been used for party political purposes and so the application failed. [1987] 1 W.L.R. 1482.

Commentary
Although the action failed it did confirm the principle established in *GCHQ* that the courts were entitled to scrutinise actions by the executive that failed to maintain legitimate expectations. The court went further than the decision in *GCHQ* in refusing to accept that its jurisdiction could be totally ousted because of dangers to national security.

Key principle: **The justiciability of a prerogative power depends on subject matter and suitability in each case.**

R. (Abbasi) v Secretary of State for Foreign and Commonwealth Affairs
A British national captured by the US Army in Afghanistan was transported to the Guantanamo naval base in Cuba and held there as an enemy combatant without access to a court, or even to a lawyer. He sought judicial review to compel the Secretary of State to make representations to the US authorities on his behalf, or to account for his failure to do so. The basis of the judicial review claim was that his detention violated his right not to be arbitrarily detained. The Divisional Court dismissed his claim and the claimant appealed.

Held: (CA) Notwithstanding the principle that an English court would not sit in judgment on the sovereign acts of a foreign state, it was objectionable that the claimant should be held in a legal black hole in a territory over which the US had exclusive control with no opportunity to challenge the legitimacy of his detention before a court or tribunal. However, no direct remedy was available to the claimant, since the US government was not before the court and would not be bound by any order it might make. The UK government had no means to compel his being brought before a court. The state had no duty to intervene to protect a citizen who was suffering injury in a foreign state. But it was within the discretion of the Secretary of State to decide whether to do so. If that discretion was exercised in a way that was irrational or contrary to legitimate expectation it might be judicially reviewable. But on the facts in the instant case all that could be required was that the Secretary of State give due consideration to a request for assistance. [2002] EWCA Civ 1598.

Commentary
The case illustrates the importance of the distinction the Court of Appeal drew in *Everett* between administrative and foreign policy decisions. The Court of Appeal observed here that foreign policy was one of the "forbidden areas".

5. THE EXECUTIVE (2)

Ministerial Responsibility

Key Principle: **It is for Parliament, in accordance with the convention of ministerial responsibility, and not the courts to require the Home Secretary to explain an administrative decision.**

Liversidge v Anderson
The plaintiff was detained under reg.18b of the Defence (General) Regulations 1939. The measure allowed administrative detention where the Secretary of State had reasonable cause to believe a person to have hostile associations. The claimant sought to compel the Secretary of State to reveal the reasons for his detention and took the matter on appeal to the House of Lords.

Held: (HL) The court could not inquire whether in fact the Secretary of State had reasonable grounds for the necessary belief. The production by the Secretary of State of an order of detention, made by him and apparently regular and duly authenticated, was a defence to the action unless the claimant succeeded in showing the order itself to be invalid. [1942] A.C. 206.

Commentary
In this case the decision was influenced by the existence of the convention. Of course in many later cases discretionary powers of ministers have been challenged successfully in court and this case marks what is generally accepted as a low point of judicial activism in the face of administrative decision-making.

Law Officers

Key Principle: **The Attorney-General alone has absolute discretion in deciding whether consent should be given to a relator action to restrain unlawful action by a public authority.**

Gouriet v Union of Post Office Workers
The executive of the Union of Post Office Workers voted in January 1977 to call for a boycott of mail to South Africa as part

of an international protest against apartheid. The claimant sought the Attorney-General's consent to act as claimant in relator proceedings for an injunction to restrain the union from taking the proposed action. The Attorney-General refused to authorise the claimant to do so, and the claimant issued a writ in his own name seeking an injunction, which was refused by the judge. On appeal he was granted an interim injunction and leave to join the Attorney-General as a defendant. He amended his pleadings at the resumed hearing to claim a permanent injunction against the union and declaration that the Attorney-General had wrongfully refused his assent. The Attorney-General sought to have the pleadings struck out on the grounds that his discretion to refuse his assent was absolute. The Court of Appeal by a majority held that it had no power to review the Attorney-General's decision, that the claimant was not entitled to a permanent injunction but could claim declarations. All parties appealed to the House of Lords.

Held: (HL) Only the Attorney-General could sue on behalf of the public to prevent public wrongs: a private individual could not do so on behalf of the public. The courts had jurisdiction to declare public rights but only at the suit of the Attorney-General. There was no power to grant an interim injunction to the plaintiff, since he had no right to sue. [1978] A.C. 435.

Commentary
It is the task of the Attorney-General to protect the public interest and as such he has power to take action against public bodies to prevent actions threatening a class of citizens. This case settled conclusively that the Attorney-General does not have to justify his decisions whether or not to assert public rights in a civil action known as a relator action. Such an action is "at the relation" of an individual who lacks standing himself. The Attorney-General's decisions in this area may not be reviewed by the courts. The ruling the *Gouriet v Attorney-General* covers all civil proceedings brought for a declaration or an injunction in respect of civil rights.

The Courts and Executive Bodies

Key Principle: **A non-governmental body which exercises public functions may be susceptible to judicial review.**

R. v Panel on Takeovers and Mergers Ex p. Datafin 1987
(For facts see p.110.)

Held: (CA) Because of its public element, the panel was amenable to judicial review although it had no statutory or prerogative basis. But there were no grounds for review. [1987] Q.B. 815.

Commentary

The great increase in the numbers of non-statutory bodies which carry out public functions has presented difficulties of legal accountability. Here the courts have shown a willingness to extend the scope of public law thus recognising that those with executive power over citizens' lives may be found outside the government, the civil service and local government.

Key Principle: **Central government and bodies which are emanations of the state for the purpose of the direct applicability of Community directives include bodies which provide a public service.**

Foster v British Gas

Female workers for British Gas, a nationalised corporation, were required to retire at 60, though their male counterparts could continue to work to 65. They complained that this offended against the EC Equal Treatment Directive, even though the relevant section of the Sex Discrimination Act 1975 did not prohibit discrimination in retirement provision. The industrial tribunal ruled that the Directive could not be relied on directly by the applicants as the corporation was not a state body. The House of Lords referred to the European Court of Justice the question of whether the corporation was a body against which the Directive was directly enforceable.

Held: (ECJ) The Directive might be relied on in a claim for damages against a body, whatever its legal form, which provided a public service under the state and as a result had special powers beyond those of normal individuals. [1991] 1 Q.B. 405.

Commentary

The jurisprudence of the European Court of Justice has an increasing impact on the approach of the courts to executive actions. With the extent of privatised bodies and the proliferation of quangos it is significant that the European Court of Justice has adopted such a wide definition of a state body.

Local Authorities

Key Principle: **Local authorities owe a fiduciary duty to their ratepayers.**

Bromley LBC v Greater London Council

The Greater London Council voted to implement the "fares fair" policy, levying a supplementary rate to subsidise public transport by reducing fares. Bromley LBC was refused judicial review of the Greater London Council decision, but the decision was reversed in the Court of Appeal. The Greater London Council appealed.

Held: (HL) The Greater London Council owed a fiduciary duty to ratepayers to have regard to their interests and were under a statutory obligation to apply business principles to the conduct of public transport and had acted ultra vires the relevant legislation and in breach of its fiduciary duty. [1983] 1 A.C. 768.

Commentary

The case establishes that before embarking on significant spending a local authority must consider the rights of interested parties.

Key Principle: **The courts will take action against corrupt practices in local authority finances.**

Porter v Magill

Westminster LBC, a Conservative-controlled local authority, adopted a policy of selling council houses and flats in marginal wards, in the expectation that home-owners would be more likely than tenants to vote Conservative. The opposition on the council alerted the district auditor and requested him to surcharge the members of the ruling group responsible for the policy under s.201 of the Local Government Finance Act 1982. The auditor found that the council's leader and others had adopted a policy with the predominant purpose of achieving electoral advantage for their party, knowing that was unlawful and had thereby caused the council to lose some £31 million. The amount was reduced on appeal to the Divisional Court, and the Court of Appeal, by a majority, held that since they had acted on what they believed to be legal advice the councillors were not guilty of wilful misconduct. The auditor appealed.

Held: (HL) The knowing or reckless use of a public power other than for the public purpose for which it had been conferred constituted wilful misconduct. The council could not lawfully sell its property to promote party electoral advantage. The facts as found by the auditor and the Divisional Court precluded the councillors' claim to have relied on legal advice. The proceedings were not punitive but compensatory and regulatory and were therefore civil rather than criminal. The art.6 requirement of an independent and impartial tribunal was satisfied by the right of appeal by way of a full rehearing in the Divisional Court. A fair-minded and informed observer would have concluded that the proceedings were fair. Appeal allowed. [2002] A.C. 357.

Commentary
The Anti Terrorism, Crime and Security Act 2001 contains stronger powers against corruption. The courts have a wide scope in ensuring what the National Audit office lists as the "economy, efficiency and effectiveness" of local authority financial practices. The terms are not clearly defined.

Key Principle: **Even broadly drafted powers of local authorities are not immune from review.**

Hazell v Hammersmith and Fulham LBC
A London borough council undertook a number of speculative transactions on the money markets with a view to making a profit. A capital market fund was set up without a decision of the members, who received no report on the transactions. In 1988 the council authorised the finance director to arrange transactions in the money market to take advantage of interest rate changes. The arrangement was questioned by the auditor and the council tried to extricate itself from the contracts it had bought. The council was advised it could undertake such activities as part of the management of its funds, but could not lawfully go into the money market business. Counsel advised

that the scale of the money market activities was too great to be lawful. The auditor applied under s.19 of the Local Government Finance Act 1982 for a declaration that the activities were unlawful and an order for rectification of the accounts. A number of banks involved in the transactions intervened in the proceedings to oppose the grant of a declaration and to defend their commercial interests. The Divisional Court of the Queen's Bench Division made the declaration and granted the order sought. The banks succeeded in part in the Court of Appeal which upheld the declaration and made no order for rectification. The auditors and the council appealed.

Held: (HL) The transactions were ultra vires and unlawful since they could not be said to be designed to facilitate the council's function of borrowing. The only underlying function to which the transactions were incidental related to previous transactions which were themselves ultra vires. The council could not rely on its charter as giving it the capacity to enter into contracts, since the charter had been granted in accordance with statute, and the council was confined to the powers conferred on it by statute. [1990] 2 W.L.R. 1038.

Commentary
The case has sparked controversy with some commentators arguing that the courts are not a suitable forum for the development of a managerial control over local authorities. The courts' intervention in local authority finance is in marked contrast to its approach to central government.

———

Key Principle: **A decision of a minister applying financial measures of a statute affecting local government finance would be subject to review only for bad faith, improper motive or manifest absurdity.**

R. v Secretary of State for the Environment Ex p. Hammersmith and Fulham LBC (see p.134)

Commentary
The courts are understandably reluctant to adjudicate in the sensitive political area of central and local government relations.

Public Interest Immunity

Key Principle: **The Crown's objection to the production of a document as evidence in legal proceedings will be allowed if it is against the public interest to produce it.**

Duncan v Cammell Laird

The submarine Thetis sank during trials and relatives of the dead sued the builders. They sought discovery of documents relating to contracts between the builders and the Admiralty and salvage reports on the submarine. The Government refused to allow discovery on the grounds that it would be against the public interest.

Held: (HL) The minister's certificate that the matter was one of national security was conclusive and could not be questioned in the courts. Public interest immunity could be claimed on both the basis of the contents of the documents and of their forming part of a class of documents which should not be disclosed. [1942] A.C. 624.

Commentary

Public interest immunity was formerly known (as in this case) as "Crown privilege". It has its origin in the Crown's original immunity from all proceedings by virtue of the royal prerogative. It followed from this that it could not be compelled to produce documents as evidence whether it was a party to the proceedings or not and whether the documents were in the Crown's possession or not. This case identified two types of claims: first, those based on the grounds that the contents of a particular document would injure the national interest, for example by endangering national security or by prejudicing good diplomatic relations; and secondly, the claim that the document is one of a class of documents which must be withheld to ensure the proper functioning of the public service. The House of Lords' judgment has been criticised because of its contention that the minister's certificate was conclusive and furthermore because the second ground on which privilege could be claimed was too wide.

Key Principle: **The court will decide as a matter of substantive law whether a claim for non-disclosure should be upheld in the public interest.**

Conway v Rimmer
A police officer was prosecuted for theft. The charge was
dismissed. However, he was dismissed from the police force
and brought an action for malicious prosecution against his
former superintendent. He sought discovery of relevant documents from the Home Office, which claimed immunity on the
basis of Crown privilege.

Held: (HL) It was for the courts, not the Crown, to decide
whether or not evidence should be withheld from a court of
law. The court had to weigh the public interest in not revealing
the contents of sensitive documents against the public interest in
a fair trial of the case. The court was entitled to inspect the
documents in private to determine whether they should or
should not be disclosed. [1968] A.C. 910.

Commentary
This landmark case indicates the transformation of the doctrine
from Crown privilege to public interest immunity since it emphasises that the court not the Crown has the final decision on
disclosure. The court further indicated that the power to examine
documents applied to contents and class claims. In *Rogers v Home
Secretary* [1973] A.C. 388, the House of Lords indicated their
objection to the use of the term Crown privilege. There Lord
Pearson said ". . . the expression Crown Privilege is not accurate,
though sometimes convenient. The Crown has no privilege in the
matter".

Key Principle: **The court's power to inspect documents for
which immunity is claimed also covers high level state policy
documents.**

Burmah Oil v Bank of England
The bank rescued the oil company from financial difficulties on
terms dictated by the Government, including the transfer to the
bank of the oil company's shares in British Petroleum. The oil
company challenged the transfer arrangement in court, seeking
a declaration that it was unconscionable and inequitable. It
sought discovery of the relevant documents held by the bank.
On Government instructions the bank resisted discovery of 62
documents. The Attorney-General intervened in the case and the

Chief Secretary to the Treasury certified that their production would be contrary to the public interest. Some of the documents related to the formulation of Government policy, others to commercial and financial information communicated in confidence. By mistake six of the documents were sent by the bank's solicitors to the oil company's solicitors and were read by them. The judge upheld the Crown's claim for privilege without having read any of the documents but gave leave to appeal. The Court of Appeal read the documents before giving judgment and dismissed the appeal. The claimants appealed to the House of Lords.

Held: (HL) Without inspection of the documents, it was impossible to decide whether the balance of the public interest lay for or against disclosure. On inspection it was apparent that none of them contained matter of such evidential value as to make their disclosure necessary for the fair disposal of the case. They were relevant but their significance was not such as to override the objections to their being disclosed. [1980] A.C. 1090.

Commentary
The significance of this case is that unlike *Conway v Rimmer* (see p.75) the documents involved were generated at high ministerial level. Furthermore, the House of Lords also showed its reluctance to acknowledge the legitimacy of class immunity. Finally, the argument that policy-making documents should be kept secret from the court because there was a need for candour in civil servants' advice given to ministers was largely dismissed. Lord Keith said: "The notion that any competent or conscientious public servant would be inhibited at all in the candour of his writings by consideration of the off-chance that they might have to be produced in a litigation is in my opinion grotesque."

***

Key Principle: **There has to be a reasonable probability not just a speculation that documents would help the claimant or damage a defendant before the court will scrutinise a claim for immunity.**

Air Canada v Secretary of State for Trade (No.2)
The British Airports Authority at the direction of the Secretary of State imposed substantial rises in landing charges at

Heathrow airport. The plaintiff airlines claimed the Secretary of State had acted ultra vires because the imposition of increases to reduce public sector borrowing was not a purpose authorised by the Airports Authority Act 1975. The Secretary of State refused discovery of communications between government ministers and ministerial briefs, having certified that it would be contrary to the public interest to produce them. The claimants claimed the documents were essential for the fair disposal of the case and invited the court to inspect them to verify that this was so. The judge ordered the documents be produced for his inspection, and the Secretary of State appealed successfully to the Court of Appeal. The claimants appealed to the House of Lords.

Held: (HL) It was for the party seeking discovery to demonstrate that the information was likely to help his own case or damage that of his opponent. This applied both at the stage of private inspection by the judge and at the stage of ordering production to the other party. On the facts, the claimants had not made out their case for the documents to be inspected. Cabinet minutes were entitled to a high degree of protection against disclosure but were not automatically immune from disclosure. [1983] 2 A.C. 394.

Commentary
Although this case does not deny the power of the courts to override claims by the executive to privilege, it does put more obstacles in the way of a litigant in his task of asking the court to order discovery. He cannot embark on a "fishing expedition".

Key Principle: **Discovery will be ordered when the rights of the litigant outweigh the possibility that a government ministry will face ill-judged or unfair comment.**

Williams v Home Office
A prisoner was placed in a so-called control unit which involved 90 days of solitary confinement followed by 90 days of limited association with other prisoners. The Prison Rules allowed the Home Secretary to authorise the removal of a prisoner from association with other prisoners for one month and thereafter from month to month. The prisoner sued the Home Office for

false imprisonment on the basis that by instituting a predetermined policy of 180 days' detention the Home Secretary had fettered his duty to review the situation before renewing the authority for his detention each month. The Home Office objected to certain documents being disclosed and claimed public interest immunity for 23 days which it claimed concerned the formulation of government policy. The Home Secretary claimed that the Home Office policy was irrelevant to the issue before the court and so discovery of the documents was unnecessary.

Held: (QB) The Home Office could not claim public interest immunity on the ground that the candour of ministers and officials might otherwise be inhibited. The action extended to issues of fact, including whether the manner by which the monthly extensions were ordered was unreasonable. The liberty of the subject was at stake. The court inspected the documents and having done so ordered that six of them be produced. [1981] 1 All E.R. 1151.

Commentary
This case is a further undermining of the candour argument. There was however an implied undertaking that the documents would not be used for any other purpose than an action against the Home Office illustrating that public interest immunity is a matter of evidence concerned with discovery of documents for litigation not freedom of information generally.

Key Principle: **Sources that need to be protected include those involving authorised bodies as well as government departments.**

D v National Society for the Prevention of Cruelty to Children
The NSPCC was informed that the respondent's baby daughter had been ill-treated and an inspector was sent to the family home. The information proved to be untrue, but the false accusation affected the respondent's health and she sought from the NSPCC the name of the informant with a view to suing the informant. She issued a writ against NSPCC claiming damages for failure to exercise reasonable care in its investigation and asked for discovery of her case file. The NSPCC resisted

discovery but it was ordered by the Master. The judge reversed the Master's decision but it was reinstated by the Court of Appeal, on the grounds that only central government had the power to refuse discovery on the ground of public interest. The NSPCC appealed to the House of Lords.

Held: (HL) The public interest required that persons who gave information about child abuse should remain anonymous, otherwise the information would dry up. The fact that the NSPCC was not under a legal duty to bring proceedings could not affect the degree of protection from discovery afforded to the NSPCC's informants. [1978] A.C. 171.

Commentary
Here by analogy with the law on police informants, the public interest required confidentiality to those who gave information to the Society which was recognised under the Children and Young Persons Act [1969]. Confidentiality is not in itself a sufficient ground for non-disclosure but is a factor which the court can take into account in determining the balance of competing public interests.

See also *Alfred Crompton v Customs and Excise* (No.2) [1974] A.C. 405.

Science Research Council v Nassé
In the course of proceedings before an industrial tribunal for alleged discrimination, a complainant sought discovery of her own performance assessments and those of two colleagues she said had been selected for promotion in preference to her. The industrial tribunal ordered discovery in this and a similar case and in both cases the employer appealed. They argued that the disclosure of the performance assessments would breach confidence, damage industrial relations and impair the efficiency of promotion procedures.

Held: (HL) It was a matter of discretion for the tribunal whether to order discovery of confidential reports or other documents relating to an employee. The tribunal should not order discovery unless it is necessary either for disposing fairly of the proceedings or for saving costs, and when exercising that discretion, in relation to confidential documents, it should have regard to the fact that the documents were confidential and the extent to which third party interests would be affected. The tribunal need not order discovery if the information could be obtained from other sources. If it was necessary for fairly disposing of the proceedings discovery must be ordered despite the confidential nature of the material. The tribunal should inspect the documents and consider whether they could be edited to exclude confidential but irrelevant parts. [1979] 3 All E.R. 673.

Key Principle: Documents arising from police complaints proceedings do not fit into a class covered by public interest immunity.

R. v Chief Constable of West Midlands Police Ex p. Wiley

The applicant was arrested and charged with robbery and shotgun offences. At his trial the prosecution offered no evidence and he complained against the police and brought an action against the chief constable. He declined to make a statement to the police under the complaints procedure without an undertaking that the information would not be used in the civil action. The chief constable declined to give the undertaking and he obtained a declaration that the chief constable had acted unlawfully in declining the undertaking. The chief constable appealed.

The second applicant was arrested following a street fight during which he had struck a plain clothes police officer. He claimed he was seriously assaulted at the police station and made a complaint. Both applicants refused to make any statements under the police complaints procedure without an undertaking that the information would not be used in a civil action. The chief constable declined to give the undertaking. Popplewell J. held that the public interest immunity attached to police complaints procedure as a class so as to prevent their disclosure and the use of information therefrom in civil proceedings. He granted the declarations sought and in the second case an injunction. The Court of Appeal dismissed the chief constable's appeals.

Held: (HL) The appeals were allowed. There was no clear justification for imposing a general class public interest immunity on all documents generated by an investigation into a complaint against the police. [1995] 1 A.C. 274.

Commentary

Earlier authorities were overruled. The decision left open the possibility of a contents claim based on the particular contents of specific documents and furthermore that a class claim might be upheld for a sub-class of documents (see *Taylor v Anderton* below). The decision was generally welcomed as underlining that the case for a class claim must be clearly set out and will not readily be accepted by the court.

Key Principle: **A class claim to non-disclosure may attach to reports of police officers investigating complaints.**

Taylor v Anderton

The plaintiff was acquitted of offences of dishonesty related to business dealings. He began proceedings against the chief constable for malicious prosecution, misfeasance in public office and conspiracy. During the proceedings he applied for production of reports prepared by investigating officers during investigations into police conduct which had taken place after his acquittal. The chief constable asserted a class claim to public interest immunity.

Held: (CA) Investigating officers should feel free to report on professional colleagues or members of the public without apprehension that their opinions might be disclosed. Public interest immunity attached to their reports. However, it was for the judge to determine whether their production was so essential to a fair disposition of the matter that the immunity should be overridden. [1995] 1 W.L.R. 447.

Key Principle: **The balancing test of public interests also applies in claims for non-disclosure in criminal proceedings.**

R. v Governor of Brixton Prison Ex p. Osman

The applicant was facing extradition to Hong Kong on charges of conspiracy, fraud and theft. Three applications for habeas corpus failed. In the course of the third application, correspondence between the Magistrates' Court and the Home Office and between the latter and the Hong Kong Government was disclosed to the parties, though not read in open court. In his fourth application for habeas corpus the applicant relied on nine items in the correspondence and sought discovery of other documents. The Secretary of State claimed public interest immunity in the documents.

Held: (DC) The extradition proceedings were criminal in nature and public interest immunity could be claimed in criminal as well as civil proceedings. That immunity had to be balanced against the weighty interest of justice. None of the nine documents disclosed any matter which required that the privilege be set aside, and since there had only been limited dissemination of the documents they should not be disclosed. The applicant was also estopped from relying on the documents as they had been found irrelevant in the previous proceedings. [1991] 1 W.L.R. 281.

Commentary
There is a dearth of direct authority for claims of non-disclosure in criminal proceedings which is scarcely surprising since as Mann L.J. stated here "Where the interests of justice arise in a criminal case touching and concerning liberty, or conceivably on occasion life, the weight to be attached to the interests of justice is plainly very great indeed". The collapse in November 1992 of the *Matrix Churchill* trial, a criminal case concerned with the export of prohibited goods to Iraq, followed the refusal of the trial judge to accept ministers' public interest immunity certificates in a criminal prosecution. This led to the setting up of the Scott Inquiry whose report (HC (1995–1996) 115) doubted whether class claims could be made in criminal cases. The government subsequently indicated that it would no longer make class claims in criminal proceedings. Courts will remain arbiters of any contents claim. In *R. v Ward* [1993] 1 W.L.R. 619 the Court of Appeal confirmed that public interest immunity applied in criminal cases. (Disclosure more generally was put on a statutory basis by the Criminal Procedure and Investigations Act 1996 (as amended).)

Key Principle: **Failure by the prosecution to disclose documents to the defence under the doctrine of public interest immunity may impair the fairness of the criminal proceedings.**

Rowe and Davis v United Kingdom (2000)
The appellants had been convicted of murder. They contended that their convictions were obtained in violation of Art.6 since

they were based on unreliable evidence from witnesses who had vindictive motives for giving evidence, were police informers or had obtained rewards. The trial judge had accepted a prosecution request not to disclose documents to the defence and had not reviewed the documents; the Court of Appeal had reviewed them and refused disclosure.

Held: (ECtHR) The applicants had been denied a fair trial and the Court of Appeal had not been able to remedy the defect of the non-inspection of the documents by the trial judge. The trial judge was best placed to decide whether non-disclosure of public interest immunity evidence would be unfairly prejudicial to the defence. A fundamental principle of a fair trial in the adversarial system was that there was equality of arms. There might be occasions when documents were not made available to the defence but this had to be "strictly necessary". (2000) 30 E.H.R.R. 1.

Commentary
The Court referred approvingly to *R. v Ward* [1993] 1 W.L.R. 619 in its judgment. The convictions of the appellants were overturned by the Court of Appeal, which held that a conviction may be unsafe even where there was no doubt about guilt but the trial process had been "vitiated by serious unfairness or significant legal misdirection" (see *R. v Rowe and Davis, The Times*, July 17, 2000). By contrast to the ruling in *Rowe v United Kingdom*, in *Jasper v United Kingdom* and *Fitt v United Kingdom* (2000) there was no violation of Art.6(1) since the defence were notified of the ex parte hearing and were allowed to present their case to the judge. The court observed in the latter cases that disclosure of relevant evidence is not an absolute right and that competing interests of national security, protecting witnesses and preserving the secrecy of police investigative methods have to be balanced against those of the accused. These considerations affect the operation of the doctrine of public interest immunity. However, a more general issue is the disclosure of prosecution evidence to the defence. It is arguable that the regime under the Criminal Procedure and Investigations Act 1996, whereby secondary disclosure is postponed until after a defence statement, may not be compatible with the Convention. This case is commonly known as the *M25 Case*. For another example of the same principle see *Atlan v United Kingdom* (Application No.36533/97) June 19, 2001.

Crown Immunity

Key Principle: The immunity of the Crown in tort is a matter
of substantive not procedural law and does not amount to a
violation of Art.6.

Matthews v Ministry of Defence
The claimant, a former serviceman, brought proceedings on the
basis that he had suffered injury as a result of exposure to
asbestos during his service in the Royal Navy. The Secretary of
State in response signed a certificate under s.10 of the Crown
Proceedings Act 1947 stating that his injury would be treated as
attributable to service for the purposes of entitlement to a
pensions award. The effect of the certificate was that the Crown
was not liable to the claimant in tort. The judge held this to be a
procedural bar incompatible with the claimant's rights under
Art.6(1) of the European Convention. The Court of Appeal held
that the bar was substantial, not procedural so that Art.6 did not
apply. The claimant appealed on the nature of the bar.

Held: (HL) Section 10 in effect substituted a system of no-fault
compensation for a claim for damages. This was substantive, not
merely procedural. It was not incompatible with Art.6(1) for the
state to substitute a no-fault compensation system for injuries
which would otherwise lead to claims in tort. [2003] 2 W.L.R.
435.

Commentary
The approach of the Strasbourg court to immunities from suit has
provoked some controversy. In *Osman v United Kingdom* the
Strasbourg Court had held that the immunity of the police from
suits in negligence violated Art.6 but it subsequently retreated
from this approach. In *Z v United Kingdom* [2001] E.C.H.R.
29392/95 it held that such immunities were matters of substantive
law on which it was not appropriate for the ECtHR to pronounce.
(See also p.41 for the reaction of the House of Lords to the *Osman*
judgment.)

6. PARLIAMENT

Key Principle: **The election of MPs is governed by statute.**

R. v Boundary Commission for England Ex p. Foot
The Boundary Commission were on the point of delivering a report under the House of Commons (Redistribution of Seats) Acts 1949–1979. Leading members of the Labour Party, and three local authorities, sought judicial review of the Commission's proposals for revised parliamentary boundaries. The grounds of review in the first application were that the commission had failed to give effect to the principle of equal representation for electors embodied in the requirement that "the electorate of any constituency shall be as near the electoral quota as possible" contained in one of the rules scheduled to the 1949 Act. In the local authorities' application it was claimed that the Commission had wrongly decided that they were bound to recommend 13 constituencies in Tyne and Wear. The Divisional Court dismissed both applications and the applicants appealed.

Held: (CA) Dismissing the first appeal, that the High Court had power to review the carrying out by the Commission of instructions given to them by Parliament. The 1949 rules had been reduced by an Act of 1958 to the status of guidelines. The work of the Commission necessarily involved subjective views so that there was a heavy burden on anyone seeking judicial review of their decisions. The Court might have made a declaration, but relief by way of an order of prohibition was not appropriate. In the second case, the assistant commissioner had in his report recorded the proposal from the local authorities that there should be 14 constituencies. He had recommended against the proposal and his report had been accepted by the Commission so there was no ground for judicial review. [1983] 1 Q.B. 600.

Commentary
The Boundary Commission was set up by an Act of Parliament with power to make recommendations for changes in boundaries of parliamentary constituencies. The requirement of proportionality in respect of size was a guideline which could not be enforced against the Commissioners. The fact that their recommendations might benefit one political party more than another was not sufficient grounds to review the recommendations.

Key Principle: **The franchise is not dependent on property. Residence for the purposes of the electoral laws means factually resident at the appropriate time.**

Fox v Stirk and Bristol Electoral Registration Officer; Ricketts v Cambridge City Electoral Registration Officer
Two students, one at Bristol and the other at Cambridge University, appealed to the local county courts against a decision of the registration officer that since they were not "resident" in the respective constituencies on October 10, 1969 they could not be included on the electoral register there. Both students had arrived for the start of term before October 10 and were living in university accommodation. In both cases the county court upheld the officers' decisions.

Held: (CA) The students were not only factually resident in the particular constituency on the qualifying date, they were also resident for the purposes of the Representation of the People Act 1948 because they had a sufficient degree of permanence in their residence. A person might be resident in more than one place and could register in those places to vote although he could only vote once at a general election. [1970] 2 Q.B. 463.

Hipperson v Newbury District Electoral Registration Officer
Seven women who were camped outside a military airfield in protest against nuclear weapons were included in the electoral register for the local constituency. At the time the women, who had lived in the camp for up to two years, were facing eviction proceedings brought by the Department of Transport and the local authority. An objection was lodged to their registration and upheld by the registration officer on the basis that the unlawfulness of their residence disqualified them from inclusion on the register. The county court upheld an appeal by the women and the objector appealed.

Held: (CA) The franchise was not based on considerations of the standard of accommodation of the would-be voter. All the women had been on the site for a considerable period and it was immaterial that they might be required to leave shortly after registration. The issue as to whether a person was resident in a particular place was a question of fact to be determined by the tribunal of fact. There were no grounds for the court to interfere. The appeal would be rejected. [1985] Q.B. 1060.

Key Principle: **Limits on spending under electoral law apply to individual constituencies. Organisations and parties can spend freely on national campaigns without infringing the law.**

R. v Tronoh Mines Ltd

During the 1951 general election campaign, a company placed advertisements which condemned Labour Party policy, with particular reference to controls on company dividends. The advertisement said Labour should be rejected in favour of "a new and strong government with ministers who may be relied upon to encourage business enterprise and initiative". The company was charged with unlawfully incurring expenses with a view to promoting the election of a parliamentary candidate in the constituency where the company had its offices and the newspaper was published.

Held: (CCC) Section 63 of the Representation of the People Act 1948, under which the company was charged, was designed to outlaw spending on adjustments supporting a particular candidate in a particular constituency. The advertisement was aimed at supporting the interests of a party in all constituencies and there was no case to answer. [1952] 1 All E.R. 697.

Commentary

The decision illustrates the different approaches to spending at constituency and national level. For a more recent case on a similar point see *Walker v Unison* [1995] S.L.T. 1226. It is argued that this favours the wealthier political parties.

Key Principle: **Freedom of speech by a political party at an election was not to be interfered with save on the most pressing grounds.**

R. (Prolife Alliance) v British Broadcasting Corporation

A registered political party was opposed to abortion. It was entitled to one party political broadcast in Wales. The broadcasting authorities refused to transmit the video it submitted which contained images of aborted foetuses. The authorities argued that the video offended against taste and decency and would breach the broadcasters' obligations under s.6(1) of the Broadcasting Act 1990 or under the agreement between the BBC and the Secretary of State. The Court of Appeal granted permission to seek judicial review and treated the hearing as a substantive appeal.

Held: (CA) Freedom of expression was a constitutional right and the court had an overarching responsibility to protect freedom of speech. It was only in very rare circumstances that a party election broadcast, which was otherwise truthful and unsensational, might properly be rejected by broadcasters on the grounds of taste, decency or public interest. A broadcast that consisted of a video graphically depicting the abortion process should not have been rejected. [2002] 3 W.L.R. 1080.

Commentary
The decision illustrates the effect of the Human Rights Act on judicial review. It is arguable that it would not have failed the test of irrationality. Laws L.J. commented that the United Kingdom was "long past the point" where a public authority's "bare demonstration of rationality or reasonableness would suffice". The Court of Appeal in effect has decided that there is a right to broadcast where one party is denied broadcasting access and others are not. In *X and Z v United Kingdom* (1971) 38 C.D. 86, the European Court of Human Rights held that Art.10 does not guarantee a right to broadcast in general terms.

Key Principle: **Members of Parliament (including members of the House of Lords) enjoy immunity from arrest for civil process.**

Stourton v Stourton
The wife of a peer of the realm brought proceedings against her husband, from whom she was separated, for the return of property belonging to her under the Married Women's Property Act 1882. The husband was ordered to return certain items of property and to complete a questionnaire from the wife. He failed to do so and she issued a writ of attachment. The peer claimed privilege against attachment.

Held: (Probate Division) Whether or not parliamentary privilege arose, and if it did what was its scope and effect, were issues to be determined by the court in accordance with the common law, not with parliamentary practice. The privilege from arrest of a Member of Parliament related only to civil process, that is to say, arrest to compel performance of a civil obligation. The wife was seeking to compel the husband to perform such an obligation, so he was protected by parliamentary privilege. [1963] P. 302.

Key Principle: **The courts will not review the internal proceedings of Parliament itself.**

Bradlaugh v Gossett
The plaintiff, Charles Bradlaugh, was elected MP for Northampton. On previous occasions he had refused to take the oath in the prescribed form. When he required the Speaker to call him to the table to take the oath, the Sergeant-at-Arms, in pursuit of a resolution of the House, prevented him from doing so. The plaintiff sought an injunction against the Sergeant-at-Arms.

Held: (QBD) The House of Commons was not subject to the control of the courts in relation to matters concerning its internal procedures. Thus, a court could not inquire into whether it was proper for the House to restrain a member from doing within the walls of the Commons something which by the general law he was entitled to do, namely to take the oath prescribed by the Parliamentary Oaths Act 1866. No action lay against the Sergeant-at-Arms for excluding a member in accordance with a resolution of the House. (1884) 12 Q.B.D. 271.

Commentary
In *A v United Kingdom* (ECtHR 17/12/2002) the European Court of Human Rights acknowledged the significance of parliamentary immunity. The applicant's MP, Michael Stern, denounced her by name in the course of a parliamentary debate on municipal housing policy, stating that her brother was in prison, giving her precise address and making extensive derogatory remarks about her conduct and that of her children. As a result she was denounced in the local press and received hate mail. She com-

plained that none of the allegations to which the MP referred had ever been substantiated or upheld by the authorities and that many of them came from neighbours motivated by racism and spite. She was unable to bring defamation proceedings against the MP, who was protected by absolute privilege. The media reports benefited from qualified privilege. The applicant complained that the MP's immunity violated her right of access to court under Art.6(1) and her right to privacy under Art.8. She also alleged discrimination contrary to Art.14. The Strasbourg court held that Parliamentary immunity pursued legitimate aims of protecting free speech in parliament and maintaining the separation of powers between legislature and judiciary. It was not a disproportionate restriction on the right of access to court as embodied in Art.6(1). The immunity of UK MPs was in several respects less sweeping than the immunity of MPs in other Council of Europe jurisdictions. It was designed to protect the interests of parliament as a whole as opposed to that of individual MPs. Victims of defamatory mis-statements in parliament were not entirely without means of redress. Where their own MP had made the offending remarks they could petition the House through any other MP to seek a retraction. Deliberately misleading statements could be punished as a contempt of the House. The court expressed sympathy with A over the MP's regrettable remarks. But to create exceptions would seriously undermine the legitimate aims which the immunity was there to pursue.

Key Principle: The courts have the power to determine the limits of the privileges of the House of Commons but the Commons have exclusive jurisdiction within those limits.

Stockdale v Hansard

Inspectors of Prisons reported to the House of Commons that at Newgate prison they had found "a book of a most disgusting nature" with "plates . . . indecent and obscene in the extreme". The reference was to a textbook on the female reproductive system written by a medical practitioner whose publisher sued for libel. The inspectors claimed that the book was never considered a scientific work but was "intended to take young men in by inducing them to give an exorbitant price for an indecent work". The inspectors pleaded parliamentary privi-lege, relying on a resolution of the House of Commons.

Held: (QB) It was no defence that the libel was part of a document which was, by order of the House of Commons, laid before the House. The court would determine whether the House had the privileges claimed. (1839) 9 Ad. & E. 1.

Commentary
Parliament later passed an Act giving immunity from action for defamation to papers or reports certified to have been printed by the authority of either House or Parliament. As a result the action was stayed, the court refusing to look behind the Speaker's certificate that the inspectors' report was subject to the Act.

Key Principle: **Art.9 of the Bill of Rights 1688: Freedom of speech and debates or proceedings in Parliament ought not to be impeached or questioned in any court or place out of Parliament.**

Church of Scientology v Johnson-Smith
In an action for libel against an MP, the claimants sought to bring evidence, including the reading of extracts from *Hansard*, of what had taken place in Parliament. The defendant said such evidence would infringe the privileges of parliamentary privilege.

Held: (QB) Parliamentary privilege extended to the examination of proceedings in the House for the purpose of supporting a cause of action, even though the cause of action itself arose out of something done outside the House. [1972] 1 Q.B. 522.

Commentary
In the case of *Prebble v Television New Zealand Ltd* [1995] 1 A.C. 321 involving proceedings in the New Zealand Parliament, the Court stressed that parliamentary privilege belonged to Parliament not the individual MP. Therefore an individual member, including one who initiated court proceedings, could not waive the privilege. This aspect of parliamentary privilege was overruled by s.13 of the Defamation Act 1996. Subsequently Neil Hamilton waived his parliamentary privilege in order to sue Mohammed Al Fayed for libel.

Key Principle: **By virtue of s.13 of the Defamation Act 1996 an MP has power to waive his protection under parliamentary privilege.**

Hamilton v Al Fayed

The claimant, a former MP, had been accused by the defendant on television of taking money in return for questions in Parliament about the defendant's business. After an investigation by the Parliamentary Commissioner for Standards, the allegations were upheld by Parliament. However the claimant sued the defendant for libel on the basis that he had not been given a proper opportunity to clear his name. The defendant sought to have the proceedings struck out as an infringement of Art.9 of the Bill of Rights in that they questioned the validity of proceedings in Parliament. The application was dismissed at first instance and in the Court of Appeal. The defendant appealed.

Held: (HL) The claimant had validly waived his parliamentary privilege under s.13 of the Defamation Act 1996. Accordingly it was academic for the court to consider whether or not the rules of parliamentary privilege would have prevented the trial of the action. S.13 gave the individual MP bringing proceedings the power to waive the protection of parliamentary privilege. Once that had been done the admission of the evidence was not open to challenge as infringing the privileges of Parliament. [2001] A.C. 395.

Commentary

Answering a defence argument in his judgment, Lord Browne-Wilkinson stated that in operating the waiver Mr Hamilton had by virtue of the 1996 Act also overridden any privilege belonging to Parliament as a whole. The trial of the defamation action concluded that the defence of justification had been made.

Key Principle: **Courts may, in construing legislation, make reference to Hansard.**

Pepper v Hart

In an action by taxpayers against the Inland Revenue, it was sought to refer to *Hansard* to clarify the meaning of the relevant Act of Parliament.

Held: (HL) Subject to any question of parliamentary privilege, reference to statements by a Minister or other promoter of the Bill should be permitted as an aid to construction where an Act was ambiguous or obscure or led to absurdity. [1993] A.C. 593.

Commentary

In the case the Attorney-General, for the Government, had argued that consulting *Hansard* would infringe Art.9 of the Bill of Rights. This argument was rejected by the Court since any such reference would not amount to an impeachment or a questioning of the freedom of speech or debate in Parliament.

Courts exercise some discretion as to applying rules of construction of statutes. This is illustrated by *R. v Secretary of State for the Environment, Transport and the Regions Ex p. Spath Holme Ltd* [2001] 2 W.L.R. 15. The Rent Acts (Maximum Fair Rent) Order 1999, made under s.31 of the Landlord and Tenant Act 1985, imposed a ceiling on fair rent increases which could be registered under the Rent Act 1977 in relation to regulated tenancies. The owners of flats which were let on such tenancies sought judicial review to quash the Order, claiming s.31 had been enacted to counter general money inflation but was being used by the Secretary of State to achieve a different purpose, namely to alleviate hardship to tenants. The Court of Appeal, after considering evidence of what was said by ministers in parliament about the section, held that the Order had indeed been made ultra vires and was invalid. The Secretary of State appealed. The House of Lords held that this was not an appropriate case for considering what had been said about the section in parliament, since the statutory language was not ambiguous, obscure or such as would lead to absurdity and there was no clear and unequivocal ministerial statement to the effect for which the applicants contended and ministerial statements in Parliament were inadmissible to identify the scope of a discretionary power as distinct from the meaning of statutory language. The 1985 Act was primarily concerned with the relationship between landlord and tenant and the protection of tenants of dwelling houses from hardship caused by excessive or increased rents, and s.31 did give the executive a reserve discretionary power which had in this case been lawfully exercised.

Delegated Legislation

Key Principle: **Considerations of fairness are not applicable in the legislative process.**

Bates v Lord Hailsham of St Marylebone
A committee acting under the Solicitors Act 1957 produced a draft order dealing with solicitors' fees. A solicitors' association brought an action for an injunction because it had not been consulted about the fees changes.

Held: (Ch D) Considerations of natural justice did not apply to the legislative function. The Lord Chancellor was under no duty to consult those who would be affected. [1972] 1 W.L.R. 1373.

Commentary
Megarry J. held that the function of making the order was legislative rather than executive or administrative. He said "I do not know of any implied right to be consulted or make objections, or any principle on which the courts may enjoin the legislative process at the suit of those who contend that insufficient time for consultation and consideration has been given". This was a controversial decision and some commentators have argued that the making of the order was an administrative rather than a legislative act and that it could be said to be in accordance with good administration for the court to impose a duty to consult in making general rules.

———————

Key Principle: **A statutory instrument is complete from the moment that it is made and laid before Parliament.**

R. v Sheer Metalcraft
Sheer Metalcraft Ltd were charged with selling excess goods in contravention of a statutory instrument. They pleaded that the instrument was invalid because the provisions of the Statutory Instruments Act 1946 and regulations made under it for the printing of statutory instruments had not been complied with.

Held: (Streatfield J.) The statutory instrument was valid and effective as soon as made or where it is required to be laid before Parliament as soon as that is done, regardless of whether the Act has been complied with. [1954] 1 Q.B. 586.

Commentary
The question of whether publication of delegated legislation is necessary for it to be valid has been a subject of much debate. On

the facts here since the instrument had been brought to the attention of the defendant by means other than publication the court did not have to decide whether publication was necessary. A further complication is that the duty to publish may be directory or mandatory depending on the parent legislation.

Key Principle: **Delegated legislation may be struck down because its provisions infringe the parent Act or a constitutional principle.**

R. v Secretary of State for Social Security Ex p. Joint Council for the Welfare of Immigrants

Asylum seekers were entitled to claim urgent cases payments amounting to 90 per cent of income support, until their claims for asylum were determined. The Secretary of State issued new regulations excluding from that entitlement those who sought asylum otherwise than on arrival in the United Kingdom and those who were awaiting appeal against rejection of their asylum claims. An asylum seeker sought judicial review of the new regulations.

Held: (CA) Rights conferred by statute were not to be cut down by subordinate legislation made under the enabling powers of a different statute. The Regulations rendered nugatory rights conferred by statute on asylum seekers and hence were unlawful. [1997] 1 W.L.R. 275.

Commentary

This case illustrates the approach taken by the courts to human rights under the common law. Since the right to claim refugee status was such a basic human right there was no need to refer to the European Convention. Simon Brown L.J. made reference to *R. v Inhabitants of Eastbourne* (1803) where Ellenborough C.J. had said that in the absence of positive law the law of humanity made it necessary to provide relief to poor immigrants to prevent them from starving. See also *Pierson v Secretary of State for the Home Department* [1998] A.C. 539, where the House of Lords held that there is a presumption that a general statutory provision does not authorise administrative acts which undermine the basic rights of citizens unless Parliament makes clear its intentions to do so.

7. JUDICIAL REVIEW—PROCEDURE

Time Limits

Key Principle: **An application for judicial review shall be made promptly and in any event within three months from the date when grounds for the application first arose unless the court considers that there is a good reason for exceeding the period within which the application shall be made. Civil Procedure Rules, Pt 54.5. Supreme Court Act 1981, s.31(6):**

> "Where the High Court considers that there has been undue delay in making an application for judicial review, the court may refuse to grant: (a) leave for the making of the application; or (b) any relief sought on the application, if it considers that the granting of the relief sought would be likely to cause substantial hardship to, or substantially prejudice the rights of, any person or would be detrimental to good administration."

Key Principle: **The time limit referred to the leave stage; although an application had to be made promptly the court had discretion to grant leave. Undue delay could include situations within the three months.**

R. v Stratford-on-Avon DC Ex p. Jackson
Application for leave to seek judicial review was delayed for nine months. The delay was caused by securing legal aid and was not the applicant's fault.

Held: (CA) Time should be extended but the Court would still have discretion to consider the delay at the substantive hearing. [1985] 1 W.L.R. 1319.

R. v Secretary of State for Health Ex p. Furneaux
Doctors were granted outline consent to run a pharmacy but an appeal by local pharmacists was allowed. Six months later, the doctors sought judicial review on the grounds that the Minister had considered information of which they were unaware. The review was quashed on the intervention of a local company which had bought the only nearby pharmacy on the strength of the Minister's decision.

Held: If an applicant for judicial review failed to apply promptly he was guilty of undue delay even if there was a reason. The court then had a discretion to refuse judicial review on the ground of substantial prejudice to the rights of another, which need to have a causal connection with the delay. [1994] 2 All E.R. 652.

Commentary
Courts have stressed the need for speed in judicial review of public authorities. They should not be kept in suspense about the legal validity of their decisions, and there are practical considerations, including the effect of uncertainty on budget decisions. The rules lay down a three-month time limit for applications. In certain circumstances applications made within three months can be dismissed for delay. There is a discretion to extend the time limit. The courts are reluctant to dismiss an application on grounds of delay where a private citizen is defending himself against an unfounded claim by a public body (*Wandsworth LBC v Winder*, see p.104).

In *R. (Burkett) v Hammersmith and Fulham LBC* [2002] 1 W.L.R. 1593 the House of Lords said (obiter) that the obligation to apply "promptly" for judicial review might not be sufficiently certain to comply with Community law and with the ECHR. It held that where the same objection affected an initial resolution to grant planning permission as would affect the eventual grant of permission it was on the date of the latter that grounds for an application for judicial review first arose. Judicial review has been subject to reform in recent years. The procedure is now set out in the Civil Procedure Rules (CPR) replacing the old Ord.53 of the Rules of the Supreme Court.

Sufficient Interest

Key Principle: **Supreme Court Act 1981, s.31(3):**

"No application for judicial review shall be made unless the leave of the High Court has been obtained in accordance with rules of court; and the court shall not grant leave to make such an application unless it considers that the applicant has a sufficient interest in the matter to which the application relates."

Key Principle: **Except in cases where the applicant clearly lacked a sufficient interest, the court should not treat the issues on standing as a preliminary one to be dealt with only at the leave stage but should consider it along with the merits of the case.**

R. v Inland Revenue Commissioners Ex p. National Federation of Self-Employed and Small Businesses Ltd

The Federation sought a declaration that the Inland Revenue had acted unlawfully in making an arrangement with Fleet Street casual printworkers that it would not investigate arrears of unpaid tax provided the casuals registered in future. It maintained this was different from the way the revenue treated other self-employed and small business people.

Held: (HL) It was necessary in determining whether an applicant had sufficient interest to identify the matter to which the application related. Sufficient interest, except in cases where there was obviously none, should be treated as a possible reason for refusal of discretionary relief, rather than as a preliminary issue or a matter of jurisdiction. [1982] A.C. 617.

Commentary

This case marked a liberalisation of the approach of the courts to leave although it clearly demonstrated that even if the applicant is granted leave he can still be shown at the substantive hearing to have no standing. The court stressed that the law should not allow a reversion to technical restrictions on *locus standi* which had been current 30 years before.

Key Principle: **Where individuals did not have sufficient interest they could not obtain it by forming themselves into an association.**

R. v Secretary of State for the Environment Ex p. Rose Theatre Trust

Developers of a site in central London discovered the remains of an Elizabethan theatre. A trust company was set up with a view to preserving the remains for public exhibition. The Secretary of State declined to list the remains as a building of historic importance. The trust sought judicial review.

Held: (DC) The Secretary of State's decision was a government decision in respect of which members of the public had insufficient interest to bring review proceedings. A member of the public did not obtain a sufficient interest by applying to the Secretary of State and receiving a reply. The members of the trust had no standing as individuals and had created none by getting together. [1990] 1 Q.B. 504.

Commentary
The court here refused to acknowledge that a number of persons who oppose an administrative decision but who individually lack standing can create sufficient interest by becoming a pressure group.

Key Principle: **Pressure groups may have standing, each case being decided on its own merits.**

R. v HM Inspectorate of Pollution Ex p. Greenpeace (No.2)
The applicant sought judicial review of the inspectorate's decision to vary the licence of the Sellafield nuclear plant to expand reprocessing of nuclear waste.

Held: (DC) The applicant was a respected body with a genuine interest in the issues raised. It had 2,500 supporters in the area where the plant was situated, who might not otherwise have an effective access to the court. The applicant had been actively involved in the consultation process relating to expansion of the plant. Accordingly, the applicant had a "sufficient interest in the matter" to be allowed to seek judicial review. [1994] 4 All E.R. 329.

R. v Secretary of State for Foreign and Commonwealth Affairs Ex p. World Development Movement Ltd
The applicants sought judicial review of the Secretary of State's decision to grant finding under s.1(1) of the Overseas Development and Co-operation Act 1980 for a project to construct a power station on the Pergau river, Malaysia. The decision had been taken against the advice of the Overseas Development Administration which had concluded it was an abuse of the statutory aid programme. The Secretary of State argued among other things that the World Development Movement did not have a sufficient interest to bring the application.

Held: (DC) Since standing went to jurisdiction it should not be treated as a preliminary issue but was to be taken in the legal and factual context of the whole case. The merits of the challenge were important and the court should take account of the importance of vindicating the rule of law, the likely absence of other challengers and the nature of the breach which was complained of. On the evidence the project had no developmental promotion purpose within s.1(1) of the 1980 Act, and the Secretary of State's decision was unlawful. [1995] 1 W.L.R. 386.

Commentary
Here the court accepted that a political pressure group may have sufficient standing dependent on the circumstances. This case applied the dicta in The National Federation of Self-Employed Case (see p.98). It stressed also that the applicants were an established organisation with a prominent role and experience in the matters under review.

Key Principle: **An individual and a group set up by statute may both have standing.**

R. v Secretary of State for Employment Ex p. Equal Opportunities Commission
The Equal Opportunities Commission wrote to the Secretary of State pointing out that the exclusion of certain part-time employees from the protection against unfair dismissal provided by the Employment Protection (Consolidation) Act 1978 discriminated against women because considerably more women than men worked part-time. The EOC claimed this infringed the EEC Treaty and Directives. The Secretary of State claimed the legislation was justifiable. On the EOC's application for judicial review the Divisional Court held that both the EOC and a part-time worker who had failed to meet the Act's qualifying conditions had standing, but refused to order the Secretary of State to introduce legislation or to declare that the United Kingdom was in breach of relevant obligations under the EEC Treaty. Both applicants appealed.

Held: (HL) The part-time worker's claim for redundancy pay ought to have been brought against her employer before an industrial tribunal and not in the Divisional Court. The EOC had a sufficient interest in the proceedings to give it standing, since its duty under the Sex Discrimination Act 1975 was to work towards the elimination of discrimination. The Secretary of State had failed to show that the exclusion of part-time workers had resulted in a greater availability of part-time work, so had failed to justify the exclusion. It would be declared incompatible with the EEC Treaty and Directives. [1995] 1 A.C. 1.

Commentary

This case illustrates the stand the court will take in cases where both an individual and a group have an interest in a given decision. In cases where a group is set up by statute to uphold a certain interest the court may prefer the group. The court is not compelled to refuse leave where the "interest" of the applicant was also shared by the general public.

Public or Private Law

Key Principle: **As a general rule public law rights must be enforced by way of judicial review in the procedure provided for in CPR 54 (formerly Ord.53) against public authorities, rather than by way of writ or originating summons.**

O'Reilly v Mackman

Four prisoners were disciplined by the prison board of visitors for offences arising out of a riot. Three brought an action against the visitors by writ in the Queen's Bench Division and one by summons in the Chancery Division seeking a declaration and injunction. The defendants' applications to strike out the actions were dismissed at first instance but allowed by the Court of Appeal. The plaintiffs appealed to the House of Lords.

Held: (HL) The reform of Rules of the Supreme Court Ord.53 had removed unfair disadvantages to applicants for judicial review which had in the past made applications for prerogative orders an inadequate remedy. Ord.53 protected decision-making public bodies against groundless, unmeritorious or tardy harassment. It would be contrary to public policy and an abuse of the process of the court for a person seeking to establish that a decision of a public authority infringed his public law to proceed by way of ordinary action and thus evade those protections. Exceptions should be decided on a case-by-case basis. [1983] 2 A.C. 237.

Commentary

The House was concerned to provide safeguards against frivolous applications in public law matters and considered therefore that Ord.53 procedure would generally be the most appropriate method. One consideration was that there was a need for a consistent treatment of such cases and this was already being developed in the Divisional Court. The House did however accept that there might be occasions where Ord.53 procedure might not be appropriate. Such situations included cases where the public law matter was collateral to another application, cases where it was raised as a defence and finally the issue should be looked at on a case-by-case basis. Subsequent cases showed that there are exceptions to this general rule of exclusivity.

Key Principle: **Where a public body has public law decision-making functions, the determination of which was a necessary precedent to a private law right, the public law decision can only be challenged by proceedings brought under CPR 54 (formerly Ord.53). Private law actions should be brought by writ.**

Cocks v Thanet DC

A homeless person who had been given temporary accommodation by this local authority started proceedings against the authority in the country court claiming that they were in breach of their duty to house him permanently under the Housing (Homeless Persons) Act 1977. A High Court judge decided that the plaintiff was entitled to proceed with the claim in the county court rather than proceed by way of application for judicial review under RSC, Ord.53. The council appealed directly to the House of Lords.

Held: (HL) Where a person claimed that a public authority had infringed his public law rights it was as a general rule contrary to public policy and an abuse of process to allow him to proceed by way of ordinary action. That rule applied where a plaintiff was obliged to impugn a public authority's determination as a condition precedent to enforcing a statutory private law right. In this case the private law matter of the statutory duty to house a homeless person arose only after the authority had determined that the person was homeless. This was a public law matter and the general rule should apply. [1983] 2 A.C. 286.

Davy v Splethorne BC

The council served the claimant with an enforcement notice under the Town and Country Planning Act 1971. He did not appeal against the notice within the statutory time-limit and so was unable to challenge it. However, he claimed that the reason he had not appealed was the council's negligent advice, and he brought proceedings by writ for damages for negligence and for an injunction ordering the council not to implement the notice and an order setting it aside. The defendants' application to have the writ struck out was dismissed at first instance, but the Court of Appeal struck out the claims for injunction and setting aside of the enforcement notice on the ground that they raised public law questions and should be brought by way of judicial review under RSC, Ord.53. The defendants sought to have the rest of the claim struck out on the same grounds.

Held: (HL) The claimant's action for damages for negligence did not raise any issue of public law since he was not seeking to impugn a determination by a public body but bringing an ordinary action in tort in respect of which the procedure of RSC, Ord.53 would be entirely inappropriate. There was no abuse of process in bringing that part of the claim by way of ordinary action rather than under RSC, Ord.53. The order of the Court of Appeal would stand. [1984] 1 A.C. 262.

Commentary

These two cases show differing conclusions being drawn by the House of Lords. These resulted from the application of the test in *O'Reilly v Mackman*: could and should the action be brought by an application for judicial review? In *Cocks* the answer was yes; in *Davy*, no.

Key Principle: **The test to be applied in deciding justiciability is whether the procedure adopted had been an abuse of process.**

Clark v University of Lincolnshire and Humberside

Because a student submitted substandard coursework the university awarded a mark of 0 per cent which meant under the rules that she could not be awarded more than a third class degree. She brought proceedings in contract against the university, claiming that the mark was outside the limits of academic convention and the authorities had failed to take account of her explanation that her hard disc had crashed on the eve of the deadline. The university claimed that such breaches of contract were not justiciable and that proceedings ought to have been brought by way of judicial review in a timely manner.

Held: (CA) Before the advent of the civil procedure rules, the bringing of such cases in the ordinary civil courts was normally barred by the rule in *O'Reilly v Mackman* since they were regarded as a way of evading the protections provided to public authorities in judicial review proceedings. The CPR now allowed the court to give summary judgment on a civil claim, thus minimising the inconvenience caused by hopeless claims. The court would no longer strike out a civil claim just because it ought to have been brought by way of judicial review. But it could still strike out for abuse of process, for example where the case was not brought promptly, even though it was brought within the limitation period. [2000] 1 W.L.R. 1988.

Commentary
The case illustrates the significant impact of the advent of the Civil Procedure Rules. Lord Woolf M.R. stated, "the intention of the CPR is to harmonise procedures as far as possible and to avoid barren procedural disputes which generate satellite litigation." See also *Carter Commercial Developments v Bedford Borough Council* (2001) All E.R. (D) 388. The court also commented on the citation of appeal court decisions dismissing applications for leave to appeal, which were not to be regarded on the same footing as Court of Appeal decisions following full argument.

Key Principle: **A public law matter could be raised as a defence in a private claim without going through judicial review procedure.**

Wandsworth LBC v Winder
The tenant of a council flat, while continuing to pay his original rent, refused to pay rent increases which he considered excessive. The council brought proceedings in the county court to recover the arrears and for possession of the flat. The tenant claimed in his defence that he was not liable to pay the arrears

because the council's resolutions raising the rent were ultra vires and void and counter-claimed for a declaration to that effect. The council applied to strike out the defence and counter-claim as an abuse of process. The judge held it to be an abuse of process and contrary to public policy to challenge the conduct of a public authority other than by way of RSC, Ord.53 procedure. The Court of Appeal by a majority allowed the appeal. The council appealed.

Held: (HL) The private citizen's recourse to the courts for the determination of his rights was not to be excluded except by clear words. Nothing in the language of RSC, Ord.53 or the Supreme Court Act 1981 could be taken as abolishing a citizen's right to challenge the decision of a local authority in the course of defending an action. [1985] A.C. 461.

Commentary
The court observed that it would be a strange use of language to call the defendant's behaviour an abuse of the court process. He had not selected the procedure to be adopted and was merely seeking to defend the proceedings brought against him on the ground that was not liable for the whole sum claimed. He put forward his defence as a matter of right, whereas in an application for judicial review, success would require an exercise of the court's discretion in his favour.

Key Principle: **Public law defences may be raised in criminal proceedings and no distinction should be drawn between claims of substantive and procedural invalidity.**

Boddington v British Transport Police
A passenger was convicted of smoking on the railway contrary to a British Railways Board byelaw which prohibited smoking in the vicinity of a no smoking sign. He was convicted and appealed by way of case stated. He wished to argue that the railway company's decision to post no smoking notices in all its carriages was ultra vires, and that the notices were invalid since they had been posted by the railway company rather by the BR Board. The Divisional Court ruled that he was not entitled to advance either defence.

Held: (HL) It would be a fundamental departure from the rule of law if an individual were liable to conviction for contravention of some rule which is itself liable to be set aside by a court as unlawful. Subordinate legislation, or an administrative act, was sometimes said to be presumed lawful until it has been pronounced to be unlawful. But that did not make the legislation valid until quashed prospectively. The true effect of the presumption was that the legislation was presumed to be good until pronounced to be unlawful, but was then recognised as never having had any legal effect at all. On the facts the railway company's action was not unlawful and the conviction would stand. [1999] 2 A.C. 143.

Commentary
The decision shows the importance the court attached to the principle that a defendant to a criminal charge ought to be able to adduce all legally relevant defences. See also *R. v Searby* [2003] EWCA Crim 1910.

Key Principle: **Private law rights can be enforced by private law action even if they involve a challenge to a public body's decision.**

Roy v Kensington and Chelsea and Westminster Family Practitioner Committee
The Family Practitioner Committee withheld fees from a general practitioner on the basis that he had failed to devote a substantial amount of time to general practice as required under the relevant National Health Service regulations. The general practitioner brought an action in the Queen's Bench Division to recover the fees. On the Committee's application the judge struck out the action as an abuse of process, as the committee's decision was a matter of public law which could only be challenged by way of judicial review under RSC, Ord.53. The Court of Appeal, however, held that the general practitioner had a contract for services with the Committee so that his proper remedy was by way of ordinary action. The Committee appealed.

Held: (HL) A litigant possessed of a private law right could seek to enforce that right by ordinary action whether or not the proceedings would involve a challenge to a public law act or decision. The general practitioner's relationship to the committee conferred on him private law rights to fees and the bringing of an ordinary action to enforce that right did not constitute an abuse of process. [1992] 1 A.C. 624.

Commentary

The claimant would not be excluded from bringing the action even if there was no contract between him and the Committee. He could sue if he had any sort of private law right. Lord Lowry referred to two different applications of the principle in *O'Reilly v Mackman*: first, a broad approach under which Ord.53 would be required if private rights were not in issue, and secondly a narrow approach which required all applicants to proceed by Ord.53 in all proceedings in which public law matters are raised, apart from the exceptions already noted. Lord Lowry, favouring the broad approach, said "unless the procedure adopted by the moving party is ill suited to dispose of the question at issue, there is much to be said in favour of the proposition that a court having jurisdiction ought to let a case be heard rather than entertain a debate concerning the form of the proceedings". This case is significant both in recognising that a single claim could be a mixture of public and private law and for moving away from a rigid approach to procedure.

In a further refinement of *O'Reilly v Mackman*, in *Joanne Elizabeth Clark v University of Lincolnshire and Humberside* [2000] 3 W.L.R. 752, the Court of Appeal held that a court would not strike out a claim in contract by a student against a university which could more appropriately be made under RSC Ord.53 solely because of the procedure which had been adopted unless it found it to be an abuse of process. The case illustrates the significant effect of the advent of the Civil Procedure Rules. For the effect of the Human Rights Act on claims against public bodies see Ch.3.

Key Principle: **Disputes over dismissal involving public authorities are rarely suitable for judicial review.**

R. v East Berkshire Health Authority Ex p. Walsh

A senior nursing officer was dismissed for misconduct by a district nursing officer and sought judicial review. The grounds of review were that the district nursing officer had no power to dismiss him and that he had been denied natural justice. The judge ruled on a preliminary point raised by the health authority that judicial review was appropriate because of the public interest in seeing that a public service acted lawfully towards its employees. The judge also ruled that it would be appropriate to allow the proceedings to continue under RSC, Ord.53 as if they had been begun by writ. The health authority appealed.

Held: (CA) An applicant for judicial review had to show that a public law right which he enjoyed had been infringed. The employee of a public body whose terms were controlled by statute might have rights in public as well as private law, but an infringement of statutory provisions giving rise to public law rights had to be distinguished from a breach of the contract of employment. The applicant was seeking to enforce a private law right under his employment contract and his application was a misuse of the judicial review procedure. The only remedy he was seeking was certiorari which was not available in a civil action so the proceedings could not be allowed to continue as if they had been begun by writ. [1985] 1 Q.B. 152.

Commentary
The mere presence of a public interest does not make the matter concerned a matter of public law. Most disputes about dismissal are private law disputes between the employer and the employee, even where the employer is a public body. They mostly belong in the industrial tribunal, not the Divisional Court.

Key Principle: **Where the applicant does not have a contract of employment, judicial review may be an appropriate way to challenge a dismissal.**

R. v Secretary of State for the Home Department Ex p. Benwell
The Dartmoor branch of the Prison Officers' Association passed a motion of no confidence in the prison governor. The motion was reported in the press. The branch chairman was warned that if he spoke to the press about the governor he would be disciplined. He was ordered to attend a meeting with the regional director of the Prison Service but because of a dispute over the expenses of the journey he did not attend. A disciplinary inquiry recommended a severe reprimand, but the Home Department gave him notice of dismissal. He appealed first to a

single adjudicating officer and then to the Civil Service Appeal Board. At both appeals details of his disciplinary record, including the warning over press interviews, were brought before the tribunal, though they should have been excluded under the terms of the disciplinary code, and the applicant was not given a chance to put his claim that he had merely told the press the result of the branch meeting. He sought judicial review.

Held: (DC) As a prison officer the applicant held the office of constable and had no private law rights that could be enforced in civil proceedings. The court had jurisdiction over the application of the code of conduct which was made under statute and prison rules. The applicant had been denied natural justice and the dismissal would be quashed. [1985] 1 Q.B. 554.

Commentary
These cases illustrate that a number of difficulties remain in deciding when CPR 54 procedure is appropriate. There is a fear of opening the floodgates if public employees are allowed to pursue employment law matters by judicial review. However, the problem of deciding which cases are appropriate is seen for example in *Council of Civil Service Unions v Minister for the Civil Service* (see p.61) which on one interpretation could be said to be an employment law matter.

Key Principle: **A choice of procedure may be based partly on whether it would be suitable for the type of claim.**

Mercury Communications Ltd v Director-General of Telecommunications
In a dispute over the terms of their licence to run a telecommunications system, the plaintiffs issued an originating summons against the Director-General seeking a declaration of the true terms of the licence. The judge dismissed the Director-General's summons to have the action struck out as an abuse of process. The Court of Appeal allowed the Director-General's appeal. The claimants appealed.

Held: (HL) The overriding question was whether the proceedings were an abuse of the court. There could not be a rigid distinction between public and private law. The Director-

General was performing public duties, but the dispute was essentially over the terms of a contract, to which the originating summons procedure was appropriate. The appeal would be allowed. [1996] 1 W.L.R. 48.

Commentary
This case represents a further move, evidenced in *Roy v Kensington and Chelsea and Westminster Family Practitioner Committee*, away from a rigid approach to the public-private law divide towards a more pragmatic approach to procedure.

Nature of the body whose decisions are to be reviewed

Key Principle: **In considering whether the matter was a public law one the court must take into account not only the source of a body's powers and duties but also their nature.**

R. v Panel on Takeovers and Mergers Ex p. Datafin Plc
The panel was the City's self-regulating mechanism for dealing with takeovers and mergers. The applicants complained about the conduct of their competitors in a take-over bid. They were refused leave to seek judicial review of the panel's decision to reject their complaint and appealed.

Held: (CA) Although the panel purported to be part of a system of self-regulation and to derive its power solely from the consent of those whom its decisions affected, it was in fact operating as an integral part of a governmental framework for regulating the City. It was under a duty to act judicially and was open to judicial review. However, on the facts there were no grounds for interfering with its decision. [1987] 1 Q.B. 815.

Commentary
English law does not offer a clear definition of what is a public body so this case is an important illustration of what the courts mean when applying the criterion of exercising a public function. There are two aspects to the definition: first the Panel's decisions were clearly seen by the Government to be part of its regulation of the City; and secondly those affected had no choice but to submit to its jurisdiction. (See cases under HRA pp.50–55).

Key Principle: **Judicial review is not available against domestic tribunals whose authority derives from contract.**

Law v National Greyhound Racing Club Ltd

The claimant, a greyhound trainer, had his licence to practice suspended for six months by the club, the sport's regulatory body. He brought an action by originating summons for a declaration that the decision to suspend him was unreasonable and unfair and thus a breach of his contract with the club. The club applied to have the proceedings struck out on the basis that they should have been brought under RSC, Ord.53. The judge dismissed the application and the club appealed.

Held: (CA) The club's authority to suspend the trainer's licence was derived from his contract with the club. Although its decisions might affect the public, the club was a domestic tribunal whose decisions were not open to judicial review. The action had been brought in the proper forum and would not be struck out. [1983] 1 W.L.R. 1302.

Commentary

Some commentators have suggested that bodies which exercise monopolistic powers should be subject to judicial review because in such instances people have no choice but to submit to their juris-diction. It was held here however that, although the Jockey Club regulated racing, it was not part of a Government regulatory scheme. In a number of similar cases involving sporting bodies it has been held that judicial review is not appropriate where a body exercises consensual jurisdiction. See also *R. v Disciplinary Committee of the Jockey Club Ex p. Aga Khan* [1993] 1 W.L.R. 909 and *Andreou v Institute of Chartered Accountants in England and Wales* [1998] 1 All E.R. 14.

R. v Fernhill Manor School Ex p. A

A girl expelled from an independent school for alleged bullying had no opportunity to answer the allegations. She sought judicial review, claiming a breach of natural justice.

Held: (DC) The rules of natural justice had not been followed, but the case fell into the private sector in which public law remedies could not provide relief. Public law remedies were not available where the legal relationship was based on contract rather than the exercise of a power derived from statute. [1993] 1 F.L.R. 620.

Commentary
A public law element does not arise simply because the action complained of is taken by a public body. Thus a senior nursing officer was denied judicial review of his dismissal by a health authority because infringement of his contract of employment was a private law matter, even though the authority was a creature of statute (*R. v East Berkshire Health Authority Ex p. Walsh* [1985] Q.B. 152). But a prison officer dismissed contrary to natural justice for alleged breach of a statutory code of conduct was entitled to judicial review of the decision (*R. v Secretary of State for the Home Department Ex p. Benwell* [1985] Q.B. 554).

Key Principle: **Decisions of officers of a nature where legislation would not encroach were not suitable for review.**

R. v Chief Rabbi of the United Hebrew Congregations of Great Britain and the Commonwealth Ex p. Wachmann
The applicant sought judicial review of a decision by the Chief Rabbi declaring him unfit to act as an orthodox rabbi.

Held: (DC) For a decision of a non-governmental body to be subject to the court's supervisory jurisdiction there had potentially to be a governmental interest in the decision-making power, in that the body was exercising, as part of a self-regulatory system, control over an activity which might otherwise be subject to statutory regulation. Parliament would not seek to control the Chief Rabbi's regulatory responsibilities should he abdicate them, as they were essentially religious functions. [1992] 1 W.L.R. 1036.

Commentary
This marks an extension of the *Datafin* (see p.110) analysis in holding that for the decision of a body not established by statute or prerogative to a be a public law matter there had to be government, not merely a public interest in the matter. Here the Government would not exercise the functions of the Chief Rabbi if he failed to do so since these were spiritual.

Key Principle: **A person dissatisfied with a decision of an ombudsman set up by statute can apply for judicial review of that decision.**

R. v Parliamentary Commissioner for Administration Ex p. Balchin

Owners of property blighted by a road scheme sought judicial review of a decision by the parliamentary Ombudsman that there was not maladministration when the Secretary of State for transport confirmed orders for a by-pass without seeking an assurance from the county council that the applicants would be adequately compensated for the effect of the road on their home.

Held: (DC) The county council had refused to buy their property for fear that other applicants would want to be similarly treated, a textbook example of fettered discretion. However, the Ombudsman had concluded "it is not for me to consider the actions of the council". He should have decided that the Department of Transport ought to have drawn the council's attention to its power to acquire blighted property and to its obligation to consider exercising it. [1997] C.O.D. 146.

Key Principle: **The court will refuse judicial review where the Ombudsman's powers are conferred by private contract rather than by statute.**

R. v Insurance Ombudsman Bureau Ex p. Aegon Life Assurance Ltd

The insurer sought judicial review of a decision by the Insurance Ombudsman Bureau, a body set up within the financial services sector for the resolution of disputes which had been re-organised by the Life Assurance and Unit Trust Regulatory Organisation (LAUTRO) responsible for regulating the carrying on of insurance business.

Held: (DC) It did not follow that because LAUTRO's decision was susceptible to judicial review, decisions of bodies set up by LAUTRO were also reviewable. The Ombudsman Bureau's powers were solely derived from contract and it could not be said that it exercised government functions. Its decisions were

therefore not reviewable. Application dismissed. *The Times,*
January 7, 1994.

Commentary
This case means that non-parties to the contract cannot take
proceedings.

Key Principle: **Decisions of officers of the House of Commons are not amenable to judicial review.**

R. v Parliamentary Commissioner for Standards Ex p. Al Fayed
The applicant sought judicial review of a decision by the
parliamentary Commissioner for Standards. He claimed that the
Commissioner had acted ultra vires in rejecting his complaint
that a government Minister had corruptly accepted payment.

Held: (CA) The responsibility for the supervision of the commissioner lay with parliament, acting through its standing
orders and the Commons Committee on Standards and Privileges. [1998] 1 All E.R. 93.

Commentary
The Commissioner's role differed from that of the parliamentary
Ombudsman because the latter's role was to investigate the actions
of government while the former was concerned with the activities
of those within Parliament.

No alternative remedy

Key Principle: **Judicial review is not normally available where there is an alternative remedy.**

R. v Chief Constable of the Merseyside Police Ex p. Calveley
Complaints were made against five police officers but the chief
constable allowed two years to go by before giving formal
notice of the complaints as required by regulations. At a
disciplinary hearing the chief constable rejected a submission
that the officers had been prejudiced by the delay because their
notes and logs relating to the matters complained of had been
routinely destroyed. The officers were found guilty and dis-

missed from the force. They gave notice of appeal under the police discipline regulations and also sought judicial review. The Divisional Court refused to hear the judicial review application before the disciplinary appeal. The officers appealed.

Held: (CA) Judicial review would be available only in exceptional circumstances where there was an alternative remedy by way of appeal. Where the basis of the application was delay, judicial review should only be granted if the delay amounted to an abuse of process. In this case, the delay had been a serious departure from the disciplinary process which justified the grant of judicial review. Judicial review should not be granted merely because it was more effective and convenient than the alternative appeal route. [1986] 1 Q.B. 424.

Key Principle: **Remedies are discretionary and may not be available even where grounds for review are found.**

Glynn v Keele University

A number of students were seen naked in the university precincts. The Vice-Chancellor, without hearing the student, punished one with a £10 fine and exclusion from the residence for the following academic year. The student was informed that he had a right of appeal, but when notice of the appeal hearing arrived he was abroad and on his return found that the appeal had been dismissed in his absence. Instead of asking for a rehearing, he issued a writ and sought an injunction restraining the university from excluding him from residence.

Held: (Ch. D) The Vice-Chancellor was acting in a quasi-judicial capacity in exercising his powers under the university statutes. The plaintiff had failed to make arrangements which would have enabled him to attend an appeal hearing and had not applied for a re-hearing of his case. There was a discretion in the court to grant an injunction where natural justice had failed. But although the plaintiff would lose the opportunity of making a plea in mitigation, the court would not do so in this case because the offence merited a severe penalty. [1971] 1 W.L.R. 487.

Ouster Clauses

Key Principle: **Statutes which preclude judicial review of administrative determinations do not apply to decisions which are nullities.**

Anisminic v Foreign Compensation Commission

The Foreign Compensation Act 1950 provided that the determination of the Foreign Compensation Commission of any application made to them under the Act should not be called in question in any court of law. The owners of property sequestrated by the Egyptian Government following the Anglo-French-Israeli invasion in 1956 claimed they were entitled to compensation but the Commission provisionally found against their claim. The owners sought a declaration that the Commission had misconstrued an Order in Council made under the Act, but the Commission claimed the court had no jurisdiction. The owners lost in the Court of Appeal but appealed to the House of Lords.

Held: (HL) The Foreign Compensation Act 1950 provided that the determination of an application to the Foreign Compensation Commission "shall not be called in question in any court of law". But this should not be construed as including everything that purported to be a determination, but was not in fact a determination because the Commission had misconstrued the provision of the Order defining their jurisdiction. It followed that the court could inquire whether or not an order of the Commission was a nullity. [1969] 2 A.C 147.

Commentary

Statutory provisions which preclude review are known as ouster clauses. This decision has been criticised as flouting the will of Parliament. The courts have shown a greater willingness to preclude review under partial ouster clauses which limit the opportunity for a decision to be challenged in the courts. Thus for example in *Smith v East Elloe RDC* [1956] A.C. 736 the House of Lords held that a compulsory purchase order was immune from judicial review after a time limit had expired. See also *R. v Secretary of State for the Environment Ex p. Ostler* [1977] Q.B. 122 where it was held that the authority of *Smith* was not affected by *Anisminic*.

8. JUDICIAL REVIEW GROUNDS—ILLEGALITY

Key Principle: **The grounds for review which already applied to powers under statute could be summarised as illegality, irrationality and procedural impropriety.**

Council for Civil Service Unions v Minister for the Civil Service
(For facts see p.61.)

Held: (HL) The grounds for judicial review of administrative action could be classified under three heads: illegality, irrationality and procedural impropriety. Others, including perhaps pro-portionality, might be added later (per Lord Diplock). [1985] 1 A.C. 374.

Commentary
Lord Diplock considered that a further development on a case-by-case basis may in the course of time add further grounds. Over the years the courts have developed an elaborate body of principles to be applied to judicial review of actions and omissions of administrators. However, there is no general agreement on a classification of grounds and de Smith has said "the task of separating them analytically in particular fact situations may be almost insuperable". The three-fold classification is itself subject to varying subdivisions and not all commentators agree on the nomenclature.

Substantive Ultra Vires

Key Principle: **For a public body to take a decision or to embark upon a decision-making process without authority or power means that it acts ultra vires or without jurisdiction.**

R. v Secretary of State for the Home Department Ex p. Leech (No.2)
A prisoner who was involved in various civil actions feared his correspondence with his solicitor was being censored under Prison Rules 1964. He applied for judicial review to quash the governor's power of censorship over letters between himself and his legal adviser as being ultra vires the Prison Act 1952. The application was refused at first instance and the prisoner appealed.

Held: (CA) A convicted prisoner retained all civil rights which were not removed either expressly or by necessary implication. The Prison Act authorised some interference with the right of confidentiality. But it was a fundamental principle that every citizen had a right of unimpeded access to a court and to a solicitor for receiving advice and assistance in that connection. Prison staff could read correspondence between prisoner and solicitor to see that it was bona fide. But for the prison to stop prisoner–solicitor correspondence under prison rule 33(3) on the ground that its contents were of inordinate length was ultra vires. [1994] Q.B. 198.

Key Principle: **Where a statutory power does not clearly authorise the infringement of a fundamental right the court will draw the inference that the intention of the statute was not to infringe that right.**

R. v Lord Chancellor Ex p. Witham

The Lord Chancellor increased the fees for issuing a writ and abolished the exemption from paying fees for litigants in person in receipt of income support. The applicant was an unemployed man in receipt of income support who wished to issue proceedings in person for defamation, for which legal aid was not available. He was not able to afford the fee and sought judicial review of the Lord Chancellor's decision.

Held: (DC) Access to the courts was a constitutional right at common law and could be abrogated only by a specific statutory provision in primary legislation. The Lord Chancellor had no power to prescribe fees so as to deny the poor access to the courts and his decision to do so was ultra vires and unlawful.

Commentary

The reasoning in this case falls under the ground of ultra vires, whereas in another case involving fundamental rights, *Ex p. Smith* (see below p.135), the ground applied was irrationality.

Error of Law, Error of Fact

Key Principle: **All errors of law are ultra vires in that the tribunal has exceeded its rightful jurisdiction.**

Anisminic v Foreign Compensation Commission
(For facts see p.116.)

Held: (HL) A determination did not include everything which purported to be a determination but was not in fact a determination because the Commission had misconstrued the Order which defined their jurisdiction. The court could consider whether or not the Commission's finding was a nullity. It was a nullity and the owners were entitled to the declaration they sought. [1969] 2 A.C. 147.

Commentary
The House of Lords here made virtually obsolete the distinction between errors of law which went to jurisdiction and those within jurisdiction. It held that all errors of law went to jurisdiction even where they were errors made in actually exercising the power rather than errors in establishing whether the power existed. The Foreign Compensation Commission had asked themselves a question they were not empowered to ask, namely the nationality of the successor in title, and had hereby made an error of law which took them outside their jurisdiction.

R. v Lord President of the Privy Council Ex p. Page
A Hull University staff member was appointed on the basis that he could not be removed without good cause before the retirement age of 67. He was made redundant and petitioned the university's Visitor (the Lord President) for a declaration that the university's decision to make him redundant was ultra vires the university's powers and thus invalid. The Visitor rejected the petition and the Divisional Court granted the applicant the declaration he sought. On appeal by the university the Court of Appeal held the Visitor's decision to be open to judicial review but decided the university had not exceeded its powers. Both sides appealed.

Held: (HL) The Divisional Court had no jurisdiction to hear the judicial review application because the Visitor's decision was not reviewable for error of fact or law in the adjudication of the dispute between the staff member and the university. Judicial review would have been available had the Visitor acted outside his jurisdiction in the sense that he did not have the power to enter into the adjudication of the dispute, or had abused his power or had acted contrary to natural justice. In any event the Visitor's decision had been correct. [1993] A.C. 682.

Commentary

Although review was denied in this case the House of Lords reaffirmed the position in *Anisminic* that all errors of law went to jurisdiction. The older view was that there could exist what was known as "an error of law on the face of the record" which arises when a body is acting within its powers but errs in law while doing so and that error appears on the face of the record of that decision. Such an error, i.e. one intra vires, is reviewable under the inherent jurisdiction of the court to control all inferior tribunals. All errors of law are now jurisdictional, although only relevant errors of law would lead to a decision being quashed. The decision left open the question whether there was a distinction in this area between decisions of administrative bodies and those of inferior courts.

Key Principle: The court may define the meaning of a statutory term applied by the administrative agency. If the meaning is inherently imprecise the court will only substitute its judgment if the agency's application of the term is so aberrant as to be irrational.

R. v Monopolies and Mergers Commission Ex p. South Yorkshire Transport Ltd

A bus company wholly owned by the South Yorkshire passenger transport authority bought certain private bus companies in its area. The Secretary of State for Trade and Industry referred the purchase to the Monopolies Commission. The Commission accepted that the reference concerned "a substantial part of the United Kingdom", on the basis that "substantial" meant "something real or important as distinct from something merely nominal", though the area was only 1.65 per cent of the total area of the United Kingdom. It recommended that the first applicant be required to divest itself to its acquisitions. The Secretary of State adopted the Commission's conclusion and its recommendation. In proceedings for judicial review the applicants challenged both decisions on the ground that such a small territorial area could not constitute "a substantial part of the United Kingdom". The judge granted their application and his decision was upheld by a majority in the Court of Appeal. The Commission and the Secretary of State appealed.

Held: (HL) The words "a substantial part of the United Kingdom" meant a part of such size, character and importance as to make it worth consideration for the purposes of the Act. In the circumstances the Commission had rightly concluded that the reference area was sufficiently worthy of consideration. There was no ground to interfere with the decisions. [1993] 1 W.L.R. 23.

Commentary
Ideally judicial review is confined to review of errors of law. In practice however it is often difficult to distinguish between errors of law and fact. A matter is generally held to be one of interpretation of fact if it is one on which reasonable persons may arrive at different conclusions on the evidence before them. The courts however may set out criteria within which the tribunal of fact must approach the matter. This case illustrates that the reviewing court will only interfere in the meaning of words where the agency has acted perversely.

Key Principle: **The reviewing court will be reluctant to intervene in matters of policy.**

Pulhofer v Hillingdon LBC
The applicants, a married couple with two young children, lived in one room on bed and breakfast terms, without cooking or laundry facilities. The local housing authority refused their application for accommodation under the Housing (Homeless Persons) Act 1977 on the ground that since they had the room they were neither homeless nor threatened with homelessness. The applicants sought judicial review of the housing authority's decision. Hodgson J., granting relief, held that no reasonable housing authority could have concluded that the accommodation in question was appropriate. The Court of Appeal allowed an appeal by the housing authority. The applicants appealed.

Held: (HL) Parliament had not qualified "accommodation" in s.1(1) of the Housing (Homeless Persons) Act 1977 by adjectives such as "appropriate" or "reasonable" and no such qualification was to be imported, nor was accommodation not accommodation because it might in certain circumstances be unfit for human habitation. What was properly to be regarded as "accommodation" was a question of fact for the housing authority, which had been entitled to find that the applicants were not homeless. Where the existence or non-existence of a fact was left to the judgment and discretion of a public body and that fact involved a broad spectrum ranging from the obvious to the debatable to the just conceivable, the court should leave the decision of that fact to the public body to which Parliament had entrusted the decision-making power unless it was obvious that the public body was acting perversely. [1986] A.C. 484.

Commentary
This case illustrates the importance attached by the courts to the sovereignty of Parliament. Reviewing courts should leave decisions on the meaning of "accommodation" to the public body to whom Parliament had entrusted the decision-making power. *Bugdaycay v Secretary of State for the Home Department* [1987] A.C. 514 shows how the courts draw distinctions between law, fact and policy. The courts were not the appropriate forum for resolving issues of policy and diplomacy, for example whether immigrants should be given asylum in the United Kingdom on the ground that they were political refugees. However the court could intervene on the issue of whether an immigrant would be in danger of persecution if deported. The immigration authorities had drawn a wrong inference from a letter showing the risk of persecution.

No evidence

Key Principle: **Lack of evidence for a decision may be ground for review.**

R. v Bedwellty Justices Ex p. Williams
Two defendants were tried for assault. The applicant testified that she had acted in self-defence, produced witnesses to substantiate her story and both defendants were acquitted. The defendants and the witnesses were later charged with conspiracy to pervert the course of justice. The applicant, unlike the other accused, sought an old style committal under s.6(1) of the Magistrates' Courts Act 1980. The prosecution called no oral evidence but showed the magistrates transcripts of police interviews in which the co-defendant and witnesses had admitted the conspiracy and implicated the applicant. On her application to quash the committal, the Divisional Court held that although there had been no admissible evidence before the justices on which the applicant could properly have been committed, it was

not the practice of the Divisional Court to exercise its discretion to order certiorari to quash a committal on the ground of inadmissibility or insufficiency of evidence. The applicant appealed.

Held: (HL) Committal for trial by jury at the Crown Court would be quashed in judicial review proceedings where the justices had failed to follow the procedure laid down by s.6(1). Committal would normally be quashed where there had been no admissible evidence before the justices of the defendant's guilt, though the court would be slow to interfere where evidence had been admissible but insufficient, which was more appropriately dealt with at trial. [1997] A.C. 225.

Commentary
This case is a further illustration of how the courts have rejected a limited theory of jurisdiction in favour of more extensive review. *Williams* opens the way for review of the evidence supporting the decision-maker's findings. Where a tribunal makes a finding of fact wholly unsupported by evidence or draws an inference wholly unsupported by any of the primary facts found by it, it may be held to have erred in point of law.

Abuse of Discretion

Administrators frequently are given discretion to act as opposed to a duty to act where action is mandatory. The following cases illustrate how the courts have tried to structure the exercise of such discretion.

Improper Purpose

Key Principle: **Administrators must not exercise their discretion for an improper purpose.**

Wheeler v Leicester CC
Three members of the Leicester rugby team were selected to play for England on a tour of South Africa. The team used a ground belonging to the council. The council questioned the club as to whether it would press the players not to take part in the tour. The club replied that it was a matter for the players whether they went on the tour, but that the club had supplied

them with material explaining the case against sporting links with South Africa. After the tour, in which the three players participated, the council banned the club for a year from using the ground. An application by club members for judicial review was refused and the applicants appealed. The Court of Appeal by a majority dismissed the appeal and held that the council was entitled, when exercising its discretionary powers, to have regard to the need to promote good race relations. The club members appealed.

Held: (HL) The council had power to consider the best interests of race relations when exercising its discretion to manage the ground. But in the absence of any unlawful or improper conduct by the club, the ban was unreasonable and a breach of the council's duty to act fairly. The council's actions were a procedural impropriety and a misuse of its statutory powers. [1985] A.C. 1054.

Roberts v Hopwood
The Public Health Act 1875 empowered Metropolitan Borough Councils to pay their employees "such . . . wages as [the council] may think fit". Poplar BC paid £4 a week to its lowest paid employees, despite a dramatic fall in the cost of living, because it believed this to be the least a local authority should pay to adult workers. The district auditor found that the payments were not wages but gratuities to the employees. Starting with the pre-war rate of wages, he added on a cost of living bonus and a further £1 as margin and surcharged the councillors for the rest. The Divisional Court upheld the surcharge, but it was overturned in the Court of Appeal. The district auditor appealed.

Held: (HL) The council's statutory discretion must be exercised reasonably. The fixing of wages without regard to existing labour conditions was not a proper exercise of the discretion. An expenditure on a lawful object might be so excessive as to be unlawful. The disallowance and surcharge would be upheld. [1925] A.C. 578.

Commentary
These cases illustrate the difficulties of defining grounds; both could also be considered as examples of irrationality (see pp.132 et seq.).

Padfield v Minister of Agriculture, Fisheries and Food
The Milk Marketing Board fixed prices at which producers had to sell their milk. Under the Agricultural Marketing Act 1958

different prices were fixed in each of the board's 11 regions, to reflect variations in transport costs between the regions. The same price differentials had been in operation for several years though transport costs had altered. South-east region producers wanted to change the differentials, but were unable to get a majority of the national board to agree. They asked the Minister to mount an inquiry under the Act but he refused. The producers applied for an order of mandamus to compel the minister to appoint the inquiry.

Held: (HL) The Minister's discretion had been conferred by Parliament so that it could be used to promote the policy and objects of the Act, which were for the court to determine as a matter of law. The Minister's discretion was not unlimited and the court was entitled to interfere if it appeared that the effect of his refusal to intervene was to frustrate the purpose of the Act. The order sought would be made. [1968] A.C. 997.

Commentary
One reason for the minister's failure to refer the complaint was that publicity might be politically damaging. This could also be seen as taking into account an irrelevant consideration (see p.128).

Congreve v Home Office
The Home Secretary increased television licence fees from £12 to £18 with effect from April 1 and instructed Post Office counter clerks not to renew licences for the period after the date the rise came into force until the rise was in force. The applicant sought in March to renew his licence which expired on March 31. The counter clerk in violation of the instruction issued him with a new licence at the old £12 rate. The Home Office wrote to him saying that the licence would be revoked unless he paid the extra £6. He sought a declaration that the threatened revocation would be unlawful, invalid and of no effect. The judge refused the declaration and he appealed.

Held: (CA) The courts would stop the Home Secretary exercising his statutory discretion arbitrarily or improperly. The applicant's licence was valid when issued and there was nothing in the legislation to prevent the holding of overlapping licences. The minister had acted unlawfully in excess of his authority. [1976] 1 Q.B. 629.

Commentary
The Minister wished to revoke the licences to avoid loss of revenue which was an improper purpose since it could be implied that power to revoke was restricted to illegal licences.

Fettering of Discretion

Key Principle: **The decision-maker can adopt a policy legitimately, but in exercising it must not exclude the merits of individual cases and prevent the authority from exercising its discretion in individual cases.**

Lavender & Son Ltd v Minister of Housing and Local Government

A gravel extraction company bought some land part of which was in an area reserved for agriculture and sought planning permission to work the site. The Ministry of Agriculture told the planning authority it had strong objections on agricultural grounds. The planning authority had no objection on amenity or highway grounds, but refused permission on grounds of prematurity and because of the Minister of Agriculture's objections. The company appealed under the Town and Country Planning Act 1962 to the Minister of Housing whose inspector concluded the land could be properly restored after extraction, but would make no recommendation because he was in no position to judge whether the reservation for agricultural use should be maintained. The Minister refused planning permission and told the applicant that it was his policy not to release land for working "unless the Minister of Agriculture is not opposed to working".

Held: (DC) The Minister was obliged to exercise his statutory discretion by giving consideration to whether on planning grounds the land could be worked. By his stated policy he had in effect inhibited himself from exercising his discretion in cases where the Minister of Agriculture had raised objection. The Minister had wrongly delegated his statutory duty to the Minister of Agriculture. [1970] 1 W.L.R. 1231.

British Oxygen Co Ltd v Minister of Technology

The company produced gases which were transported in small or large road tankers, in hydrogen trailers towed by tractors or in metal cylinders. It sought industrial development grants for new transporters but the Board of Trade decided all the tankers were ineligible as "vehicles", that the hydrogen trailers and cylinders were also ineligible because they were essentially means of storage, and it would not exercise its discretion to make grants for the cylinders which cost less than £25 each. The company asked the court to determine whether the equipment was "machinery or plant" and thus eligible for grant.

Held: (HL) The tankers and hydrogen trailers were not "machinery or plant", and thus were not eligible for grant. The cylinders might be eligible for grant, but the Minister had a discretion not to make a grant. He could adopt a policy or make a limiting rule as to the future exercise of his discretion, provided he listened to any applicant who had something new to say. The declaration was refused. [1971] A.C. 610.

Commentary

It is more difficult to apply this principle where an authority has to deal with a large number of applications. Lord Reid said,

> "What the authority must not do is to refuse to listen at all. But a Ministry or large authority may have had to deal already with a multitude of similar applications and then they will almost certainly have evolved a policy so precise that it could well be called a rule. There can be no objections to that provided the authority is always willing to listen to anyone with something new to say".

Failure to Exercise Discretion

Key Principle: **A public body cannot undertake by contract or some other form of agreement not to exercise a discretionary power.**

Ayr Harbour Trustees v Oswald

Harbour trustees were empowered by Parliament to take land necessary for their undertaking. The respondent's land was to be taken and compensation assessed by an arbiter. Before the arbiter decided, the trustees lodged a minute stating that the conveyance should restrict their use of the land so as to allow continued access by the respondent to the harbour. The arbiter found £4,900 payable for unrestricted use by the trustees, but only £2,786 if the trustees' use was restricted. The respondent wanted the full compensation.

Held: (HL) Under their special Act of Parliament, the trustees had power at any time to build on the land and destroy the respondent's access to the harbour. In any event the trustees were not competent to dispense with the future exercise of their powers. Full compensation would be paid. [1883] 8 A.C. 623.

Commentary

The covenant the trustees sought to make was ultra vires. Parliament had to be assumed to have conferred the powers of compulsory purchase on the grounds that it would be for the public good. An authority cannot bind itself not to use those powers.

Improper Delegation

Key Principle: **When a statute has delegated a function to an administrative authority it cannot delegate that function to another body.**

Carltona Ltd v Commissioners of Works
A food factory was requisitioned under defence regulations. The owners challenged the requisition decision because it gave a reason not mentioned in the regulation and the requisitioning authority had not brought their minds to bear on the question, and had they done so could not possible have concluded as they did.

Held: (CA) Parliament had given the executive the discretion to decide when a requisition order should be made under the regulation. No court could interfere with that discretion if exercised properly. [1943] 2 All E.R. 560.

Commentary
The court here accepted that except for those occasions where statute expressly demands that a Minister acts personally his powers are going to be exercised on his behalf by senior civil servants. Lord Green M.R. stated: "The whole system of departmental organisation and administration is based on the view that Ministers being responsible to Parliament will see that important duties are committed to experienced officials. If they do not do that Parliament is the place where complaints must be made against them." In *R. v Secretary of State for the Home Office Ex p. Oladehinde* [1991] 1 A.C. 254 the House of Lords held that often when a civil servant takes action he is acting as the alter ego of a Minister and there is no delegation.

Irrelevant Considerations

Key Principle: **If a public body takes an irrelevant consideration into account or fails to take note of a relevant consideration in making a decision, the decision will be ultra vires.**

Bromley LBC v Greater London Council
The Greater London Council voted to implement the "fares fair" policy, levying a supplementary rate to subsidise public transport by reducing fares. Bromley LBC was refused judicial review of the GLC decision, but the decision was reversed in the Court of Appeal. The GLC appealed.

Held: (HL) The GLC owed a fiduciary duty to ratepayers to have regard to their interests and were under a statutory obligation to apply business principles to the conduct of public transport and had acted ultra vires the relevant legislation and in breach of its fiduciary duty. [1983] 1 A.C. 768.

Commentary
This case could also be seen as one decided on grounds of fettering of discretion since the GLC had (per Lord Diplock) regarded itself as irrevocably committed to carry out the reduction in fares whatever the cost to rate payers because that was in the election manifesto of the majority party.

See also the House of Lords decision in *R. v Warrington Crown Court Ex p. RBNB (a company)* [2002] 1 W.L.R. 1954.

Key Principle: **The decision-maker has a "margin of appreciation" within which he may decide whether or not to take into account certain considerations in coming to a decision.**

R. v Somerset CC Ex p. Fewings
Land held for amenity purposes by the council in the Quantock Hills was part of an area of outstanding natural beauty. The council voted to ban stag-hunting over the land. Representatives of the Quantock Staghounds sought judicial review. The judge held that the majority of the council had voted because of moral repugnance to hunting which was not relevant to the exercise of the powers under the Local Government Act 1972 which they claimed to be exercising in imposing the ban. The council appealed.

Held: (CA) The council had failed to take account of the objects of the statute under which they claimed to be acting. As local authority landowners, as opposed to private landowners, they were subject to an overriding statutory constraint. They had not exercised their power to promote the benefit of the area and had not been entitled to make their decision on the ground relied on. The Court of Appeal also held that the council was entitled to take into account the "cruelty argument". [1995] 1 W.L.R. 1037.

Key Principle: **Public opinion or public petition are irrelevant considerations in sentencing decisions.**

R. v Home Secretary Ex p. Venables

The applicants murdered a small child when they were 10 and were sentenced to be detained during Her Majesty's pleasure. The trial judge reported to the Secretary of State that a minimum of eight years detention was needed to satisfy the requirements of retribution and deterrence. The Lord Chief Justice set a tariff of 10 years. The Secretary of State invited representations as to the appropriate length of the tariff. He informed the applicants that he had received petitions and correspondence and expressions of opinion supplied by a national newspaper, in support of a long or whole-life tariff. He then fixed a tariff of 15 years as appropriate to satisfy the requirements of retribution and deterrence. The applicants sought judicial review of the decisions. The Divisional Court quashed the decisions. Both sides appealed unsuccessfully to the Court of Appeal and thence to the House of Lords.

Held: (HL) A sentence of detention during Her Majesty's pleasure was not the same as a mandatory life sentence imposed on an adult murderer. It required the Secretary of State to consider from time to time whether continued detention was justified. He might set a provisional and reviewable tariff. But his decision that under no circumstances would it be varied was unlawful and contrary to his duty to take account of the child's welfare. The Secretary of State was acting as a sentencing judge, and natural justice required him to ignore as irrelevant public petitions or public opinion as expressed in the media. In giving weight to public protests to the detriment of the applicants, the Secretary of State had misdirected himself and his exercise of discretion had been unlawful. [1998] A.C. 407.

Commentary

The courts have categorised considerations which decision-makers are faced with as falling broadly into three categories: those which they must not take into account because they are irrelevant, those which must be taken into account because they are relevant and those which decision-makers may have regard to if they judge it appropriate. *Fewings* and *Venables* provide examples of these categories.

9. JUDICIAL REVIEW GROUNDS— IRRATIONALITY

Key Principle: **A decision-maker in whom a discretionary power is vested must not exercise that power in a way that no reasonable body would.**

Associated Provincial Picture Houses Ltd v Wednesbury Corp.
The Sunday Entertainments Act 1932 empowered local authorities to licence Sunday cinema opening "subject to such conditions as the authority may think fit to impose". The corporation granted a Sunday licence to the company on condition that nobody under the age of 15 was admitted. The company sought judicial review.

Held: (CA) The local authority had not acted unreasonably or ultra vires. The court was only entitled to review the exercise of so unlimited a power with a view to seeing whether the authority had taken account of matters it ought not to have taken into account, or disregarded matters it should have taken into account. [1948] 1 K.B. 223.

Commentary
Lord Green said that taking irrelevant considerations into account and exercising a discretionary power for an improper purpose would constitute unreasonable actions (see Ch.8). However, unreasonableness is also in itself an invalidating factor. Apart from irrelevant considerations and improper purpose Lord Green said that "if a decision on a competent matter is so unreasonable that no reasonable authority could ever come to it then the courts can interfere" but this would require "something overwhelming". According to Lord Green, irrationality is a comprehensive term so it does cover behaviour which might also be described as illegal. In *Council for Civil Service Unions v Minister for the Civil Service (GCHQ case)* (see p.61) Lord Diplock had in contrast confined the term "irrationality" to the rather extreme cases and used the term "illegality" to conduct which has in other cases been called unreasonable.

In practice it is difficult to challenge a decision on grounds of unreasonableness alone. Where an applicant succeeds it is usually in connection with improper purpose and/or irrelevant considerations. This category comes closest to challenging the merits of a decision and it might be felt that if it were a straightforward road to success the court was vetoing powers conferred by Parliament on public authorities and substituting its own view for that of the authority to which discretion was given.

Wheeler v Leicester CC
(For facts see p.123.)

Held: (HL) The council had a statutory power to consider the best interests of race relations when managing the ground, but in the absence of any unlawful or improper conduct by the club, the 12-month ban was unreasonable and a breach of the council's duty to act fairly. The council's actions were a procedural impropriety and the ban would be quashed. [1985] A.C. 1054.

Commentary
The Court of Appeal and the House of Lords found different applications of the irrationality principle. In the Court of Appeal Ackner L.J. considered the council's decision was not one that no reasonable local authority could have taken, however in the House of Lords, Lord Roskill considered the council's decision was within *Wednesbury* unreasonableness in that it had applied pressure beyond persuasion. This case can be considered under a number of heads including improper purpose and taking irrelevant considerations into account.

Key Principle: **In its application to local authority decisions the Wednesbury test means that the decision-maker must have acted with manifest absurdity.**

Secretary of State for Education v Tameside MBC
A Labour local education authority proposed to introduce comprehensive secondary schooling. Its plans were approved by the Secretary of State for implementation in September 1976. The matter was an issue in local elections which were won by the Conservative Opposition. The new administrative body changed the plans so as to retain three grammar schools which would have gone comprehensive. The Secretary of State directed the authority to carry out the original plan as to change it would be too disruptive and obtained a writ of mandamus to that effect in the Divisional Court. The order was overturned on appeal and the Secretary of State appealed.

Held: (HL) The Secretary of State was not entitled to require the authority to abandon their policy because he disagreed with it. He could give a direction only if the authority were acting unreasonably in what they were entitled to do. There had been no proper ground for intervention against the change of plan. [1977] A.C. 1014.

R. v Secretary of State for the Environment Ex p. Hammersmith and Fulham LBC

The Secretary of State acting applied the Local Government Finance Act 1988 to impose limits on the amount of Community Charge which could be levied by designated councils. Twenty-one councils were designated, and 19 sought judicial review of the decision to designate, on the grounds that the Secretary of State had failed to have regard to the individual spending needs of the individual authorities and had designated only those authorities with high-standard spending assessments. Judicial review was refused in the Divisional Court and in the Court of Appeal. The councils appealed.

Held: (HL) The Secretary of State's decision to designate particular authorities was based on principles of general application as to what as a matter of political opinion constituted excessive spending. The application of those principles only to authorities with high standard spending assessments did not contravene the legislation. The authorities had no legitimate expectation that the Secretary of State would only prevent them spending above what any reasonable authority would incur. The Secretary of State's power under the Act involved the exercise of a political judgment which was not open to challenge on grounds of irrationality short of bad faith, improper motive or manifest absurdity. [1991] 1 A.C. 521.

Commentary

The council had applied on grounds of illegality, irrationality and procedural impropriety. The House of Lords showed concern that the courts would not be embroiled in the political arena in deciding that the Secretary of State's decision involved the exercise of political judgment which was subject to approval by the House of Commons. The two cases above confirm that the courts take the view that to be unreasonable there must be a decision which no reasonable authority could take. The test is not what the court considers reasonable. The decision here follows the earlier case of *R. v Secretary of State for the Environment Ex p. Nottinghamshire*

CC [1986] A.C. 240 where the House of Lords held that where a decision concerned matters of public expenditure approved by resolution of the House of Commons, then it was unconstitutional for the court to apply *Wednesbury* grounds of irrationality. The decision would have to be so absurd that the decision-maker "must have taken leave of his senses".

Key Principle: **The more substantial the interference with human rights the more ready will the court be to apply Wednesbury standards of unreasonableness.**

R. v Ministry of Defence Ex p. Smith

It was government policy that homosexuality was incompatible ible with service in the armed forces and that personnel known to be homosexual or engaging in homosexual activity would be administratively discharged. The applicants were serving members of the armed forces administratively discharged of homosexuality. They challenged by way of judicial review the decision to discharge and the policy on which it was based, as irrational, contrary to Art.8 of the European Convention on Human Rights and in breach of the EEC Equal Treatment Directive. The Divisional Court dismissed the applications and the applicants appealed.

Held: (CA) An administrative decision made in the context of human rights would require proportionately greater justification to satisfy the court that it was within the range of responses open to a reasonable decision-maker. The test of irrationality was sufficiently flexible to cover all situations, but the court would show greater caution where the nature of the decision was esoteric, policyladen or security-based. The lawfulness of the applicants' discharge fell to be assessed as at the date it occurred. The policy was supported by Parliament and the leaders of the armed forces whose advice had not been invalidated by any other evidence. Neither the EEC Treaty nor the equal treatment directive addressed discrimination on the ground of sexual orientation. The applications were dismissed. [1996] Q.B. 517.

Commentary

This case indicates that the courts are increasingly ready to apply a lower threshold of unreasonableness where human rights are involved although on the facts they found against the applicants. In *Smith v UK* and *Grody v UK* (2000) the Strasbourg court held there had been victims of Arts 8 and 13.

10. PROCEDURAL IMPROPRIETY, OTHER GROUNDS

Key Principle: **The rules of natural justice have to be observed where there is a duty to act judicially and this duty is not confined to the procedure of a court of law but exists where any body of persons has legal authority (arising from statute or common law or contract) to determine questions affecting the rights (not only legal rights) of others.**

Ridge v Baldwin

The chief constable of Brighton was tried for conspiracy to obstruct the course of justice. During the trial he was suspended from office. He was acquitted but the judge told him he had lacked the "professional and moral readership" the public was entitled to expect. Using its powers under the Municipal Corporations Act 1882 the borough watch committee voted to dismiss him, forfeiting his pension rights. He had not been invited to appear before the committee, which confirmed its decision at a subsequent meeting at which he was represented. He sought judicial review to challenge the dismissal as a breach of natural justice.

Held: (HL) The watch committee was in breach of the principles of natural justice as well as of the statutory regulations governing police discipline. The watch committee had three possible courses of action: dismissal, requiring the chief constable to resign or reinstating him. It was contrary to natural justice to decide the issue without hearing the chief constable. Natural justice was not confined to situations where a judicial or quasi-judicial function was being exercised. [1964] A.C. 40.

Commentary

This landmark decision is a recognition of the impact of decisions of administrative bodies on people's lives.

Procedural Ultra Vires

Key Principle: **Where Parliament has laid down a procedure which should be followed before a body can exercise its powers, the body will be acting ultra vires if it does not follow the procedure.**

Agricultural Training Board v Aylesbury Mushrooms Ltd
The Board was established under the Industrial Training Act 1964, which provided for prior consultation by the Ministry of Labour with interested organisations. Consultations were organised, in which the National Farmers Union took part, and an invitation was sent to, but not received by, a branch of the union, the Mushroom Growers. Association, which was unaware that the board was being established. The Board was duly established and claimed to regulate training of mushroom growers. The Association made formal application for its members to be excluded. The Board issued a summons to determine whether the Minister had complied with his duty of consultation before making the order establishing the Board, and if not, what the consequences were.

Held: (DC) The Minister was under a duty to consult the Association. Consulting the union would have constituted consultation with its constituent parts, had not the Minister tried to consult the Association directly. Without communication and the consequent opportunity of responding, there could be no consultation. The result of the failure to consult was that the Board had no authority over mushroom growers as such. [1972] 1 W.L.R. 190.

Commentary
Lord Diplock in *Council of Civil Service Unions v Minister for the Civil Service* (see p.61) recognised two aspects to procedural impropriety. First, failure to observe procedures laid down in the relevant statute and secondly, failure to follow the common law principles of natural justice. Specified procedural requirement may fall into two sorts, mandatory or directory. However, it is not always possible to distinguish them and a minor breach of a mandatory requirement will not necessarily be significant.

Natural Justice

Key Principle: **A person cannot incur the loss of liberty, property or livelihood unless he has an opportunity of a fair hearing.**

Cooper v Wandsworth Board of Works
Under the Metropolis Local Management Act 1855 the Board of Works had power to alter or demolish a house where the

builder had neglected to give notice of his intention to build seven days before proceeding to lay or dig the foundations. The plaintiff had given only five days' notice before starting to build. The house was already built up to the second storey when late one evening council workers came and razed it to the ground. The builder brought an action in damages for the house, claiming that the Board had improperly exercised its power by acting without notice and failing to give him an opportunity to be heard.

Held: (CCP) A person could not be deprived of his property without a hearing. The council's statutory power to demolish did not empower them to do so without giving the builder an opportunity of being heard. (1863) 14 C.B. (N.S.) 180.

Key Principle: **The content of a right to a hearing may vary according to the circumstances of the case.**

McInnes v Onslow-Fane

The plaintiff applied for a boxing manager's licence but was refused without an oral hearing. The boxing board of control gave him no reasons for refusal. He sought a declaration that the board had acted in breach of natural justice and unfairly.

Held: (Ch. D) The court was entitled to intervene to ensure natural justice. But the case did not involve an existing right, nor had the plaintiff any legitimate expectation of success. The board was under a duty to reach an honest conclusion without bias but was under no obligation to give reasons, nor to grant an oral hearing. The application would be dismissed. [1978] 1 W.L.R. 1520.

Key Principle: **No one can be a judge in their own cause.**

Dimes v Grand Junction Canal Co

A dispute over the ownership of part of the Grand Junction Canal led the canal company to apply for an injunction before the Vice-Chancellor against a landowner who was obstructing navigation. The injunction was granted and on appeal the Lord

Chancellor confirmed it. It later emerged that the Lord Chancellor held shares in the company worth several thousand pounds. The landowner appealed to the House of Lords.

Held: (HL) The appeal would be allowed. Because of his interest, the Lord Chancellor was disqualified from sitting as a judge in the case and his decision was thus voidable and must be reversed. Despite his disqualification, the Lord Chancellor was still competent to grant leave to appeal to the House of Lords in the case. [1852] 3 H.L. Cas. 759.

Commentary
This is the leading case on matters involving possible bias arising out of a pecuniary interest. The Lord Chancellor could not have been supposed to have been influenced by his interest in the company but it was important that the rule that no one should be a judge in his own cause should be seen to be upheld.

R. v Gough
The defendant was convicted of conspiring with his brother to commit robbery. The brother had been discharged at the committal stage, but after the defendant had been convicted and sentenced he made a scene in court and was recognised by one of the jury as her next door neighbour. The defence raised with the judge the possibility of bias but he held he was *functus officio*. The Court of Appeal dismissed the defendant's appeal and he appealed to the House of Lords.

Held: (HL) The test to be applied in all cases of apparent bias was whether in all the circumstances of the case there appeared to be a real danger of bias such that justice required the decision should not stand. The only category of case where bias would be assumed was where the tribunal had a pecuniary or proprietary interest in the subject-matter of the proceedings. The appeal would be dismissed. [1993] A.C. 646.

Commentary
In cases such as these involving non-pecuniary interest the words "real danger" should be taken to denote a possibility not a probability.

R. v Inner West London Coroner Ex p. Dallaglio
Two mothers who had lost children when the Marchioness pleasure boat sank after a collision in the Thames became

involved in a dispute with the coroner while the inquest was adjourned pending the outcome of criminal proceedings. One of the mothers applied unsuccessfully for an exhumation order, having been denied an opportunity to see her son's body. She believed the hands had been cut off her son's body for identification purposes. The coroner expressed a belief that she had been psychologically affected by grief and was not acting rationally. The two mothers took the story to a newspaper and the coroner met journalists in an attempt to set the record straight. In the course of that meeting he described one of the women as "unhinged" and displayed hostility to her. The coroner later wrote to the relatives of all the victims asking whether they wanted the inquest reconvened. He subsequently refused to remove himself on grounds of bias or to resume the inquests, on the grounds that only a minority of families wanted resumption. An application by the mothers for judicial review was refused in the Divisional Court and they appealed.

Held: (CA) Where there was a challenge to a court for bias, and the court expressly disavowed any suggestion of actual bias, it was necessary to consider whether there was a real danger that the decision-maker was unconsciously biased. The applicant had to demonstrate not that there was a real possibility that the coroner's decision would have been different but for the bias, but that the real danger of bias had affected the decision. The coroner's use of the word "unhinged" indicated a real possibility that the coroner had unconsciously become biased and the inquest should be resumed before a different coroner. [1994] 4 All E.R. 139.

Key Principle: **If a direct interest, including a non-pecuniary interest, of a person in a judicial capacity can be shown, the court is not required to inquire whether there was any real likelihood of bias.**

R. v Bow Street Magistrate Ex p. Pinochet (No.2)

The former Chilean dictator was arrested in London under extradition warrants requested by Spain. The warrants charged various crimes against humanity, including murder, hostage-taking and torture. The Divisional Court quashed the warrants on the basis that a former head of state was immune from arrest and extradition proceedings in the United Kingdom in respect of acts committed while he was head of state. The prosecutor appealed to the House of Lords. Amnesty International obtained leave to intervene in the proceedings and was represented by counsel. By a majority of three to two, the House of Lords allowed the appeal and restored the warrant. Lord Hoffmann, who was part of the majority, was an unpaid director and chairman of Amnesty International Charitable Trust Ltd, whose objects included the abolition of torture, extra-judicial execution and disappearance. The applicant petitioned to have the decision set aside for apparent bias on the part of the judge.

Held: (HL) The fundamental principle that a man might not be a judge in his own cause applied if the judge's decision would lead to the promotion of a cause in which he was involved together with one of the parties. Although the judge could not personally be regarded as having been a party to the appeal, Amnesty International and the charitable trust were both parts of a movement working towards the same goals. A judge who was involved, whether personally or as a director of a company, in promoting the same causes in the same organisation as was a party to the suit should be disqualified. [1999] 2 W.L.R. 272.

Commentary
This case extends the special category of automatic disqualification for apparent bias to instances where the judge's interest was neither financial nor proprietary. The House noted that the case was highly unusual.

Key Principle: **There is no difference between the common law test of bias and the requirements under Art.6 of an independent and impartial tribunal.**

Porter v Magill
Lady Shirley Porter and other leaders of the Conservative council in Westminster were found by an auditor to have been acting unlawfully by targeting the sale of council houses in key wards with the primary purpose of improving their party's chances of retaining its majority. The auditor surcharged Porter and her associates, and was upheld by the Divisional Court, which set the surcharge at £26m. The Court of Appeal, however,

quashed the auditor's order on the grounds that the Divisional Court had inconsistently exonerated some of the defendants. The matter went on appeal to the House of Lords. Among other things the defendants claimed that the auditor's inquiry had been unfairly conducted, accusing him of bias.

Held: (HL) The auditor's role required him to act as investigator, prosecutor and judge, but the defendants' right to an independent and impartial tribunal was met by the right of appeal by way of a full rehearing. The appropriate test for apparent bias was whether a fair-minded and informed observer, having considered the relevant facts, would conclude that bias was a real possibility. That although the auditor had made public his provisional findings in advance of the final decision, such a progress statement was appropriate given the public interest in the matter and the defendants had failed to show a real possibility of bias. [2002] A.C. 357.

Commentary
In *Lawal v Northern Spirit Ltd* [2003] I.C.R. 856 the House of Lords "unanimously endorsed" the approach in *Porter v Magill*. Lord Steyn observed, "The principle to be applied is that stated in *Porter v Magill*, whether a fair-minded and informed observer, having considered the given facts, would conclude that there was a real possibility that the tribunal was biased." In this case it was held that public confidence in the administration of justice might be undermined by the practice whereby leading counsel sat as part-time judges in the Employment Appeal Tribunal. Counsel might have sat as a judge with one or more of the lay members of the panel before which he was appearing. The practice should be discontinued.

Key Principle: **If there was genuine doubt about the real danger of bias then the matter should be resolved in favour of disqualification. It would however be as wrong for a judge to accede to a tenuous objection as it would be for him to ignore one of substance.**

Locabail (UK) Ltd v Bayfield Properties Ltd
Various applications for permission to appeal raised common questions about disqualification of judges (whether judge, lay

justice or juror) for bias. The court delivered a judgment on the general principles and then considered the applications individually.

Held: (CA) On the authorities, where the judge had an interest in the outcome of the case he would be automatically disqualified if the outcome of the case before the judge could realistically and directly affect the judge's interest. In *Pinochet* the House of Lords had extended the rule to a limited class of non-financial interests. Further extension of the present rule on automatic disqualification would be undesirable. A judge might also be disqualified and his decision set aside in all the circumstances there was a real danger (or possibility) of bias. It would very often be appropriate to enquire whether the judge knew of the matter relied on as appearing to undermine his impartiality, because if it was shown that he did not know of it the danger of its having influenced his judgment was eliminated and the appearance of possible bias was dispelled. Solicitors who were judges should, before embarking on the trial of any assigned civil case, conduct a careful conflict search within their firm. It was always inappropriate for a judge to use intemperate language about subjects on which he had adjudicated or would have to adjudicate.

Commentary
There are now a series of cases which set out the test for the appearance of bias. Cases of actual bias which inevitably provide good grounds for challenging a decision are rare. Cases of serious apparent bias will also provide grounds for a successful challenge unless the court is satisfied that there was no actual bias.

Key Principle: **The duty to act fairly applies to a prison governor when exercising disciplinary functions.**

Leech v Parkhurst Prison Deputy Governor
A prisoner was penalised for a disciplinary offence. The proceedings were carried out in breach of natural justice but the prison authorities claimed the Secretary of State had no power to quash the guilty finding. The application was refused in the Divisional Court, but leave to appeal was granted by the Court of Appeal, which rejected judicial review on the sole ground

that it was bound by *R. v Deputy Governor of Camphill Prison Ex p. King* [1985] Q.B. 735.

Held: (HL) An essential characteristic of the rights of the subject, even in prison, was a right of recourse to the courts unless some statute provided otherwise. No provision in the Prison Act 1952 derogated from that principle in relation to the governor's exercise of disciplinary powers. The adjudication would be quashed and *R. v Deputy Governor of Camphill Prison Ex p. King* [1985] Q.B. 735 overruled. [1988] A.C. 533.

Key Principle: **Availability of legal representation is a matter of discretion.**

R. v Board of Visitors of HM Prison, the Maze Ex p. Hone
A prisoner facing disciplinary proceedings before the Board of Visitors was refused legal representation and sought judicial review.

Held: (HL) Natural justice did not automatically require that a prisoner facing disciplinary proceedings be legally represented. The application would be rejected. [1988] A.C. 379.

Commentary
This case emphasises the flexibility of the application of the principles of natural justice. A Board of Visitors should exercise its discretion to allow legal representation if the nature, complexity and seriousness of the offence and the nature of the penalty require it. Furthermore, in exercising discretion whether to allow legal representation, the Board of Visitors must not fetter themselves for example by adopting a policy that legal representation would never be allowed. Each case must be looked at on its merits.

Key Principle: **Hearings before prison governors should be conducted in accordance with the principles of natural justice and this may require allowing witnesses to be called and hearsay evidence to be excluded.**

R. v Hull Prison Board of Visitors Ex p. St Germain (No.2)

Prison visitors hearing disciplinary proceedings against prisoners following a riot refused to allow certain witnesses to be called on behalf of the prisoners and admitted statements by prison officers who were not called to give evidence. The Divisional Court refused judicial review, but that decision was reversed in the Court of Appeal and the matter was remitted to the Divisional Court for hearing and determination.

Held: (DC) Most of the applications would be granted for unfairness in refusing to exercise the discretion to allow witnesses to be called and to refuse to admit hearsay evidence. [1979] 3 All E.R. 545.

Commentary

The duty to act fairly can be applied in a range of contexts and does not necessarily mean that a judicial process should be adopted. Compare *R. v Commissioner for Racial Equality Ex p. Cottrell & Rothon* [1980] 1 W.L.R. 1580 where the Court of Appeal held that the Commission was under no obligation to provide an opportunity for cross-examination of witnesses whose evidence underpinned its decision to issue a non-discrimination notice against the applicant firm of estate agents.

Key Principle: **A party to any proceedings has the right to know the opposing case in advance, but this does not necessarily mean a detailed case.**

R. v Gaming Board for Great Britain Ex p. Benaim and Khaida

The applicants, French nationals, bought the Crockford's gaming club and sought a certificate of consent from the board to enable them to apply for a licence under the Gaming Act 1968. The Board heard the applicants and rejected their application, without giving reason. They complained to the Court of Appeal that they had been unfairly treated contrary to the requirements of natural justice.

Held: (CA) The Board's statutory duty was to act fairly by giving an applicant sufficient indication of the objections to him to enable him to answer them. The Board was not obliged to disclose the sources of its information or give reasons for concluding that a certificate should be refused. [1970] 2 Q.B. 417.

Commentary
This case emphasises that the right to know the opposing case is not an unqualified one. An administrative body may be required to keep its sources confidential and as long as it acted with "substantial fairness" only the general nature of charges may be presented.

Key Principle: **There is no absolute right to an oral hearing.**

Lloyd v McMahon
A group of Liverpool councillors were asked to make written representations as to why they should not be surcharged by the district auditor for having wilfully refused to set a rate. They did so and were surcharged. The Divisional Court dismissed their appeals on the basis that they had had sufficient opportunity to rebut the case against them. They refused to give oral evidence to the Divisional Court, whose decision was upheld by the Court of Appeal. The councillors appealed on the basis that the auditor's failure to offer an oral hearing nullified his decision.

Held: (HL) The auditor had not acted unfairly nor had the councillors been prejudiced by the decision not to hear them. [1987] 1 A.C. 625.

Commentary
Per Lord Bridge, the so-called rules of natural justice are not engraved on tablets of stone.

Key Principle: **An express statutory provision excluding a duty to give reasons does not exclude a duty to disclose the substance of the case.**

R. v Secretary of State for the Home Department Ex p. Fayed
Two brothers, prominent businessmen born in Egypt, had been granted indefinite leave to remain in the United Kingdom. They applied for naturalisation. The Secretary of State issued a news release indicating that the applications were regarded as especially difficult and sensitive. He refused both applications and declined to give reasons for his decisions. The judge dismissed

the brothers' judicial review applications on the ground that the statute entitled the Secretary of State to dispense with any requirement to give reasons. On appeal by the applicants.

Held: (CA) The Secretary of State was not relieved by the statute of the obligation to act fairly, which required that, before reaching his decision, he should inform an applicant of the nature of matters weighing against granting his application and give him an opportunity of addressing them. [1998] W.L.R. 763.

Commentary
It clearly is often pointless to give someone a right to make representations if they do not know the case against them. Disclosure of evidence adverse to the applicant is therefore an aspect of natural justice. *Ex p. Fayed* illustrates that the duty of disclosure may be an ongoing one.

Legitimate Expectation

The above cases illustrate how the courts have moved away from a rigid concept of procedural fairness and have developed a more flexible, pragmatic approach. One new development has been the recognition of the concept of legitimate expectation. In *GCHQ* (see p.61) Lord Roskill likened it to the right to be heard and stressed that it can take many forms. There are however, many senses to "legitimate expectation". Some of the most common are listed below.

Key Principle: **The existence of a legitimate expectation did not mean that officials were prevented from changing policies.**

Findlay v Secretary of State for the Home Department
Under the Criminal Justice Act 1967 the Home Secretary could release a prisoner on licence if the Parole Board so recommended. In 1983 the Home Secretary adopted a new policy of refusing to release on licence drug traffickers and violent offenders sentenced to more than five years' imprisonment. The Home Secretary did not consult the board on the formulation of the new policy but subsequently consulted it as to the precise way of achieving that policy. Four prisoners affected by the policy sought to challenge it by way of judicial review, claiming

they had suffered loss of expectation of parole. The Divisional Court failed to agree, and their appeal was dismissed by the Court of Appeal.

Held: (HL) A convicted prisoner could legitimately expect no more than that his case would be examined individually in the light of any policy which the Home Secretary might lawfully adopt. [1998] A.C. 318.

Commentary
There is a constitutional issue at stake here since if administrators were not free to change policies and practices their discretion would be fettered and their responsibilities to the public as a whole hampered. The most that a convicted prisoner could expect in this situation was that his case would be examined individually in the light of whatever policy was in operation at the time, provided the policy was lawfully exercised under the statute. Here there was a limited legitimate expectation. By contrast in *R. v Secretary of State for Health Ex p. United States Tobacco* [1992] Q.B. 353 the Court held that the applicant manufacturer of snuff had no legitimate expectation at all. The manufacturer had been given a government grant, the terms of which it had observed, but subsequently production was banned by the government. The Court held that Ministers were entitled to such changes of policies in the public interest.

Key Principle: **Where a public authority has said it will follow a certain procedure those potentially affected have a legitimate expectation that it will carry out its promise.**

Attorney-General of Hong Kong v Ng Yuen Shiu
The applicant had entered Hong Kong illegally from Macau in 1976. Until 1980 the government had followed a "reached base" policy which allowed illegal immigrants to stay once they had reached the urban areas without being arrested. The policy was abandoned in 1980 and the government announced plans to deport illegal immigrants to China. Those who had entered from Macau made representations and it was announced that they would all be interviewed and each case considered on its merits. The applicant was detained and ordered to be removed without having the opportunity of making representations. He

was refused judicial review but the appeal court granted an order of prohibition. The Attorney-General appealed.

Held: (PC) Where a public authority promised to follow a particular procedure before making a decision, it should follow that procedure provided it was lawful. The applicant had been wrongly denied an opportunity to state his case and the removal order would be quashed. Certiorari not prohibition was the appropriate order. [1983] 2 A.C. 629.

Key Principle: **An administrative body may create a legitimate expectation by publishing proposed procedures.**

R. v Secretary of State for the Home Department Ex p. Khan

A Home Office circular advised people who wished to adopt a child from abroad that the Home Secretary would allow a child to enter despite immigration rules provided certain specified criteria were met. The circular said the Home Secretary would in such cases check with the Department of Health whether the adopters were suitable. The applicant and his wife, who were settled in England, wished to adopt a relative's child who lived in Pakistan. The Home Office did not follow the procedure in the circular, but refused the application, applying criteria for deciding whether to admit for settlement children who were already adopted by persons settled in the United Kingdom. The applicants were refused judicial review and appealed.

Held: (CA) The applicants had a reasonable expectation that the procedure set out in the circular would be followed. The Home Secretary had acted unfairly and unreasonably in not applying the procedure to them. Appeal allowed. [1984] 1 W.L.R. 1337.

Council of Civil Service Unions v Minister for the Civil Service

(For facts see p.61).

Commentary
Here legitimate expectation of the right to be heard arose from a regular practice which the applicants could expect to continue.

The courts have not fully resolved the question of whether there is a legitimate expectation of the right to continue to enjoy a benefit.

Key Principle: **A legitimate expectation of making representations may not be allowed in cases of prior misconduct.**

Cinnamond v British Airports Authority

Six car-hire drivers had been touting for business at Heathrow Airport for several years despite a string of convictions for loitering. Their prices were higher than black cab drivers, and the authority used its powers under the Airports Authority Act 1975 to tell them in writing that they would not be allowed on the Airport save as bona fide passengers. The drivers were refused a declaration that the authority had acted unlawfully, and appealed.

Held: (CA) The ban on their entry was "calculated to facilitate the discharge" of the authority's duties, and it had the power to bar them. The drivers' previous convictions deprived them of a legitimate expectation that they would be heard before the ban was imposed. [1980] 1 W.L.R. 582.

Key Principle: **A public body can only be bound by acts and statements of its employees and agents if they had actual or ostensible authority.**

South Bucks DC v Flanagan

A solicitor in private practice represented a council which was bringing prosecutions for breaches of two enforcement notices. At the magistrates' court the solicitor agreed to discontinue the prosecutions. The council then applied for an injunction to enforce compliance with the original notices.

Held: (DC) The council was entitled to seek an injunction. The solicitor had no actual or ostensible authority and it was not within the usual authority of a solicitor appointed to prosecute to agree to withdraw the original notices. [2002] 1 W.L.R. 2601.

Commentary

There is a developing jurisprudence on legitimate expectation at common law where fairly strict requirements are set out. In *Josie*

Rowland v Environment Agency [2003] 1 All E.R. 624 the claimant failed to persuade the court that the implementation of the HRA and the greater protection to property afforded under Protocol 1 Art.1 meant that these requirements should be relaxed. Lightman J. held that an ultra vires defence to the application of the principle of legitimate expectation could not be overcome by recourse to the ECHR. Any expectation of the claimant did not constitute a possession and even if it did the interference here was lawful.

Key Principle: **Once a claimant has established legitimate expectation s/he must show it would be unfair of the public body to resile from giving effect to it.**

R. v North East Devon Health Authority Ex p. Coughlan

A severely disabled patient sought judicial review of a decision by the respondent health authority to close the property where she was living. When she had moved to the property from another hospital which was being closed, the patient had been told she would have a home there for life. The judge found that the decision to break the promise was equivalent to a breach of contract and could be done only where overriding public interest demanded it. The health authority had failed to establish this. It had wrongly treated the promise as a promise to provide care regardless of the place of care. There had been insufficient consultation. The health authority appealed.

Held: (CA) The proper test was whether the need judged to exist by the health authority to move the patient to a local authority facility was such as to outweigh its promise that she would have a home for life at the property. There was no overriding public interest to justify the closure decision in breach of the promise. The unfairness amounted to an abuse of power. The property was the applicant's home which required to be respected under Art.8 of the European Convention. The health authority was not justified under the convention in seeking to deprive the patient of a home. Breach of the convention could amount to a free-standing ground of review. [2000] 2 W.L.R. 622.

Commentary

Woolf L.C.J. spoke of at least three kinds of possible unfairness by a public body: irrational failure to take its representations into account; procedurally unfair failure to provide the citizen affected by its decision to resile from its representation with an opportunity for consultation; and unfairness where there is no overriding interest that would justify the body in resiling from its representation that a substantive benefit would be forthcoming. It is now acknowledged that with the recognition of the doctrines of legitimate expectation and abuse of power there is no place in planning law for the private law doctrine of estoppel. Even though the HRA was not then in force the court was willing to invoke Art.8.

Duty to Give Reasons

Key Principle: **Where there is a duty under statute to give reasons to an individual affected by an administrative decision the test of the adequacy of the reasons given is whether the applicant has been substantially prejudiced by the deficiency in the reason given.**

Save Britain's Heritage v Number 1 Poultry Ltd

The owners of a group of listed buildings in the City of London proposed to build a new development on the site. The stated policy of the Secretary of State was that listed buildings capable of economic use should not be demolished. The local authority rejected the scheme but the Secretary of State held that the new building was so meritorious that it should go ahead. Objectors sought to quash the Secretary of State's decision on the grounds that he had failed to give sufficient reasons and had misdirected himself as to the effect of his policy relating to consent for demolition of listed buildings. The judge dismissed the application but the Court of Appeal found for the objectors. The owners appealed.

Held: (HL) It was for the objectors to show that they had been prejudiced by the absence of sufficient reasons. The Secretary of State's policy was not absolute, but could be overridden in special circumstances. There had been no flaw in the decision-making process and the appeal would be allowed. [1991] 1 W.L.R. 153.

Key Principle: **The common law may impose a duty to give** reasons on administrative bodies in order to make their decisions effectively reviewable.

R. v Civil Service Appeal Board Ex p. Cunningham

The applicant was dismissed from his job as a prison officer. As a prison officer he was precluded from claiming unfair dismissal to an industrial tribunal, so he appealed to the Civil Service Appeal Board, which recommended reinstatement. The Home Office refused to comply with the recommendation and substituted a payment of £6,500 without indicating how the sum had been arrived at. The applicant succeeded in obtaining judicial review. The Board appealed and the applicant cross-appealed on the basis that the award was irrational.

Held: (CA) The Board's appeal would be dismissed. The judge had correctly held that the Board was under a duty to give outline reasons for the size of award. Procedural fairness required a quasi-judicial body to give sufficient reasons to enable parties to know that it had addressed the issues and had acted lawfully. The applicant's cross-appeal would be allowed because in the absence of adequate explanations it was so far below what he could reasonably have expected as to be irrational. The case would be remitted to the Board for compensation to be reconsidered. [1992] I.C.R. 816.

Commentary

The Court of Appeal here acknowledged there may, in the absence of a statutory requirement, be a common law requirement for natural justice to be satisfied by the giving of outline reasons for a decision. It should, however, be noted that the Court was not creating a general duty for administrative bodies to give reasons. That may depend on the nature of the decision being given. This category overlaps with procedural impropriety.

———————

Key Principle: **Procedural fairness may require a duty to give reasons.**

R. v Secretary of State for the Home Department Ex p. Doody

Four convicted murderers were told the minimum term they could expect to serve as life prisoners before being considered for parole. They sought judicial review of the Home Secretary's decision on the basis that they ought to have been consulted and that the Minister could not set periods greater than those recommended by the trial judge and the Lord Chief Justice.

Held: (HL) The Secretary of State was obliged to tell the applicants the judicial recommendations on their case and allow them an opportunity to make representations as to the term, but that the Secretary of State was not obliged to abide by the judicial recommendations, provided he gave reasons for so doing. Procedural fairness required that reasons should be given. [1994] 1 A.C. 531.

Commentary

Lord Mustill said that he could have come to the same decision in relation to the duty to give reasons by the reasoning made in *Cunningham*. This is now the leading case on the duty to give reasons and could be said to have indicated there was a general duty on the part of administrators to give reasons for decisions. However in *R. v Higher Education Funding Council Ex p. Institute of Dental Surgery* [1994] 1 W.L.R. 242 the court stressed that the requirement will depend on the circumstances of each case. There the court reviewed the law on the duty to give reasons for administrative decisions, linking it to the requirement of fairness. It identified two strands of cases: those such as *Doody* where the nature of the process itself called in fairness for reasons to be given and *Cunningham* where something peculiar to the decision or a "trigger factor" called for reasons to be given. It does not mean that differing tests of fairness should be applied. In other words the requirements of fairness will vary with the process to which they are being applied. It rejected the argument that in *Cunningham* and *Doody* it was the judicial or quasi-judicial nature of the decision-making that required the duty to give reasons.

Key Principle: **There is no general rule of public law that reasons should be given for decisions by administrators, but if a just decision cannot be given without the provision of reasons, they should be given.**

R. v Ministry of Defence Ex p. Murray

An army sergeant pleaded guilty to wounding before a court martial and brought forward evidence to show that he had 20 years of previously exemplary service and that the offence had been partly caused by the effects of treatment for malaria. Without giving reasons, the court martial rejected this evidence, sent him to prison for six months, reduced him to the ranks and dismissed him from the army. He sought judicial review.

Held: (DC) While there was no general duty to give reasons, fairness would in some cases require that reasons be given, though an application for judicial review would be unlikely to succeed where the reasons were capable of being readily inferred. Fairness here demanded reasons and the court martial decision would be quashed. *The Times*, December 17, 1997, [1998] C.O.D. 134.

Commentary
Lord Bingham C.J. set out fully the principles concerning the duty to give reasons. He drew on the reasoning in *Cunningham, Wilson, Doody* and the *Institute of Dental Surgery* case. The case illustrates that the general proposition that there is no duty to give reasons is close to being overtaken by the number of recognised exceptions. The Freedom of Information Act 2000 requires public authorities covered by the legislation to adopt a publication scheme in devising which they must have regard to the public interest in the publication of reasons for decisions they have made.

Key Principle: **Since the coming into force of the Human Rights Act there is an enhanced duty to give reasons so as to make a statutory provision compliant with the ECHR.**

R. v (1) Dr Graham Feggetter (2) Mental Health Act Commission Ex p. John Wooder
The applicant who had been convicted of manslaughter was detained at a secure mental hospital. A second opinion appointed doctor (SOAD) under Pt IV of the Mental Health Act 1983 said that he should be given medical treatment for a psychiatric condition against his will. The Mental Health Act Commission refused to give reasons for the SOAD's decision. The applicant sought a declaration that a SOAD should provide him with written and adequate reasons.

Held: (CA) The decision to administer medical treatment to a competent non-consenting adult patient fell into the category of cases where the subject-matter was an interest so highly regarded by the law that fairness required reasons to be given as of right. With the coming into force of the Human Rights Act the time had come to declare that fairness required a decision by a SOAD that sanctioned the violation of a competent adult patient's autonomy to be accompanied by reasons. Such reasons should be disclosed to the patient unless the SOAD or the Responsible Medical Officer properly considered that such disclosure would be likely to cause serious harm to the physical or mental health of the patient or any other person. [2002] 3 W.L.R. 591.

Commentary

The Mental Health Act 1983 contained no express obligation to give reasons. The court held that the issue is no longer determined by the common law. The passage of the Human Rights Act means that a duty to give reasons may be implied into a statute, particularly where a provision enables an authority to sanction the violation of the autonomy of a competent adult patient. Brooke L.J. stated that "the fact that the critical decision is made by a doctor in the exercise of his clinical judgment and by a tribunal following a more formal process, cannot . . . be allowed to diminish the significance of the doctor's decision". By contrast in the *Dental Surgery* case (above) special expertise was considered a possible justification for not giving reasons. Commentators have speculated whether as a result of this case the kinds of situations where a duty to give reasons may be implied may include those where other Convention Articles such as Art.10 are engaged.

In *English v Emery Reimbold & Strick Ltd* [2001] W.L.R. 2409 the Court of Appeal heard three cases in which the ground of appeal was that the judge had not given adequate reasons to explain the conclusions. The nature of the duty to give reasons would vary depending on the case but the essential requirement was that the terms of the judgment should enable the parties and any appellate tribunal readily to analyse the reason that was essential to the judgment.

Proportionality

Key Principle: **Proportionality is not a distinct ground of judicial review.**

R. v Secretary of State for the Home Department Ex p. Brind
The Secretary of State made orders under the Broadcasting Act 1981 banning television and radio stations from broadcasting

the words spoken by spokesmen of organisations proscribed under anti-terrorism legislation. Broadcasters sought judicial review of the orders as being outside the Secretary of State's powers among other reasons because the ban was disproportionate to its ostensible object of preventing intimidation by the organisations concerned. The application was dismissed by the Divisional Court and by the Court of Appeal. The broadcasters appealed.

Held: (HL) The court would not apply the doctrine of proportionality because that would mean substituting its own judgment of what was needed to achieve a particular object for that of the Secretary of State who had been given that duty by Parliament. The appeal would be dismissed. (1991) 1 A.C. 696.

Commentary
Their Lordships had differing reasons for rejecting proportionality as a distinct ground of review. Lord Bridge agreed with Lord Roskill that there might be scope for such a ground in the future but it was not appropriate in the present case. Lord Ackner considered it would involve a review of the merits of a decision. Lord Lowry did not see a cause for regret that proportionality was not a part of the English common law since first, Parliament entrusted discretion to elected decision-makers; secondly, judges were not equipped to apply such a ground and thirdly, stability and relative certainty in administrative decisions would be jeopardised. Lord Templeman noting that the European Convention on Human Rights required proportionality to be considered said that the decision was not disproportionate to the damage which the restriction was designed to prevent but nor did it breach *Wednesbury* principles. The Human Rights Act 1998 requires courts determining rights under the European Convention on Human Rights to take into account the jurisprudence of the Strasbourg court (see Ch.3). This is stimulative further development of the doctrine of proportionality in the common law.

Proportionality is now part of the law of the United Kingdom. In *Ex p. Daly* the House of Lords considered the overlap between proportionality and the traditional grounds of review (see p.41). A court may now have to consider proportionality in the sense of the "relative weight accorded to interests and considerations".

Key Principle: **In cases where Articles of the European Convention on Human Rights are engaged the court must follow the proper decision-making structure.**

R. (SB) v Governors of Denbigh High School

The respondent school allowed Muslim pupils to wear the shalwar kameeze, comprising loose trousers and a sleeveless smock. The claimant appeared in a jilbab, a form of dress effectively concealing the shape of her arms and legs, but this was regarded as a violation of the school's uniform policy and she was not allowed to attend school wearing it. She sought judicial review of the school's decision to exclude her, claiming violation of her right to manifest her religion under Art.9(1) of the European Convention on Human Rights.

Held: (CA) The school had failed to follow the proper decision-making structure, which required that it ask first whether the claimant had a right qualifying for protection under Art.9(1), whether subject to justification under Art.9(2) such a right had been violated and, if so, whether the interference was prescribed by law, whether the interference had a legitimate aim and was necessary in a democratic society for achieving that aim so as to justify the interference under Art.9(2). The school had failed to show that the restriction on her dress was necessary. However, if the school on reconsideration could justify its stance under Art.9(2) there would be no breach of the claimant's human rights. [2005] EWCA Civ 199; [2005] 1 W.L.R. 3372.

Commentary

The case shows that freedom to manifest religious belief is subject to certain limitations. The judgment cannot be taken to imply that the school should necessarily have come to a different decision. The court stressed that the situation in England and Wales was different from that in Turkey in that the latter was a secular state. However Brooke L.J. said, "Nothing in this judgment should be taken as meaning that it would be impossible for the school to justify its stance if it were to reconsider its uniform policy in the light of this judgment and were to determine not to alter it in any significant respect." Mummery L.J. said ". . . it would still be possible for the school on a structured reconsideration of the relevant issues, including the Article 9 right of a person in the position of the claimant, to justify its stance on the school uniform policy. If it could, there would be no breach of the Article 9(1) right."

11. POLICE ACCOUNTABILITY AND POWERS

Office of Chief Constable

Key Principle: The police have a duty to enforce the law but Chief Officers have a wide discretion as to the chosen means to carry out that duty. The courts will only intervene where a policy decision amounted to an abandonment of the duty.

R. v Metropolitan Police Commissioner Ex p. Blackburn

The police decided as a matter of policy not to enforce in London gaming clubs the statutory requirement that the games played there should not favour the banker. The applicant, a private citizen, was refused an order of mandamus to compel the police to enforce the law. He appealed, and while his appeal was pending the police announced they had changed their policy. The commissioner contended before the Court of Appeal that there was no duty to enforce the law and that since the appeal was a criminal cause or matter, the court had no jurisdiction.

Held: (CA) The commissioner had a public duty to enforce the law, which he could be compelled to perform. Though he had a discretion not to prosecute, his discretion to make policy decisions was not absolute. The case was not a criminal cause or matter and the court had jurisdiction. [1968] 2 Q.B. 118.

Commentary
The distinguishing feature of this case was that the Commissioner had decided not to prosecute a whole class of offences. Judicial review lies in such an extreme case of the exercise of discretion by the police.

R. v Chief Constable of Devon and Cornwall Ex p. Central Electricity Generating Board

The Central Electricity Generating Board was investigating the possibility of building a nuclear power station on a farm in Cornwall. The farm owners refused to allow the CEGB surveyors onto the land and pickets prevented access. The Board obtained an injunction against the farm owners and began surveying the land. There were further protests, and further injunctions were obtained against the protesters. Others took their places and prevented the Board from completing the survey, an offence under the Town and Country Planning Act 1971. The Board sought the assistance of the Chief Constable to enable it to perform its statutory duties, but the latter declined, saying a "more definitive mandate" would be needed where there was no breach of the peace and no unlawful assembly. An application for a writ of mandamus to instruct the Chief Constable to remove the protesters was dismissed in the Divisional Court and the CEGB appealed.

Held: (CA) The police had power to remove demonstrators where there was a breach of the peace, or a reasonable apprehension that there might be a breach of the peace. The objectors were deliberately breaking the law by obstructing the survey, and the Board was entitled to use the minimum necessary force to exercise its powers. It was for the Board and the police to exercise their respective powers, but the court would not interfere by way of judicial review with the chief constable's decision not to intervene. [1982] Q.B. 458.

Commentary
The court was here reluctant to intervene since the chief constable was able to point to good grounds for a policy decision not to apply the law in a particular case.

Key Principle: **The police do not owe a general duty to identify an unknown criminal even though their failure to do so created a foreseeable risk to a class of potential victims.**

Hill v Chief Constable of West Yorkshire
The plaintiff's daughter was murdered by the so-called Yorkshire Ripper, Peter Sutcliffe. She brought an action against the police, alleging that the daughter's death had been caused by their negligent failure to capture Sutcliffe sooner.

Held: (HL) The police owed no general duty of care to identify or apprehend an unknown criminal, nor was there an individual duty of care to persons who might suffer as a result of crimes committed by a criminal who had not been apprehended. [1989] A.C. 53.

Commentary
The House of Lords was of the opinion that if the police were held
to owe a duty of care to potential victims of crime this would
hamper investigations because they would be required to justify
and explain every step they took. In *Osman v United Kingdom*
[1999] 29 E.H.R.R. 245 the European Court of Human Rights
considered this aspect of police immunity from civil suit. It was
alleged that the police and social services had failed to prevent the
murder of a schoolboy's father by a teacher despite warnings of
the latter's suspicious behaviour. The immunity of the police, so
the applicants argued inter alia, was a breach of the right of access
to the court under Art.6(1). The Court agreed with this argument.
Subsequently the Strasbourg Court retreated from the position
in *Osman* (see p.41).

Legal Basis of Police Powers

Key Principle: **The Crown retains a prerogative power to
keep the peace.**

**R. v Secretary of State for the Home Department Ex p.
Northumbria Police Authority**
The Home Secretary made provisions for the supply from a
central store of plastic bullets and CS gas to police forces. Chief
constables could buy supplies with the approval of their police
authority. But if the authority looked likely to refuse approval,
the riot control equipment could be bought directly from the
central store. The Northumbria police authority challenged the
scheme on the grounds that the Home Secretary had no power
to maintain a central store or to supply police forces without the
approval of their authority, save in serious emergency. The
Divisional Court held the Home Secretary had no power under
the Police Act 1964 to act as he had, but could do so under the
royal prerogative. Both sides appealed.

Held: (CA) The Home Secretary was empowered by the Police
Act to keep a store. Police authorities did not have an exclusive
right to provide police with equipment and the Home Secretary
could do so without the relevant authority's approval. The
Home Secretary had authority to act at all times, and not only in
emergency to keep the peace. That power existed by virtue of
the Police Act or in the alternative under the prerogative which
existed in the Middle Ages and had never been surrendered by
the Crown. [1989] 1 Q.B. 26.

Commentary
In this case an ancient prerogative to maintain the peace was
recognised by the courts as existing alongside the statute governing
police matters. The court was here demonstrating its reluctance to
intervene in politically controversial areas involving police powers.

Arrest

For a valid arrest to be made it is necessary not only for there to
be a power of arrest but also for the correct procedure to be
followed. Powers of arrest are now codified in the Police and
Criminal Evidence Act (Pt III) as amended by the Serious
Organised Crime and Police Act 2005, but to a very large extent
this draws on common law principles and in addition common
law powers and other specific statutory powers remain.

Key Principle: **Police and Criminal Evidence Act 1984, s.28(1):**

> "Subject to subsection (5) below, where a person is arrested,
> otherwise than by being informed that he is under arrest, the arrest
> is not lawful unless the person arrested is informed that he is
> under arrest as soon as is practicable after his arrest."

Key Principle: **For an arrest to be valid the fact of arrest has
to be made clear and the person has to be compulsorily
detained.**

Alderson v Booth
A motorist was told by a police constable: "I shall have to ask
you to come to the police station for further tests." Later he
appeared before magistrates on a charge under a section of the
Road Safety Act 1967 which required an arrest. The motorist
told the magistrates he had gone voluntarily to the police
station, and the justices decided he had not been arrested, since
the words used by the constable lacked the necessary element of
compulsion. The prosecutor appealed.

Held: (DC) An arrest could be carried out by any form of
words indicating compulsion. Very clear words were preferable

such as "I arrest you". Whether or not the defendant had been arrested was a decision of fact for the magistrates with which the court would not interfere. [1969] 2 Q.B. 216.

Commentary
The importance of procedure is indicated here. Since the motorist reasonably believed that compliance with a request to accompany the officer was voluntary then an arrest had not been made. Arrest means a deprivation of liberty.

Key Principle: **The reason for arrest must be made known. Police and Criminal Evidence Act, s.28:**

> "(3) Subject to subsection (5) below, no arrest is lawful unless the person arrested is informed of the ground for the arrest at the time of, or as soon as is practicable after, the arrest. (4) Where a person is arrested by a constable, subsection (3) above applies regardless of whether the ground for the arrest is obvious."

Key Principle: **The reason given for arrest must be the real reason.**

Christie v Leachinsky
The plaintiff was told he was being arrested under the Liverpool Corporation Act 1921 for unlawfully possessing a bale of cloth. The police had no power to arrest for the relevant offence without warrant because the Act only allowed arrest where the person's name and address were not known. The claimant was tried for larceny and acquitted. He sought damages against the police for false imprisonment. The police claimed that at the time of the arrest they reasonably suspected the claimant of having stolen or unlawfully received the cloth.

Held: (HL) The claimant had not been told the true reason for his arrest, but had been given a different reason which was not a ground for arrest without warrant. Accordingly he was entitled to damages for false imprisonment. [1947] A.C. 573.

Key Principle: **The question whether the real reason for the arrest had been given was a question of fact.**

Abbassy v Commissioner of Police for the Metropolis
The claimants were in a car which was stopped by four police officers after being driven inconsiderately. The driver refused to satisfy one of the police officers about the ownership of the car and was arrested. The police officer gave the reason for the arrest as "unlawful possession". The passenger tried to stop the police taking the driver away and was herself arrested for obstruction and assault. Both were acquitted at trial and sued the police for assault and battery, false imprisonment and malicious prosecution. The judge ruled that the driver's arrest had been unlawful because the police officer's explanation of the arrest was insufficient. The jury found that the first claimant had been assaulted before arrest. The police appealed.

Held: (CA) The judge should have left to the jury as a matter of fact the issue whether or not the police officer's explanation was sufficient. That part of the case should be retried. [1990] 1 W.L.R. 385.

Commentary
The police must give the reason for the arrest but that they do not have to use precise or technical language. *Christie v Leachinsky* (see p.164) still provides clear guidance on the information which should be provided upon arrest.

Key Principle: **There is no requirement under s.28 PACE for the officer who gave the grounds of arrest to be the arresting officer.**

Harbhajan Singh Dhesi v Chief Constable of the West Midlands Police
The claimant and his brother were on their way home from a public house when they encountered a group of men who had already been reported to the police for fighting. Police arrived and spoke to the claimant who ran away with his brother. A police dog was brought to the scene and, after a struggle, the claimant and his brother were arrested and charged with affray. The claimant agreed in court to be bound over and in later

proceedings for wrongful arrest was awarded only a small amount of damages. He appealed on a number of grounds, including that his arrest did not comply with s.28 of PACE in that he was given grounds for arrest by an officer other than the one who arrested him.

Held: (CA) There was no need to write into s.28 of PACE a requirement that the grounds of arrest had to be given by the arresting officer. The importance of s.28 was to ensure that a person knew he was under arrest and the reasons for the arrest. *The Times*, May 9, 2000.

Commentary
This case illustrates the pragmatic approach which is taken to s.28. In practice also it may be possible to rectify initial failings. Thus in *Lewis v Chief Constable of South Wales* [1991] 1 All E.R. 206 the complainants had not been informed of the reasons for their arrest until they arrived at the police station. There they were detained for a further five hours before being released without charge. The Court of Appeal upheld the ruling of the trial judge that their arrests were only unlawful for the time (10 minutes and 23 minutes) they were held without being given reasons. They were not therefore unlawfully detained for the time they were held at the station.

Key Principle: **The behaviour of the arrestee may be a ground for delay in giving the reason for the arrest.**

Director of Public Prosecutions v Hawkins
The defendant was arrested for assaulting a police officer. He struggled during the arrest, assaulting three officers. At no time was he told the reason for his arrest. He was charged with the assaults which occurred during the struggle. The magistrates accepted that there was no case to answer because the police had failed to inform the defendant of the reason for his arrest as soon as practicable so that the arrest was unlawful and the arresting officers had not been acting in the execution of their duty. The DPP appealed by way of case stated.

Held: (DC) The police were under a duty to state the ground of arrest as soon as practicable. But they were also under a duty to maintain the arrest until the arrested person could be informed. The failure of the police after the arrest to inform the defendant of the grounds made the arrest unlawful by s.28(3) of the Police and Criminal Evidence Act 1984. However, the reason for the delay was the defendants' behaviour and at the relevant time so far as the charge was concerned it was not practicable to give the reason. The fact that the arrest had subsequently become unlawful did not retrospectively make the actions of the arresting officers unlawful. The appeal would be allowed. [1988] 1 W.L.R. 1166.

Commentary

The court acknowledged that the police have some leeway as to the time of informing the arrestee that he is under arrest. The lawfulness of the arrest was only affected when the police had failed to give the reason for arrest when it was practicable to do so. In *Murray v Ministry of Defence* [1988] 1 W.L.R. 692 the House of Lords held that delay by soldiers in Northern Ireland in informing a woman of the fact of her arrest was acceptable. The European Court of Human Rights subsequently found no breach of the Convention.

Key Principle: **Police and Criminal Evidence Act, s.24 as amended by Serious Organised Crime and Police Act 2005:**

> "(1) A constable may arrest without warrant: (d) anyone whom he has reasonable grounds for suspecting to be committing an offence. (2) If a constable has reasonable grounds for suspecting that an offence has been committed, he may arrest without a warrant anyone whom he has reasonable grounds to suspect of being guilty of it."

Key Principle: **Reasonable suspicion requires answering "yes" to the following questions: "Did the arresting officer suspect the person to be guilty?" (a subjective test) and "was there a reasonable cause for suspicion?" (an objective test).**

Castorina v Chief Constable of Surrey

The claimant was a former employee of a company that was burgled. Detectives who had concluded that the burglary was an inside job arrested her, held her for four hours and then freed her without charge. She brought an action for wrongful arrest. The judge awarded her damages on the basis that the police did not have sufficient material to found a reasonable suspicion that she was the burglar. The police appealed.

Held: (CA) On the facts the arresting officers had reasonable cause to suspect the claimant. The appeal would be allowed. [1988] N.L.J. 180.

Commentary
Reasonable suspicion is not defined in PACE and here again the court seemed to be giving guidance that only a fairly low level of suspicion was required.

This case was decided on the original version of the 1984 Act which confined the power of arrest to "arrestable offences". The concept of an "arrestable offence" in s.24 of PACE was abolished by the 2005 Act which also repealed s.25 of the 1984 Act concerning general arrest conditions.

Key Principle: **Reasonable suspicion on the part of an arresting officer must have a material basis, not merely a reaction to instructions from a senior officer.**

O'Hara v Chief Constable of the Royal Ulster Constabulary
The plaintiff was arrested by a detective constable of the Royal Ulster Constabulary under the Prevention of Terrorism Act 1984. The constable had been told at a briefing that the claimant had been involved in a murder, but had no other basis for suspecting the claimant, who was eventually released without charge. The claimant claimed damages for wrongful arrest. The trial judge held that the constable had a reasonable suspicion of the claimant's involvement in the murder. The claimant appealed.

Held: (HL) Grounds for suspicion did not have to be based on the officer's own observations but could arise from information he had received, even if it was subsequently shown to be false, provided that a reasonable man, having regard to all the surrounding circumstances, would regard them as reasonable grounds for suspicion. A mere order by a superior officer to arrest would be insufficient to afford reasonable grounds for suspicion. Appeal dismissed. [1997] A.C. 286.

Commentary

The court here was moving closer to the test for reasonable suspicion contained in Art.5(1)(c) of the ECHR. There has to be evidence to establish the reasonable basis of the suspicion. Although the case turns on the interpretation of s.12(1) of the Prevention of Terrorism Act 1984 it also provides authority for the interpretation of sections of PACE 1984 and other statutes where reasonable suspicion is the ground upon which a police constable's discretion can be exercised.

Key Principle: **There is no common law power to detain for questioning without arrest.**

Rice v Connolly

The defendant was seen by a police officer in an area where there had been several break-ins. He refused to give his name and address, nor would he accompany the officer to a police box unless arrested. He was convicted of obstructing the officer in the execution of his duty. He appealed.

Held: (DC) Every citizen had a moral or social duty to assist the police, but there was no such legal duty, and the defendant in refusing to answer the police officer's questions was within his common law rights. He had not "wilfully" obstructed the policeman, even though his attitude made it more difficult for the officer to carry out his duty. [1966] 2 Q.B. 414.

Commentary

This pre-PACE case gives guidance on the borderline between legitimate and illegitimate disobedience to police orders or requests. Three tests must be satisfied if liability for an offence under what is now s.89 of the Police Act 1996 is to be made out. First, the officer must be acting in the execution of his duty; secondly, the defendant must do an act which made it more difficult for the officer to carry out that duty; and thirdly, the defendant must have acted wilfully. The case must now be set in the context of the abrogation of the "right to silence" in CJPOA 1994 (see p.174). It must be stressed that the citizen who does not co-operate in police questioning under certain conditions incurs only possible evidential consequences not civil or criminal liability for failure to respond.

Key Principle: **Refusal to answer police questions accompanied by abusive language may give grounds for arrest for obstruction.**

Ricketts v Cox
Police officers looking for youths responsible for a serious assault approached the defendant early one morning and questioned him. He was unco-operative, abusive and hostile and tried to walk away from the officers. He was convicted of obstructing the police in the execution of their duty and appealed.

Held: (DC) On the facts there was no doubt that he had committed the offence. (1981) 74 Cr.App.R. 298.

Commentary
The feature that was present in *Ricketts v Cox* but not in *Rice v Connelly* was abusive language and behaviour by the defendant. This arguably is the lowest level of behaviour which could qualify as obstructive.

Key Principle: **The police may be acting in the course of their duty in using minimal restraint in detaining to ask questions without an arrest.**

Donnelly v Jackman
The defendant was approached by a police officer in the street who wanted to ask him about a recent offence. The defendant ignored the officer's request to stop. The officer touched the defendant on the shoulder intending to stop him to speak to him, but not to charge or arrest him, and the defendant struck the officer. He was convicted of assaulting a constable in the execution of his duty. He appealed.

Held: (DC) The police officer was not acting outside the ambit of his duties in trying to stop the defendant in order to speak to him. The conviction would stand. Not every trivial interference with a citizen's liberty amounted to a course of conduct sufficient to take an officer out of the course of his duties. [1970] 1 W.L.R. 562.

Collins v Wilcock

The defendant and another woman, a known prostitute, were seen apparently soliciting men in the street. The defendant refused to be questioned by police and tried to walk away. When an officer tried to restrain her she scratched her arm and was arrested and charged with assaulting an officer in the execution of her duty. She was convicted and appealed.

Held: (DC) It was unlawful for a police officer to use force to try to stop and detain another person without using the power of arrest. Police could caution suspects under the Street Offences Act 1959 but had no power to stop and detain a woman to implement the system of cautioning. The police officer had not been acting in the course of her duty when she tried to restrain the defendant, and the conviction would be quashed. [1984] 1 W.L.R. 1172.

Commentary

These two cases illustrate the scope of the test to be applied to establish if the officer is acting in the execution of his duty in making physical contact with a citizen. In *Collins* there had been an unjustified detention by the police officer since the relevant statute, the Street Offences Act 1959, did not authorise detention. The test set out in that case was whether taking into account the nature of his duty, his use of physical contact in the face of non-co-operation persisted beyond generally acceptable standards of conduct. In *Donnelly*, which was referred to in *Wilcock*, Talbot J. had said not every trivial interference with a citizen's liberty amounted to a course of conduct sufficient to take the officer out of the course of his duties.

Breach of the Peace

Key Principle: **At common law power to arrest is available to a constable and a private citizen where either a breach of the peace is committed in the presence of the person making the** arrest; or where the arrestor reasonably believes that such a breach will be committed in the immediate future by the person arrested although he has not yet committed any breach; or where a breach of the peace has been committed and it is reasonably believed that a renewal of it is threatened.

R. v Howell

Police were called to a disturbance in the street during the early hours outside a house where a party was taking place. They asked a group including the defendant to move on. The defendant among others swore at the police and was told he would be arrested for disturbing the peace if he continued. The defendant argued with the policeman and a fight developed. He was charged with resisting arrest. At trial the defendant submitted that there was no case to answer because the prosecution had failed to show that any violence had been used before the arrest and because the defendant had merely used reasonable force to resist unlawful arrest. The defendant was convicted and appealed.

Held: (CA) A constable or a private citizen could arrest without warrant if he reasonably and honestly believed that a breach of the peace was about to be committed. Where an arrest was made for an anticipated breach of the peace it was enough for a valid arrest for the constable to say the arrest was for "breach of the peace". Threat of violence was sufficient to constitute a breach of the peace. [1982] Q.B. 416.

Commentary

The ingredients of a breach of the peace may also give rise to arrest powers under PACE, but the private citizen under PACE cannot lawfully arrest on the basis of reasonable belief that an offence may occur. In addition the public order offences under POA and CJPOA give specific powers of arrest to constables and the elements of the statutory offences will overlap with the factors involved in breach of the peace. (See Ch.12). The Serious Organised Crime and Police Act 2005 gives increased powers of arrest to citizens, see now PACE s.24A.

Albert v Lavin

The defendant jumped a bus queue, several of whom objected. A plain clothes police constable tried to prevent the defendant getting on the bus. There was a struggle and the constable pulled him away from the queue. The constable said he was a police officer but the defendant did not believe him and struck him several times. The constable arrested him for assaulting a constable in the execution of his duty. The magistrates held that the defendant's reaction to being prevented from boarding the bus was a continuing breach of the peace. Though he genuinely believed the constable was not a police officer he had no reasonable grounds for that belief. If he had been unlawfully detained he had used only reasonable force to effect his release. The man appealed.

Held: (HL) Every citizen had a right to prevent a breach or threatened breach of the peace. Reasonable steps to do so could include detaining the peace-breaker against his will. The defendant's assault on the constable would not have been justified even had the constable not been a policeman, so it was irrelevant whether he had acted in the belief that he was not. [1982] A.C. 546.

Key Principle: **The police may arrest for obstruction those who ignore their request for action aimed at avoiding a threat of immediate and imminent violence.**

Moss v McLachlan

Striking miners on their way to picket in Nottinghamshire were stopped at a road block where police told them to turn back on the grounds that they feared a breach of the peace. The miners tried to push through the police cordon and were arrested for obstructing the police in the execution of their duty. They were convicted and appealed by way of case stated.

Held: (DC) The police honestly and on reasonable grounds feared a breach of the peace if the miners were allowed to proceed. They were therefore acting in the execution of their duty in stopping the pickets. A constable who apprehends a breach of the peace is under a duty to prevent it. It could not be held that the police could only stop the men if it was clear from their words and deeds that they intended a breach of the peace. The defendants had been rightly convicted. [1985] I.R.L.R. 76.

Commentary
The case illustrates the important connection between the lawfulness of an arrest and the requirements of obstructing the police in the execution of their duty, now s.89 of the Police Act 1996.

Key principle: **In cases of apprehended breach of the peace where the police are entitled to use their preventive power any detention of individuals must be proportionate to the aim of preventing the breach occurring.**

R. (Laporte) v Chief Constable of the Gloucestershire Constabulary
The police stopped several busloads of protesters on their way to a demonstration at a US airbase against the preparations for the Iraq war. The vehicles were escorted back to London without being allowed to stop. The Administrative Court held that though the arrest of the passengers was unlawful it was legitimate for the police to prevent them getting to the airbase. They appealed on the basis that the Administrative Court had applied the wrong test in determining whether the action was lawful under arts 10 and 11 of the European Human Rights Convention.

Held: (CA) Though the police were entitled to intervene to prevent an anticipated breach of the peace, it was not a proportionate response to escort the passengers back to London without stopping. A less drastic way of dealing with the threat should have been chosen. [2004] EWHC 253.

Commentary
Moss v McLachlan was applied in relation to the features of the situation which allowed the police to exercise their preventive powers. The case sets limits on the period of "transitory detention".

Right to Silence

Key Principle: **S.34, Criminal Justice and Public Order Act 1994:**

"(1) Where, in any proceedings against a person for an offence, evidence is given that the accused—(a) at any time before he was charged with the offence, on being questioned under caution by a constable trying to discover whether or by whom the offence had been committed, failed to mention any fact relied on in his defence in those proceedings . . . (d) the court or jury, in determining whether the accused is guilty of the offence charged, may draw such inferences from the failure as appear proper."

Key Principle: **Legal advice not to answer questions at police interview will not in itself amount to sufficient reason for not mentioning relevant matters which may be later relied on by the defendant.**

R. v Condron

Heroin addicts were arrested on drug charges. Their solicitor considered them unfit to answer questions because of their withdrawal symptoms, and advised them to say nothing at interview. The police doctor considered them fit. They gave no answers at interview. At trial, it was submitted the jury should be told not to draw adverse inferences from the interview evidence because they had refused to answer on legal advice. The judge directed that it was a matter for the jury whether or not to draw adverse inferences.

Held: (CA) There was no rule that legal advice not to answer questions precluded the drawing of inferences under s.34. Trial judges should direct juries that before drawing inferences from silence the jury should be satisfied that that the accused's failure to mention facts could only sensibly be attributed to the accused having fabricated the evidence subsequently. The advice given by a solicitor may be taken into account by the jury in deciding whether the reason given for remaining silent at interview was reasonable. There were flaws in the judge's directions but the conviction was not unsafe. [1997] 1 W.L.R. 827.

Commentary

Legal advisors have difficult options to weigh up when faced with defendants who may be emotionally or physically vulnerable and thus arguably not in a position to be interviewed. If the suspect follows advice to remain silent, adverse inferences may be drawn at trial. In *Condron v United Kingdom* (2001) 31 E.H.R.R. 1, the European Court of Human Rights held that the trial judge had not properly directed the jury on the issue of the applicants' silence during police interviews and therefore there was a breach of Art.6. The trial judge had drawn the jury's attention to the applicants' explanation for their silence being based on the advice of their solicitor. However, he did so in terms which left the jury at liberty to draw an adverse inference notwithstanding that it might have been satisfied as to the plausibility of the explanations. The Court reiterated the point made in *Murray v UK* that the right to silence could not be considered an absolute right. See also *R. v Cowan* [1996] Q.B. 373 and *R. v Argent* [1997] 2 Cr.App.R. 27. See also *Beckles v United Kingdom* 36 E.H.R.R. 13.

Art.6: Right to a fair trial

Murray v United Kingdom
The applicant had been found guilty of aiding and abetting unlawful imprisonment after being arrested in an IRA safe house. He was interviewed without a solicitor and remained silent. The trial judge informed the applicant that because of his failure to account for his presence at the house, and because he had not given evidence at trial, he had drawn adverse inferences under the Criminal Evidence (Northern Ireland) Order 1988. The applicant claimed that his rights under Art.6 had been violated.

Held:

(1) In view of the fact that remaining silent had serious consequences at the trial the pressure on the defendant to speak to the police was sufficiently great to warrant the presence of a lawyer. The failure to secure the solicitor's presence therefore was a breach of Art.6(3)(c).

(2) The right to remain silent under police questioning and the privilege against self incrimination are generally recognised international standards which lie at the heart of the notion of fair procedure under Art.6. But these immunities were not absolutes. (1996) 22 E.H.R.R. 29.

Commentary
The Strasbourg Court thus refused to declare that the drawing of inferences from silence was necessarily a violation of the constitutional principle of the right to a fair trial. It emphasised that a conviction based wholly or mainly on the accused's silence would be incompatible with Art.6 but that on the facts of the case it was

proper to allow inferences to be drawn from the defendant's failure to respond to police questioning. In the circumstances the delay of 48 hours in giving the accused access to a lawyer was however significant although the Court declined to make a ruling that a refusal to allow a solicitor to be present during police interviews was always a violation of Art.6. The United Kingdom Government has now amended ss.34, 36 and 37 of the Criminal Justice and Public Order Act to provide that inferences should not be drawn from a refusal to respond to police questions where the suspect has not been allowed access to legal advice. In *Beckles v United Kingdom, The Times*, October 15, 2002 the Strasbourg court held that the fact that a trial judge leaves a jury with the option of drawing an adverse inference from an accused's silence during police interviews or at trial is not itself incompatible with the right to a fair trial. The fairness can be determined only in the light of all the factors in the case, including the terms of the judge's directions to the jury. The fact that the judge had failed to give appropriate weight to the accused's explanation for his silence was a violation of Art.6.

Key Principle: **Where answers are given in the course of compulsory proceedings their use by the prosecution at a subsequent criminal trial may violate Art.6.**

Saunders v United Kingdom

A company chief executive was questioned by Department of Trade inspectors investigating a takeover battle. He was obliged by law to answer their questions on pain of up to two years' imprisonment. The inspectors recommended prosecution and transcripts of his interrogation by the inspectors were used against him at trial.

Held: (ECtHR) The use of the transcripts at trial violated the applicant's right not to be forced to incriminate himself. The right was primarily concerned with respecting the will of the accused to remain silent. (1996) 23 E.H.R.R. 313.

Commentary

The Court saw no inherent objection to legislation which compels parties to answer questions in the course of non-judicial inquiries but "the public interest cannot be invoked to justify the use of answers compulsorily obtained in a non-judicial investigation to incriminate the accused during trial proceedings". It did not extend to evidence which might be obtained by compulsion but was independent of the suspect's will, such as breath samples. In the wake of this decision the Attorney-General issued guidelines designed to prevent the Crown from using what were known as items of "derivative evidence" obtained in extra-judicial investigations. The Youth Justice and Criminal Evidence Act 1999 Sch.3 has amended those provisions such as s.434 of the Companies Act 1985 which formerly purported to render admissible in subsequent criminal proceedings evidence procured by compulsion during investigations. Subsequently the applications of Saunders' three co-defendants succeeded on identical grounds at Strasbourg, see *ILJ, GMR and AKP v United Kingdom, The Times*, October 13, 2000. In *R. v Allen* [2001] U.K.H.L. 45 the House of Lords considered the application of the privilege against self-incrimination to tax proceedings in two separate cases. The defendants ran companies in Jersey. The first defendant's companies were involved in contravening sanctions against the South African apartheid regime. He was convicted of revenue offences connected with the sanctions-busting. The second defendant was convicted of evading corporation tax on property deals. The first defendant asserted that his rights under Art.1 of the First Protocol had been violated by tax statutes which deemed his company's profits to be his for tax purposes, the second that he had been deprived of a fair trial by being obliged to answer questions about his financial affairs under the threat of criminal sanctions. Their appeals were rejected by the Court of Appeal and they appealed to the House of Lords which held that the deeming provisions in the tax statute were well within the margin of appreciation allowed to the government. For the purpose of tax-collection states were entitled to require citizens to declare income and could impose sanctions for non-compliance. It followed that the revenue's requests for information did not constitute a breach of the right against self-incrimination. The defendant had given false information in response to the Revenue's inquiries, so any inducement to disclose that he might have been offered could not infringe his rights under Art.6.

In *Attorney-General's Reference (No.7 of 2000)* [2001] 1 W.L.R. 1879 the Court of Appeal held that the privilege against self-incrimination did not cover pre-existing documents obtained by compulsion but existing independently of the will of defendant. In that case a bankrupt had been threatened with a penalty under the Insolvency Act 1986 if he did not hand over books and papers relating to his estate. He was charged under the criminal law. Article 6 was not infringed by the use of these compulsory powers.

Questioning—Detention—Confessions

Key Principle: **Police and Criminal Evidence Act 1984, s.76:**

> "(2) If, in any proceedings where the prosecution proposes to give in evidence a confession made by an accused person, it is represented to the court that the confession was or may have been obtained—(a) by oppression of the person who made it; or (b) in consequence of anything said or done which was likely, in the circumstances existing at the time, to render unreliable any confession which might be made by him in consequence thereof, the court shall not allow the confession to be given in evidence against him except in so far as the prosecution proves to the court beyond reasonable doubt that the confession (notwithstanding that it may be true) was not obtained as aforesaid."

Key Principle: **Oppression is to be given its dictionary meaning.**

R. v Fulling
The prosecution at the defendant's trial sought to adduce a confession she had made after persistent questioning. She wanted the judge to exclude the confession under s.76 of PACE on the basis that the prosecution had not proved it was not obtained by oppression. The judge ruled that oppression meant something over and above the oppression normal to police custody and dismissed her application. She appealed.

Held: (CA) The word "oppression" was to be given its ordinary dictionary meaning of "the exercise of authority in a burdensome harsh or wrongful manner; unjust or cruel treatment of subjects". It was thought that most invariably this would involve some impropriety by the interrogator. [1987] 1 Q.B. 426.

Commentary
This case amplifies the non-exhaustive definition of oppression contained in s.76(8): "In this section oppression includes torture, inhuman or degrading treatment and the use or threat of violence

(whether or not amounting to torture)". The test as set out in *Fulling* on its face could mean that any breach of the Act or Codes could amount to oppression. However, this wider interpretation has been precluded by the courts since it is stressed in *Fulling* that impropriety on the part of the police was required before the section could apply. In *Hughes* (see below) it became clear that the terms "wrongful and improper" required an element of deliberate abuse of power or bad faith. Furthermore, in practice the courts have reserved this section for the most serious acts of misconduct by the police, thus although bad faith is a necessary precondition it is not a sufficient one. The exercise of discretion under PACE, s.78 is more usually applied to deliberate misuse of police power. The stress on the state of mind of the alleged oppressor rather than the effect on the detainee has been the subject of academic criticism.

Key Principle: **The test under PACE, s.76(2)(b) requires both "something said or done" and "circumstances existing at the time" to have a causal effect on making any confession so obtained unreliable.**

R. v Harvey
The defendant, who was a psychopathic alcoholic of low intelligence, was charged with murder. With her lesbian lover, she had been present when the murder occurred. Both women were arrested close to the scene of the crime. On arrest, in the presence of the defendant, the other woman confessed to the crime. The following day the defendant confessed. The other woman retracted her confession, became a Crown witness, but died before the trial. At trial the only evidence against her was the confession. The defence sought to have the confession excluded.

Held: (CCC) The judge was not satisfied beyond reasonable doubt that the confession was not obtained as a result of the defendant's having heard her lover's confession. The defendant's confession would be excluded and the jury instructed to acquit. [1988] Crim. L.R. 241.

Commentary
The application of the "two limbs of the reliability" test is set out in this case. There are two aspects, namely "something said or

done" (here hearing the first confession of the lover) and "in the circumstances existing at the time" (here the mental state of the defendant). In practice the section is frequently reserved for the vulnerable defendant, i.e. one whose mental or emotional state makes what is said or done likely to affect the reliability of any confession made under those circumstances. Another feature of the test is that there is no need for police impropriety.

R. v Goldenberg
A heroin addict requested an interview five days after his arrest on a charge of conspiracy to supply drugs. At the interview he gave information about his heroin supplier. His counsel argued at trial that the interview might be unreliable because the admissions were made to get bail and he might be expected to say anything to feed his addiction.

Held: (CA) The words "said or done" in s.76(2)(b) do not include anything said or done by the person making the confession. (1988) 88 Cr.App.R. 285.

Commentary
Here in a controversial decision the Court held that the "something said or done" cannot be something self-inflicted by the defendant.

Key Principle: **Police and Criminal Evidence Act 1984, s.78:**

"(1) In any proceedings the court may refuse to allow evidence on which the prosecution proposes to rely to be given if it appears to the court that, having regard to all the circumstances, including the circumstances in which the evidence was obtained, the admission of the evidence would have such an adverse effect on the fairness of the proceedings that the court ought not to admit it. (2) Nothing in this section shall prejudice any rule of law requiring a court to exclude evidence."

Key Principle: **A breach or breaches of PACE particularly s.58 or the Code in the absence of bad faith on the part of the police may lead to exclusion of confession evidence if it has caused the defendant to confess.**

R. v Samuel

The defendant was arrested for armed robbery. His request to see a solicitor was refused under s.58 of PACE. He was questioned and confessed to two burglaries but denied robbery. He was charged with the burglaries but his solicitor was denied access. The defendant was again questioned and eventually confessed to the robbery, whereupon he was charged and allowed to see his solicitor. He appealed on the grounds that the judge should have ruled the final interview inadmissible.

Held: (CA) The denial of access by the police could not be properly continued once the defendant had been charged so that there was no power to prevent the defendant consulting a solicitor after he had been charged. In any event the police had to show that there were reasonable grounds to believe that the solicitor would deliberately or accidentally warn other suspects or hamper the recovery of property. There were no grounds for thinking that the respected and experienced solicitor involved would do so. The conviction would be quashed. [1988] 1 Q.B. 615.

Commentary

In this case the Court of Appeal held that in failing to allow access to a solicitor "the appellant was denied improperly one of the most important and fundamental rights of the citizen". Here it was significant that the appellant was not a persistent criminal and was thus less likely to be able to handle the interview without legal advice. S.58 allows delay in access to a solicitor if certain conditions are met. Following the Serious Organised Crime and Police Act 2005 such delay may be lawful in the case of indictable offences replacing the qualifying factor of serious arrestable offences.

Key Principle: **The presence or absence of bad faith on the part of the police will affect the exercise of the court's discretion to exclude confession evidence obtained by a breach of PACE or the Codes.**

R. v Alladice

The defendant was interviewed by police after an armed robbery and according to them admitted involvement. He was asked if he wanted a solicitor and said he did though he refused to sign to that effect. He was convicted and appealed on the basis that his admissions ought to have been excluded because he had been denied access to a solicitor.

Held: (CA) Though s.58 had been breached, there was no suggestion of oppression and no reason to believe the absence of a solicitor rendered the confession unreliable. The judge had rejected the allegation that the police had invented his confession. The conviction would be upheld. (1988) 87 Cr.App.R. 380.

Commentary
The factor which distinguished this case from *Samuel* was that the appellant was criminally experienced who knew his rights regardless of the presence of a solicitor. In addition the court considered that the absence of bad faith on the part of the police was significant thus suggesting obiter that a deliberate breach of s.58 will certainly lead to exclusion under s.78.

R. v Mason
The defendant was arrested for setting fire to a motor car. During questioning police officers untruthfully told him his fingerprints had been found on glass fragments in the car. They told the same lie to his solicitor. The solicitor advised him to explain any involvement he had in the incident, and the defendant confessed that he had got a friend to do it. The judge held the confession admissible and the defendant appealed.

Held: (CA) The confession ought to have been excluded. The judge had failed to take account of the deception practised on the defendant's solicitor, whose duty it was to advise the defendant unfettered by false information from the police. [1988] 1 W.L.R. 139.

Commentary
This is another illustration that deliberate misuse of police power in investigating an offence will render a confession inadmissible.

R. v Hughes
The defendant was convicted of deception and handling on the basis of admissions made at interview. He had been arrested on a Saturday afternoon in winter and taken to a police station more than 100 miles away where he was put into a cold cell. He

asked for a duty solicitor but was wrongly told none was available. He said he would be interviewed without a solicitor. In the course of the interview he made damaging admissions. He appealed on the basis that his admissions should have been excluded under s.78(1) of PACE.

Held: (CA) S.78 required consideration first of the circumstances in which the interview came to be conducted, then the question whether its admission would have an adverse effect on the fairness of the trial. The judge was satisfied that the appellant genuinely consented to be interviewed, even though he was not aware of the true state of affairs, because he was cold and unhappy. The judge had to balance the interests of the prosecution and those of the defence in deciding where justice lay. [1988] Crim. L.R. 519.

Commentary
Here the Court of Appeal also considered the operation of the oppression test and considered that denial of legal advice due to a misunderstanding not bad faith on the part of the police could not lead to exclusion under this section. Here as in *Mason* the cases do not make it clear when s.78 and when s.76(2)(b) is appropriate for deliberate malpractice.

Key Principle: **Serious and substantial breaches of PACE and Code C should lead to exclusion of evidence obtained thereby.**

R. v Canale
The defendant was interviewed by police in connection with a series of robberies. At two interviews he allegedly admitted providing the robbers with a shotgun and driving the get-away vehicle. Contrary to the PACE Code of Practice, these interviews were not contemporaneously recorded, nor was any reason recorded for failing to do so. Two subsequent interviews were recorded contemporaneously and at them the defendant made similar admissions. At trial, the defendant sought to exclude the interviews but the judge admitted them. The defendant then gave evidence that the admissions at interview had been made as a result of a trick. He was convicted and appealed on the basis that the conviction was unsafe and unsatisfactory.

Held: (CA) Because of the absence of a contemporary record of the first two interviews, the judge had been deprived of the very evidence he needed to enable him to decide whether the interviews were admissible. The jury, too, had been deprived of evidence which would have enabled them to decide the truth of the defendant's story. The police officers had flagrantly and deliberately breached the code and the judge should have used his discretion to keep out the interviews. [1990] 2 All E.R. 187.

Commentary
This case is an example of the difference between ss.76(2)(b) and 78. The former was considered not to be appropriate since as the appellant had been in the Parachute Regiment he was not in the same position as a vulnerable defendant faced with police questions.

Key Principle: **Article 6 may be violated where the state employs a method of interrogation which evades statutory safeguards.**

Allan v United Kingdom
The applicant was suspected of murder and maintained his right to silence at interview. He was placed in a cell under covert video surveillance with an informer who had been coached by the police to try and obtain a confession. Recordings made in the cell were admitted at trial and he was convicted.

Held: (ECtHR) The right to silence and the privilege against self-incrimination were primarily designed to protect against improper compulsion by the authorities and the obtaining of evidence through coercion or oppression in defiance of the will of the accused. But the scope of the right was not confined to cases the will of the accused had been directly overborne by coercion or in some other way. The right was at the heart of the notion of a fair procedure and served to protect the suspect's freedom to choose whether to speak or to remain silent when questioned by the police. The subterfuge used by the authorities effectively undermined the suspect's freedom of choice. In all the circumstances, the right to silence had been undermined to such an extent as to violate Art.6 of the Convention. [2002] 36 E.H.R.R. 143.

Commentary
This case is evidence of a robust approach to the privilege against self-incrimination. The Strasbourg court held that the informant

was acting as an agent of the state and that the defendant's right to silence had been violated. The court emphasised that the circumstances of each case would determine whether Art.6 had been violated. In this instance the alleged admissions were not "spontaneous and unprompted statements volunteered by the applicant, but were induced by the persistent questioning of [the informer] who, at the instance of the police, channelled their conversations into discussions of the murder in circumstances which can be regarded as the functional equivalent of interrogation, without any of the safeguards which would attach to a formal police interview, including the attendance of a solicitor and the issuing of the usual caution."

Exclusion of Non-confession Evidence

Key Principle: **There is no discretion for a court to exclude evidence that is relevant solely on the grounds that there has been some impropriety in the way it has been obtained.**

Jeffrey v Black

Two drugs squad officers arrested the defendant for stealing a sandwich in a pub. He was charged and the officers searched his lodgings where they found cannabis. At his trial for possession of cannabis the justices found the defendant had not consented to his room being searched and ruled the evidence inadmissible because the police had had no authority. The prosecutor appealed.

Held: (CA) The police officers should either have obtained the defendant's consent or a search warrant. As it was their entry and search was unlawful and the drug evidence had been irregularly obtained. However, the test whether evidence was admissible was whether it was relevant and not whether it had been properly obtained. The drug evidence was relevant and the magistrates were wrong to exclude it. [1978] Q.B. 490.

Key Principle: **There is no common law discretion to exclude evidence solely on the grounds that it has been obtained by entrapment.**

R. v Sang

Two defendants were charged with conspiring to pass forged banknotes. At trial their counsel sought to establish that the facts alleged against them came about through the activities of an *agent provocateur*. The judge ruled that he had no discretion to exclude evidence for that reason. The defendants then changed their plea and were sentenced. The Court of Appeal upheld the judge's ruling. One of the defendants appealed.

Held: (HL) The judge always had a discretion to exclude evidence if its prejudicial effect outweighed its probative value. But apart from admissions and confessions and evidence obtained from the accused after commission of the offence, there was no discretion to exclude evidence even if it had been obtained improperly or unfairly. The fact that the evidence was the result of an *agent provocateur*'s activities was no reason to exclude it. [1980] A.C. 402.

Commentary
This case confirmed that entrapment was not a defence and that if the discretion was used to exclude evidence this would amount to a procedural device to circumvent a matter of substantive law. In addition the House was whittling down the discretion to exclude evidence at all under the common law to cases where the prejudicial effect would outweigh the probative value. The following cases however indicate a more robust stand on the part of the courts to exclude evidence to protect rights.

Key Principle: **Impropriety in the obtaining of evidence, including entrapment, may be a factor leading to the exclusion of evidence under s.78 of PACE.**

R. v Christou; R. v Wright
Undercover police officers set up a bogus jewellery shop which bought stolen goods. The aim was to recover stolen goods and obtain evidence against those who had either stolen or dishonestly handled the goods. The defendants were among those who sold stolen goods to the shop. At their trial, the judge refused a defence submission that the evidence ought to be excluded either because it had been obtained by a trick or because in the course of their bogus dealings the police had questioned the men without first having cautioned them contrary to Code C of the Codes of Practice. The judge concluded that admission of the evidence would not affect the fairness of the trial under s.78

of the Police and Criminal Evidence Act 1984. The defendants appealed.

Held: (CA) The judge had properly exercised his discretion. Code C was intended to protect suspects who were vulnerable to abuse or pressure from police officers and applied where a suspect was being questioned by an officer acting as such for the purpose of obtaining evidence. Here there was no question of pressure or intimidation and the parties were on equal terms. It would be wrong for police officers to adopt an undercover pose or disguise in order to circumvent the requirements of Code C. [1992] 1 Q.B. 979.

R. v Smurthwaite

In two separate cases a man had made arrangements with what he thought was a contract killer to have his wife murdered. In both cases the supposed contract killers were undercover police officers who tape-recorded their meetings. Both were convicted and contended on appeal that any prosecution evidence which came from an *agent provocateur* or was obtained by a trick should be excluded under s.78 of the Police and Criminal Evidence Act 1984.

Held: (CA) The judge had no discretion to exclude otherwise admissible evidence merely because it had been obtained improperly or unfairly. It remained a substantive rule of law that entrapment or the use of an *agent provocateur* was not of itself a defence to a criminal charge. The tape recordings were an accurate and unchallenged record of the offences being committed and had properly been admitted in evidence. [1994] 1 All E.R. 898.

Commentary

These cases confirm that s.78 had not altered the substantive rule of law whereby entrapment or use of an *agent provocateur* is not a defence to a criminal charge. However, entrapment is not irrelevant to a consideration of whether to use the discretion to exclude under s.78. The court must consider whether in all the circumstances the obtaining of the evidence in that way would have an adverse effect on the fairness of the proceedings. This involves considering fairness to the public as well as fairness to the accused.

R. v Khan (Sultan)

The defendant was convicted of involvement in importing heroin. The evidence against him came from an electronic listening device installed by the police in a private house visited by the defendant. He appealed against conviction on the basis that the evidence should have been excluded under s.78 of the Police and Criminal Evidence Act 1984.

Held: (HL) There was no right of privacy in English law. Relevant evidence remained admissible, despite being obtained improperly or unlawfully, subject to the court's discretion to exclude it. Although an apparent breach of Art.8 of the European Convention on Human Rights could be relevant in considering whether to exclude evidence, it was not determinative *per se*, as an appellant's rights were safeguarded under s.78 which provided for a review of the admissibility of evidence. [1996] 3 W.L.R. 162.

Commentary
In *Khan v United Kingdom, The Times*, May 23, 2000, the Strasbourg Court found that the use at the applicant's trial of secretly taped material amounted to a violation of Art.8 but not of Art.6.

Key Principle: **In cases of entrapment similar principles are applied under s.78 of the Police and Criminal Evidence Act 1984 and under Art.6 of the ECHR.**

R. v Looseley: Attorney-General's Reference (No.3 of 2000)
L was convicted of supplying a Class A controlled drug. R., an undercover police officer, had been given L's name and address as a dealer and telephoned L who agreed to supply him on three separate occasions. In the second case, that of X, the judge ordered proceedings to be stayed as an abuse of the process of the court. Undercover police officers were offering to sell contraband cigarettes on a housing estate. They sold cigarettes to X and then asked if he could procure heroin for them. X said he was "not into heroin" but got hold of drugs from another source and sold them to the undercover officers.

Held: (HL) In cases of entrapment a useful guide was to consider whether the police did more than present the defendant with an unexceptional opportunity to commit a crime. The court must ask the central question which was whether the actions of the police were so seriously improper as to bring the administration of justice into disrepute. If there has been an abuse of state power then the appropriate remedy is a stay of prosecution rather than the exclusion of evidence under s.78 L had been rightly convicted and the judge correct to stay the indictment of X. [2001] 1 W.L.R. 2060.

Commentary
The judgment demonstrated strong judicial recognition of the dangers of excessive police behaviour in cases of entrapment and the need for courts to protect citizens. Their Lordships considered that their judgment was compatible with *Teixeira de Castro v Portugal* [1999] 28 E.H.R.R. 101.

Powers of Entry, Search and Seizure

Key Principle: **Under the common law the police may seize articles which may be evidence of grave offences irrespective of whether the officer is lawfully on the premises at the time.**

Chic Fashions (West Wales) Ltd v Jones
The claimant's premises were searched by police looking for stolen goods. The warrant authorised a search for goods stolen from a particular manufacturer. The search revealed no goods from that manufacturer, but the police seized other goods which they believed might have been stolen. They eventually accepted the claimant's explanation and returned the goods. The claimant sued the chief constable for damages for trespass. The County Court judge gave judgment for the claimant and the chief constable appealed.

Held: (CA) Where a constable entered a house on a search warrant for stolen goods he could seize any goods which he reasonably believed to be stolen, whether or not they were specified in the warrant. The appeal would be allowed. [1968] 2 Q.B. 299.

Ghani v Jones
Police inquiring into a woman's disappearance searched her father-in-law's house without a warrant and took away his passport and those of his wife and daughter. The passport-holders, who were Pakistanis, brought an action for the return of their passports to allow them to visit Pakistan. The police

maintained that the passports might be evidence if and when they arrested those responsible for the woman's disappearance. They were ordered to return the passports and appealed.

Held: (CA) The police had power to seize evidence of grave offences, under the common law, and it did not depend on the officer being lawfully on the premises. The police had not shown reasonable grounds for believing that the documents were material evidence, and would be ordered to return them forthwith. [1970] 1 Q.B. 693.

Commentary
The law relating to searches and seizure is now largely contained in PACE but s.19(5) of PACE states "The powers conferred by this section are in addition to any power otherwise conferred". If this includes common-law powers then cases such as these cover the law relating to trespassing constables. Following the amendments to PACE made by the Serious Organised Crime and Police Act 2005 (see p.168) certain powers of search are triggered by indictable offences not arrestable offences.

In *R. (Rottman) v Commissioner of Police for the Metropolis* [2002] 2 W.L.R. 1315 the House of Lords held that ss.18 and 19 of PACE 1984 applied only to domestic offences and that they had no application in this case, an extradition case. They held that a police officer who arrested a person on his premises pursuant to a warrant of arrest had power at common law to search the premises and seize any goods or documents which he believed to be material evidence in relation to the crime for which he was being arrested. There was no indication that the 1984 Act was intended to revoke the common law power exercisable after the execution of a warrant for arrest for an extradition offence. This common law power was not contrary to Art.8 of the ECHR since it was clear, had a legitimate aim and was proportionate to that aim.

Additional powers of search and seizure are contained in the Criminal Justice and Police Act 2001.

12. FREEDOM OF ASSEMBLY

Public Meetings

Public Meetings in Private Places

Key Principle: **The police may enter and remain on private premises if they have reasonable grounds for believing that if they were not present a breach of the peace might occur.**

Thomas v Sawkins
Some 600 people attended a meeting in the Caerau library to protest against the Incitement to Disaffection Act. Police officers were refused admission but insisted on entering it and remaining there during the meeting. One of the convenors of the meeting brought an information against a police sergeant that he had unlawfully assaulted him.

Held: (DC) The officers were entitled in the execution of their duty to prevent the commission of any offence or breach of the peace, to enter and remain on the premises. [1935] 2 K.B. 249.

Commentary
This is a controversial decision. Commentators have argued that its scope should be limited to those situations where a meeting has been advertised as public and the police have reasonable grounds for believing that a breach of the peace will occur if the police are not present. That is to say it would not allow police to enter private premises to attend a meeting which is not advertised as open to the public. Furthermore, although the court's decision appears to allow entry by the police before the offence is imminent compare this formulation with that in *R. v Howell* (see p.172) where the Court of Appeal held that the power of the police only arises if a breach of the peace is imminent.

Public Meetings in Public Places

Key Principle: **On the highway anyone has the prima facie right to pass or repass along it and to make any necessary stops such as for rest. But people have no right to stop on the highway unreasonably.**

R. v Clarke (No.2)
The field secretary of the Campaign for Nuclear Disarmament
led a crowd through the streets during a demonstration against
the Greek royal couple. He was convicted of inciting persons to
commit a public nuisance by obstructing the highway and
sentenced to 18 months' imprisonment. He appealed.

Held: (DC) The judge had failed to direct the jury on the
question of whether granted obstruction there was unreasonable
use of the highway. He had told the jury that if there was
physical obstruction then the defendant was guilty. The appeal
was allowed. [1964] 2 Q.B. 315.

Commentary
This case illustrates the application of the common law offence of
public nuisance in blocking the highway. It illustrates that the
disruption involved must amount to unreasonable use of the
highway for liability to be incurred. A similar interpretation has
been applied to the application of the Highways Act (see *Nagy v
Weston*, p.194).

Key Principle: **Highways Act 1980, s.137:**

> "(1) If a person, without lawful authority or excuse, in any way
> wilfully obstructs the free passage along a highway he shall be
> guilty of an offence . . ."

Key Principle: **Mens rea in this offence does not require
knowingly doing a wrongful act.**

Arrowsmith v Jenkins
The defendant addressed a public meeting in the street in Bootle
and attracted a crowd which blocked the road for five minutes,
until police with her assistance cleared a path for vehicles. She
was accused of wilfully obstructing the highway and was
convicted by justices. She appealed on the grounds that the
prosecution had failed to establish a knowingly wrongful act on
her part.

Held: (DC) A person who without lawful authority or excuse did an act which caused obstruction was guilty of an offence. *Mens rea* in the sense that a person would only be guilty if she knowingly did a wrongful act could not be inferred from the words "wilfully obstructs". [1963] 2 Q.B. 561.

Commentary
This decision gives a great deal of licence to the police. It is arguable that the defendant intended to cause an obstruction but describing such conduct as wilful has incurred much criticism.

———————

Key Principle: **To commit an offence the user of the highway must act unreasonably.**

Nagy v Weston
A hot-dog seller parked in a lay-by near a bus stop for five minutes and refused to move on when asked by a police officer to do so. He was convicted of wilfully obstructing the highway and appealed on the ground that for an obstruction to be wilful it must lack lawful authority or reasonable excuse.

Held: (DC) Appeal dismissed. Excuse and reasonableness were really the same. It was a question of fact in each case whether the defendant had used the highway unreasonably. [1965] 1 W.L.R. 280.

Hirst and Agu v Chief Constable of West Yorkshire
Members of an animal rights group who protested outside a fur shop were convicted by justices of obstructing the highway. On appeal to the Crown Court, it was held that their actions were not incidental to lawful use of the highway so the conviction should stand. They appealed by case stated.

Held: (DC) Justices should consider whether there was an obstruction, whether it was deliberate and then whether it was without lawful authority or excuse. This embraced activities otherwise lawful in themselves which might or might not be reasonable in all the circumstances mentioned in *Nagy v Weston*. The courts recognised a right to demonstrate and should allow freedom to protest on issues of public concern. (1986) 85 Cr.App.R. 143.

Commentary
These two cases mark some liberalisation from the decision in
Arrowsmith. The stress on the purpose of the obstruction and the
reminder in *Hirst* and *Agu* that the courts should have regard to
the freedom to demonstrate suggest that using an assembly as a
means of protest may amount to a reasonable use of the highway.

Key Principle: **A breach of the peace will arise if an act is
done or threatened to be done which either harms a person or
in his presence his property or is likely to cause such harm or
which puts a person in fear of such harm.**

Piddington v Bates
In the course of a strike, the front and back entrances of a print-
works were picketed. A police officer declared that only two
pickets were needed at the back door, whereupon the defendant
tried to pass to go to the back entrance to join the two pickets
there and was arrested. The defendant was convicted of
obstructing the police officer and appealed.

Held: (DC) The mere statement by a constable that he anticipated a breach of the peace was not enough to justify his taking
action to prevent it. But that on the facts there was a real danger
of a breach of the peace and the defendant had been rightly
convicted. [1961] 1 W.L.R. 162.

Commentary
The vagueness of the definition of breach of the peace (see *Howell*,
p.172) means that is at times employed to deal with a public order
problem on occasions where the statutory powers might not be
suitable. Here, in effect, the courts sanctioned the police placing a
limit on the number of pickets when there was no statutory
maximum number. (See also *Moss v MacLachan*, p.173).

Key Principle: **Trade Union and Labour Relations (Consolidation) Act 1992, s.220:**

"(1) It is lawful for a person in contemplation or furtherance of a
trade dispute to attend—(a) at or near his own place of work, or (b)

if he is an official of a trade union, at or near the place of work of a
member of the union whom he is accompanying and whom he
represents, for the purpose only of peacefully obtaining or communicating information, or peacefully persuading any person to work
or abstain from working."

Key Principle: **Injunctions may be granted if pickets carry
out for which there is no statutory immunity.**

Thomas v National Union of Mineworkers (South Wales Area)
South Wales miners joined the national strike on March 12, 1984,
but in November a few returned to work. The collieries where
they worked were picketed by 50 to 70 strikers, who threatened
them as they were driven across the picket line. They sought
injunctions restraining unlawful picketing.

Held: The attendance of some 50 to 70 strikers each day
shouting abuse at the claimants could not be picketing for the
purpose of peacefully persuading them not to work. The working miners were entitled to enjoy their right to use the highway
without unreasonable harassment. [1986] Ch. 20.

Commentary
Here although no obvious civil offence such as assault was being
perpetrated the court was in effect extending the definition of an
existing tort. Mass picketing was "unreasonable interference with
the plaintiff's right to use the highway".

Key Principle: **There is a general presumption in favour of
protecting the exercise of free lawful expression in public and
private.**

Hubbard v Pitt
Campaigners opposed to the gentrification of part of north
London picketed local estate agents, who sued for nuisance and
libel and obtained an injunction restraining the picketing. The
plaintiffs appealed.

Held: (CA) Dismissing the appeal (Lord Denning dissenting)
that the injunction should continue until trial. The injunction

was not too wide, and there was a serious issue to be tried *per* Lord Denning M.R.). The rights to demonstrate and protest are rights which it is in the public interest that individuals should possess and exercise. [1976] 1 Q.B. 142.

Commentary
Lord Denning's comments are often cited as illustrating the close relationship of freedoms of speech and assembly.

Key Principle: **Public Order Act 1986, s.4:**

> "(1) A person is guilty of an offence if he (a) uses towards another person threatening, abusive or insulting words or behaviour, or (b) distributes or displays to another person any writing, sign or other visible representation which is threatening, abusive or insulting, with intent to cause that person to believe that immediate unlawful violence will be used against him or another by any person, or to provoke the immediate use of unlawful violence by that person or another, or whereby that person is likely to believe that such violence will be used or it is likely that such violence will be provoked."

Key Principle: **The meaning of the word "insulting" is a matter of fact, not law, and it should be given its natural meaning.**

Brutus v Cozens
The defendant disrupted play at Wimbledon when a South African was playing. As a protest against apartheid, he and others distributed leaflets to the crowd while preventing play. They were acquitted of insulting behaviour because the justices held that their behaviour had not been insulting. The prosecutor appealed to the Divisional Court, which held that the justices' findings established insulting behaviour. The defendant appealed.

Held: (HL) The meaning of "insulting" was not a question of law. It was an ordinary English word. It was not unreasonable for the tribunal to conclude that the defendant's behaviour had not been insulting. The defendant's behaviour was deplorable but it did not insult the spectators. [1973] A.C. 854.

Commentary
In disagreeing with the Divisional Court's interpretation of the word insulting, namely that which affronted others, the House of Lords observed that Parliament had to solve the difficult question of how far freedom of speech or behaviour must be limited in the general public interest. It considered (per Lord Reid) that "it would have been going much too far to prohibit all speech or conduct likely to occasion a breach of the peace because determined opponents may not shrink from organising or at least threatening a breach of the peace in order to silence a speaker whose views they detest".

Key Principle: **Such violence means immediate unlawful violence.**

R. v Horseferry Road Metropolitan Magistrate Ex p. Siadatan
The applicant laid an information against Penguin Books, the publishers of *The Satanic Verses*, claiming that it contained abusive and insulting writing whereby unlawful violence would be provoked. The magistrates refused a summons on the grounds that the applicant had failed to demonstrate a likelihood of immediate violence. The applicant sought judicial review.

Held: (DC) Dismissing the application, that of two possible readings of a penal statute the courts should adopt the alternative that limited the scope of the offence created, and the magistrate had correctly refused to issue the summons.

Commentary
This case confirms that s.4 is to be applied primarily in a public order context in stressing the requirement of immediacy so that the insulting language has to be used as part of a public demonstration.

Key Principle: **Public Order Act 1986, s.5:**

"(1) A person is guilty of an offence if he (a) uses threatening, abusive or insulting words or behaviour, or disorderly behaviour, or (b) displays any writing, sign or other visible representation which is threatening, abusive or insulting, within the hearing or sight of a person likely to be caused harassment, alarm or distress thereby . . . (3) It is a defence for the accused to prove . . . (c) that his conduct was reasonable . . ."

Key Principle: **The test of awareness is subjective, so to succeed the prosecution must show that the accused is aware of the threatening, abusive or insulting nature of the display, etc. The test of reasonableness under s.5(3)(c) is objective.**

DPP v Clarke, Lewis, O'Connell and O'Keefe

Anti-abortion campaigners were charged with threatening behaviour for showing placards of aborted foetuses outside a clinic. The justices decided that on an objective test the behaviour of the campaigners was not reasonable, but that on the balance of probabilities none of them intended to be threatening, abusive or insulting. They dismissed the informations and the prosecutor appealed.

Held: (DC) The justices had applied the right tests and the appeal would be dismissed. The defendants were unaware that those seeing the foetus placards would find them threatening. [1992] Crim. L.R. 60.

Commentary

S.5 is one of the most controversial of the new sections of the POA 1986 since it criminalises behaviour which was formerly thought to be too trivial to incur criminal liability, "mere horseplay" in the words of one commentator. This decision makes the prosecution's task more difficult in needing to establish that the defendant was aware his behaviour was likely to cause harassment, etc. However, on the other hand it gives a narrow interpretation to the term reasonable in accepting that it will depend upon what a bench of magistrates considers reasonable.

Key Principle: **A police officer may be a person who is caused harassment, alarm or distress under s.5(1).**

DPP v Orum

The defendant was drunk and arguing in the street with his girlfriend in the early hours. Two police officers arrived and one of them told the defendant to be quiet. The defendant told the police officer to go away and threatened to hit him. He was arrested for causing a breach of the peace and kicked and hit the other constable as he was being put into the police car. He was then charged under s.5 of the Public Order Act 1986. The justices found that a police officer could not be a person who could be caused harassment, alarm or distress and dismissed the charge. The prosecutor appealed.

Held: (DC) It was a question of fact whether a police officer was a person who could be caused harassment, etc. The justices were wrong to find that the officer could not be such a person. [1989] 1 W.L.R. 88.

Key principle: **Public Order Act 1986, s.14:**

"(1) If the senior police officer, having regard to the time or place at which and the circumstances in which any public assembly is being held or is intended to be held, reasonably believes that—(a) it may result in serious public disorder, serious damage to property or serious disruption to the life of the community, or (b) the purpose of the persons organising it is the intimidation of others with a view to compelling them not to do an act they have a right to do, or to do an act they have a right not to do, he may give directions imposing on the persons organising or taking part in the assembly such conditions as to the place at which the assembly may be (or continue to be) held, its maximum duration, or the maximum number of persons who may constitute it, as appear to him necessary to prevent such disorder, damage, disruption or intimidation."

Key principle: **Discomfort to others may not amount to intimidation.**

Police v Lorna Reid

Demonstrators outside the South African embassy shouted slogans and waved their fingers at guests arriving for a reception. A chief inspector decided that this amounted to intimidation and required the demonstrators to move to another location. The defendant refused to comply with this condition and was charged with an offence under s.14(5).

Held: The metropolitan stipendiary magistrate held that no offence had been committed since there had been no valid ground for imposing the condition. Causing someone to feel uncomfortable would not be intimidation. (1987) Crim. L.R. 702.

Commentary
The number of reported cases on s.14 is small. One example is *Broadwith v Chief Constable of Thames Valley Police* (2002) Crim. L.R. 924. There the stipendiary magistrate had been entitled to conclude that the conditions imposed by the chief constable in relation to a public assembly had been sufficiently clear. Although the appellant was on his own when he attempted to walk along a road which he had been told was closed he was still part of a public assembly within the meaning of s.14(5).

Key Principle: **Public Order Act 1986, s.14A:**

"(1) If at any time the chief officer of police reasonable believes that an assembly is intended to be held in any district at a place on land to which the public has no right of access or only a limited right of access and that the assembly: (a) is likely to be held without the permission of the occupier of the land or to conduct itself in such a way as to exceed the limits of any permission of his or the limits of the public's right of access; and (b) may result (i) in serious disruption to the life of the community, or (ii) where the land, or a building or monument on it is of historical architectural, archae-ological or scientific importance in significant damage to the land, building or monument, he may apply to the council of the district for an order prohibiting for a specified period the holding of all trespassory assemblies in the district or part of it as specified."

Key Principle: **Public Order Act 1986, s.14B(2):**

"A person who takes part in an assembly which he knows is prohibited by an order under section 14A is guilty of an offence."

Key Principle: **The common law recognises that an assembly on the public highway may be lawful thereby upholding the right to freedom of peaceful assembly contained in Art.11(1) of the European Convention on Human Rights.**

DPP v Jones
The defendants took part in a peaceful, non-obstructive assembly on a highway on which trespassory assemblies had been forbidden under s.14A of the Public Order Act 1986. Magistrates convicted them of trespassory assembly. On appeal, the Crown Court held there was no case to answer since a peaceful, non-obstructive assembly was part of the public's limited rights of access to the highway. The Director of Public Prosecutions succeeded in the Divisional Court. The defendants appealed.

Held: (HL) The public had the right to use the public highway for passing and repassing and any uses ancillary thereto which were usual and reasonable. That right did not include the holding of a peaceful assembly on the highway, even if it caused no obstruction. The Crown Court had erred in holding that there was no case to answer and the matter would be remitted for rehearing. [1999] 2 W.L.R. 625.

Commentary
In this case the House of Lords observed that it was undesirable in theory and practice for activities on the highway to count as trespass although they were not counted as breaches of criminal law. Lord Irvine indicated the extent to which the European Convention on Human Rights influenced the judgment in noting that if an assembly on the public highway was always a trespass "then there is not even a prima facie right to assembly on the public highway in our law". New controls on public protest have been introduced by the Serious Organised Crime and Police Act 2005.

Key Principle: **Section 14 Public Order Act 1986:**

"(1) If the senior police officer, having regard to the time or place at which and the circumstances in which any public assembly is being held or is intended to be held, reasonably believes that— (a) it may result in serious public disorder, serious damage to property or serious disruption to the life of the community, or (b) the

purpose of the persons organising it is the intimidation of others
with a view to compelling them not to do an act they have a right
to do, or to do an act they have a right not to do, he may give
directions imposing on the persons organising or taking part in the
assembly such conditions as to the place at which the assembly
may be (or continue to be) held, its maximum duration, or the
maximum number of persons who may constitute it, as appear to
him necessary to prevent such disorder, damage, disruption or
intimidation."

Key Principle: **Ultra vires conditions included in a s.14 notice
may be severed without invalidating the whole of the notice.**

Director of Public Prosecutions v Jones

The prosecutor appealed from magistrates who dismissed a
charge of failing to comply with a condition imposed by a senior
police officer under s.14 of the 1986 Act. The defendant, an
animal rights protester, had established at trial that the senior
police officer had no power to impose certain particular conditions contained in a notice to demonstrators taking part in a
public assembly. These included that participants disembark in
a particular area and take a particular route to the demonstration, and that they leave by a designated route. Those conditions
related to public processions rather than public assemblies. The
defendant claimed that the defects were sufficient to invalidate
the entire notice.

Held: (DC) There was nothing unfair in being prosecuted for
breach of a severable condition, and it was not unfair to sever
conditions. The impugned conditions could be severed without
invalidating the notice. [2002] EWHC 110 (Admin).

Commentary

The test for severability set out by the House of Lords in *Director
of Public Prosecutions v Hutchinson* [1990] 2 A.C. 783 was relied
on here. It should be noted that the Anti-Social Behaviour Act
2003 amended the definition of a public assembly in the Public
Order Act 1986 so that an assembly may consist of "a gathering of
two or more persons" as opposed to the previous definition of 20
or more persons.

Preventive Justice

Magistrates have power to bind over persons under the Justices of the Peace Act 1361, Magistrates Courts Act 1980, and the common law. A binding over order can be imposed even if the breach of the peace has not occurred. The overriding duty of the police and magistrates to preserve the peace justifies preventive methods to avert disorder even if this means interfering with someone who is not about to commit a breach of the peace or do or join an illegal act but who is likely to be made an object of insult or injury by others who are about to break the peace.

Key Principle: **A group of persons acting lawfully are not to be regarded as acting unlawfully when others make threats to cause a breach of the peace.**

Beatty v Gilbanks
Members of the Salvation Army marched in procession through Weston-super-Mare, with no intention of breaching the peace, but knowing that they might be opposed by other persons organised in a "Skeleton Army" in a way which would lead to a breach of the peace committed by those others. Salvation Army leaders were arrested and convicted of unlawful assembly. They appealed.

Held: (DC) The appellants had not been guilty of unlawfully and tumultuously assembling to the disturbance of the peace, and therefore could not be convicted of unlawful assembly. (1882) 9 Q.B.D. 308.

Key Principle: **The principle expressed in Beatty v Gilbanks may be limited if a policeman on the spot had reasonable grounds for believing that dispersing a lawful assembly was the only way of preventing a breach of the peace.**

Duncan v Jones
A communist activist was about to address a crowd outside a labour exchange when she was forbidden to do so by a police officer. She persisted in trying to hold the meeting and

obstructed the officer's attempts to prevent her. Neither she nor any of the persons present at the meeting committed, incited or provoked a breach of the peace. The court found that the officer reasonably apprehended a breach of the peace would occur if she did address the meeting. She was found guilty of wilfully obstructing the officer in the execution of his duty and appealed.

Held: (DC) It is the duty of a police officer to prevent breaches of the peace which he reasonably apprehends. The appellant was therefore guilty of obstructing the officer in the execution of his duty. [1936] 1 K.B. 218.

Commentary
Lord Hewart C.J. considered that "the somewhat unsatisfactory case of *Beatty v Gillbanks*" was not in point. However, the speaker was here arrested not because of her conduct but because the police feared possible violence from the audience.

Redmond-Bate v DPP
The appellant was convicted of obstructing a police officer in the execution of his duty. She was one of three women preaching from the steps of Wakefield Cathedral in front of a hostile crowd. A police constable feared a breach of the peace and asked the women to stop preaching. They were arrested when they refused. The appellant appealed on the grounds that it was unreasonable for the constable to believe, in the light of what he perceived, that she was about to cause a breach of the peace.

Held: (DC) The reasonableness of the constable's action stood to be judged objectively. The court had to decide whether, in the light of what he knew and perceived at the time, it was reasonable to fear an imminent breach of the peace. The critical question for the constable, and in turn for the court, was where the threat was coming from, because it was there that the preventive action had to be directed. The appellant's conviction would be overturned. [1999] Crim. L.R. 998.

Commentary
This case is an example of a trenchant rights-based approach by the court in sharp contrast with *Duncan v Jones*. An officer had no right to call upon a citizen to desist from lawful conduct. Free speech was not confined to the inoffensive, but extended to the irritating, the contentious, the eccentric, the heretical, the unwelcome and the provocative provided it did not tend to

provoke violence. The situation perceived by the constable did not justify him in apprehending a breach of the peace, and much less a breach of the peace for which the women would be responsible.

Key Principle: **Magistrates have powers to bind persons over to keep the peace when there is reasonable apprehension of a future breach of the peace.**

Lansbury v Riley
The appellant was a supporter of women's suffrage and the court was satisfied that he had been inciting others to commit breaches of the peace in the cause of women's suffrage and intended to carry on doing so. He was bound over by the metropolitan magistrate and appealed.

Held: (DC) The court could order him to enter into recognisances and to find sureties for his good behaviour or be imprisoned in default of doing so. It was not essential to the exercise of the court's jurisdiction to make such orders that the conduct of the defendant should have caused any individual person to go in bodily fear. [1914] 3 K.B. 229.

Commentary
Since binding over orders can be imposed even if the breach of the peace has not happened, the common law and statutory powers have been challenged under the ECHR. In *Steel v United Kingdom* (1999) 5 B.H.R.C. 339, the challenge under Arts 5, 6, 10 and 11 failed. The Court held, inter alia, that the detention following the refusal to be bound over was an infringement of the applicant's freedom of expression justified by the need to maintain the authority of the judiciary. However in *Hashman and Harrup v United Kingdom, The Times*, December 1, 1999, the United Kingdom was held to be in breach of Art.10. The case arose out of orders binding two hunt saboteurs to keep the peace. The principle issue in the case was whether the interference with the applicants' freedom of expression was prescribed by law, that is whether it met the criterion of foreseeability. The case was distinguished from *Steel* in that there the proceedings were in respect of breaches of the peace which were later found to have been committed. In the instant case given the lack of precision it could not be said that what the applicants were being bound over not to do must have

been apparent to them. The case thus illustrates that the binding over orders of magistrates where the breach of the peace has not yet occurred may have to be exercised more cautiously.

Key Principle: **It is not a necessary ingredient of the common law offence of breach of the peace for a disturbance on private property to affect members of the public outside that property.**

Robert McQuade v Chief Constable of Humberside Police

M had been arrested to prevent a breach of the peace at his home following a quarrel with his wife. He brought an action for wrongful arrest. He argued that he was on private property with his wife and no member of the public was affected by the incident. The judge considered previous authorities and found the police liable. The Chief Constable appealed.

Held: (CA) The judge had misunderstood *McConnell & Anor v Chief Constable of Greater Manchester Police* [1990] 1 W.L.R. 364. It was recognised in *McConnell* that the presence of a member or members of the public was a highly relevant factor in the offence of a breach of the peace but that was different from the proposition that there was a requirement that the disturbance affected a member of the public. *McConnell* was binding authority that it was not necessary for a breach of the peace that members of the public outside private property were affected by the disturbance. Special care had to be taken in such cases because the police officer called to the scene did not require a warrant, was entering private property and there was no public order element. The judge's conclusion that there was a legal requirement for there to be a disturbance to the public was an erroneous conclusion and his order was set aside. [2002] 1 W.L.R. 1347.

Commentary

The court also stated that, previous authorities apart, it was contrary to public policy that an act that constituted a breach of the peace in a public or private place where members of the public were affected ceased to be a breach of the peace if only the participants in the act were affected.

13. FREEDOM OF EXPRESSION

R. v Secretary of State for the Home Department Ex p. Brind
(For facts see p.12).

Held: (HL) The European Convention on Human Rights was
not part of English law. Though it might be resorted to in order
to resolve ambiguity or uncertainty in the provisions of a
statute, no such ambiguity existed here, and there was no
presumption that the Secretary of State had to apply the
Broadcasting Act in accordance with the Convention. The
appeal would be dismissed. [1991] 1 A.C. 696.

Commentary
This formal banning power is rarely exercised. More frequently a
form of self-imposed censorship is employed within the broadcasting hierarchy. The Board of Governors of the BBC is appointed by
the Government. Under the Broadcasting Act 1990 the Independent Television Commission must set up a code to ensure impartiality in programmes.

Defamation

Key Principle: **A local authority or central government may
not sue for defamation.**

Derbyshire CC v Times Newspapers Ltd
(For facts see p.6).

Held: (HL) Uninhibited public criticism of an elected body
was vital in a democracy. The threat of libel actions would
inhibit legitimate criticism. It was contrary to the public interest
for central or local government institutions to have any common
law right to sue for libel. The action would be struck out. [1993]
A.C. 534.

Commentary
The House held that in the field of freedom of speech there was no
difference in principle between English law and Art.10 of the
Convention.

Key Principle: **A Press Conference is a public meeting and protected by qualified privilege under the Defamation Act 1952.**

Turkington (practising as Mccartan Turkington Breen) v Times Newspapers Ltd

A firm of Belfast solicitors sued a newspaper for a report of a press conference at which statements were made about their conduct of the defence of a British soldier accused of murder. They complained that the article impugned their professional competence. At trial it was not disputed that the words in the article were defamatory of the claimants and the plea of fair comment in the defence was abandoned. The only defence was statutory qualified privilege, bestowed on newspapers by s.7 of the Defamation Act (Northern Ireland) 1955. The claimants were awarded damages of £145,000. The Northern Ireland court of appeal reduced the damages to £75,000. The defendants appealed to the House of Lords.

Held: (HL) The press conference was a public meeting within the meaning of the Act. Restriction of press freedom had to be proportionate and no more than necessary to promote the legitimate object of the restriction. There was nothing in the nature of a press conference which took it outside the ordinary meaning of "public meeting". A press release was handed out at the meeting to save time and to provide the press with a reliable record. Its contents were as much part of the proceedings of the press conference as if they had been read aloud during the meeting. Anything said one-to-one, after the general press conference had broken up, would not form part of the meeting and could not be the subject of a privileged report, unless it repeated the effect of what had been said at the meeting or written in the press release. The appeal would be allowed and the case remitted for rehearing. [2001] 2 A.C. 277.

Commentary

The case was heard just after the implementation of the Human Rights Act but the judgment was not based predominantly on Art.10 or the HRA. Lord Steyn invoked the First Amendment to the United States constitution.

Confidentiality

Key Principle: **The equitable doctrine of breach of confidence is independent of other legal rights.**

Duchess of Argyll v Duke of Argyll

After eight years of marriage the Duke sued for divorce on grounds of the Duchess's adultery. The marriage was dissolved in 1963. The Duchess published articles in a Sunday newspaper which included details of the Duke's personal conduct and financial affairs. The following year she sought interlocutory injunctions to restrain the Duke from giving to *The People* newspaper details of her private life, personal affairs or private conduct communicated to the Duke during the marriage.

Held: (Ch D) A contract of confidence could be implied and a breach of contract or trust or faith could arise independently of any right of property. The court would act to restrain a breach of confidence independently of any right at law. Communication between husband and wife would be protected against breach of confidence. The Duchess's adultery did not entitle the Duke to publish the confidences of their married life. [1967] Ch. 302.

Commentary

An action based on breach of confidence was here extended to domestic secrets. In *Coco v AN Clarke Ltd* (1969) R.P.C. 41, Megarry K.J. had set out the requirements for such an action as:

1. The information itself must "have the necessary quality of confidence about it".

2. The information must have been imparted in circumstances importing an obligation of confidence.

3. There must be an unauthorised use of that information to the detriment of the party communicating it. The following cases show the extension of these principles to other areas. This judgment illustrates that although there is no substantive law protecting privacy in Britain private confidences may be protected from publication.

Attorney-General v Jonathan Cape Ltd
(For facts, see p.2).

Held: (QB) The court had power to restrain publication in breach of confidence of information about the views of individual ministers expressed at Cabinet meetings, but there were no details of cabinet discussions in the diaries which required to be protected from publication. There was no ground in law which required the advice given by senior civil servants and ministerial observations on their capacities to remain confidential. [1976] Q.B. 752.

Commentary
Lord Widgery C.J. said "I cannot see why the courts should be powerless to restrain the publication of public secrets, while enjoying the Argyll powers in regard to domestic secrets . . . in my judgment the Attorney-General has made out his claim that the expression of individual opinions by Cabinet ministers in the course of Cabinet discussion are matters of confidence, the publication of which can be restrained by the court when this is clearly necessary in the public interest". However, he acknowledged that there must be a time limit after which the confidential character of the information and the duty of the court to restrain publication will lapse. The court should only intervene in the clearest of cases where the continuing confidentiality of the material has been demonstrated. This, 10 years after the events described, was one of the less clear cases and restraint on publication was not appropriate.

Key Principle: **The degree of disclosure of confidential information must be justified in the public interest.**

Francome v Mirror Group Newspapers
Unidentified persons tapped the telephone of a well-known jockey and made a recording said to show that he had broken the rules of racing. Two journalists from the *Daily Mirror* approached the jockey with the tapes to confirm their authenticity. The jockey and his wife obtained an injunction restraining publication of the tapes and ordering that the newspaper disclose their source. The judge ordered a speedy trial. The newspaper appealed against the injunction and the order to disclose.

Held: (CA) It was not necessary in the interests of justice that the newspaper be forced to disclose its source since a speedy trial had been ordered. Publication of the tapes would prejudice the jockey's claim at trial and the injunction should be continued until trial, but its terms should be varied so that the newspaper could disclose the information obtained to the police or the jockey club. [1984] 1 W.L.R. 892.

Commentary
This case illustrates the attitude of the court to what is sometimes referred to as the iniquity defence. There may be a public interest in disclosing wrongful behaviour but this does not necessarily mean that this should be through the media. Limited publication to the police or some other authority, here the Jockey Club, may be appropriate. Another factor which Sir John Donaldson M.R. referred to in giving judgment was the claim by the editor of the *Daily Mirror* that it was expedient to break the law in obtaining the information. The editor accepted that publication would be an offence under s.5(b) of the Wireless and Telegraphy Act 1949. The occasions when the "moral imperative" required breaking a law would be extremely rare and "it was almost unheard of for compliance with the moral imperative to be in the financial or other best interests of the persons concerned".

Key Principle: **The court may apply equitable remedies to restrain unfair exploitation of a confidential fiduciary relationship.**

Schering Chemicals v Falkman Ltd
Schering manufactured Primodos, a pregnancy-testing drug suspected of causing birth abnormalities. It was withdrawn from the market. The company hired Falkman Ltd to train its executives in presenting its point of view about the drug in public. In the course of the training sessions Schering revealed information in confidence to Falkman. Two actions by parents on behalf of affected children were begun. One of the instructors on the training course made a film with Thames Television about the case. The film contained information which had been given in confidence, but which the instructor claimed was also available from publicly available sources. Schering obtained an injunction against publication. The defendants appealed.

Held: (CA) Both Falkman Ltd and the instructor were under a fiduciary obligation to maintain the confidence placed in them.

Thames Television knew how the instructor had come by the information and so could not take advantage of his breach of duty. Lord Denning dissented on the basis that the public interest in knowing about Primodos outweighed the makers' private interest in preventing discussion of it. [1982] 1 Q.B. 1.

Commentary
This majority judgment has been much criticised. It could be argued that it gives more weight to business confidences than media freedom and is a controversial example of prior restraint. Lord Denning said that the press is not to be restrained in advance from publishing whatever it thinks right to publish. But the majority view was "The law of England is indeed as Blackstone declared a law of liberty; but the freedoms it recognises do not include a licence for the mercenary betrayal of business confidences".

Developing a Right to Privacy

Key Principle: **The common law does not recognise a tort of privacy.**

Kaye v Robertson
A newspaper reporter and photographer invaded the hospital room of a television actor when he was recovering from serious head injuries, violating hospital instructions. The actor obtained an injunction requiring the newspaper to refrain from publishing the interview and photographs the journalists had obtained. The newspaper editor and the publisher appealed.

Held: (CA) There was no right of action for breach of a person's privacy. [1991] F.S.R. 62.

Commentary
Glidewell L.J. stated "the facts of the present case are a graphic illustration of the desirability of Parliament considering whether and in what circumstances statutory provision can be made to protect the privacy of individuals". Bingham L.J. stated "this case nonetheless highlights, yet again, the failure of both the common law of England and statute to protect in an effective way the personal privacy of individual citizens". But although there was an invasion of privacy the court decided it could do nothing. This case has now to be considered in the light of *Douglas v Hello!* (see

below). The court reviewed the existing law on privacy. Referring to *Kaye v Robertson*, Brooke L.J. stated that in contrast to the uncompromising position of the Court of Appeal in that case "both academic commentary and extra-judicial commentary by judges over the last 10 years have suggested from time to time that a development of the present frontiers of the breach of confidence action could fill the gap in English law which is filled by privacy law in other countries". This commentary was given a boost recently by the decision of the European Commission of Human Rights in *Earl Spencer v United Kingdom* (1998) 25 E.H.R.R. C.D. 105, and by the coming into force of the Human Rights Act 1998. Sedley L.J. in *Douglas v Hello!* concluded that the QC for the actors "has a powerfully arguable case to advance at trial that his two first named clients have a right to privacy which English law will today recognise and where appropriate, protect". He saw privacy as "a qualified right recognised and protected by English law". Regard had also to be given to Art.10 although this did not have a presumptive priority over other rights. In *Secretary of State for the Home Department v Wainwright*, *The Times*, January 4, 2002 the Court of Appeal held that since at common law there was no tort of invasion of privacy and because the conduct complained of occurred before the coming into force of the Human Rights Act, the Act did not apply to introduce a right of privacy retrospectively.

Key Principle: **There is no free-standing right to privacy in English law but such a right may exist if there is a pre-existing legal relationship including contract.**

Douglas v Hello!

Two Hollywood stars, Michael Douglas and Catherine Zeta Jones, gave exclusive publication rights in their wedding pictures to *OK!*, a celebrity magazine, retaining a veto over publication of particular photographs. All photography other than by the magazine's own photographer was banned: guests were searched for cameras on arrival, and the couple's employees signed undertakings that they would not take pictures at the wedding. Despite these precautions, photographs were taken surreptitiously at the wedding, and it came to the couple's notice that *Hello!*, a rival celebrity magazine, planned to publish them. It was not clear whether the photographs had been taken by a guest, an employee or an intruder. The claimants obtained an injunction to prevent the publication of the photographs pending trial of an action against *Hello!*, who then appealed.

Held: (CA) If the photographs had been taken by a guest or an employee, *Hello!* might rely on the existing law of confidence on the basis that the photographer had either acted (if an employee) in breach of contract, or (if a guest) in breach of confidence. However if the photographs had been taken by an intruder who was not under an obligation of confidence towards the couple, there was no relationship of trust on which the existing law could bite. In those circumstances the law recognised that it had to protect not only those whose trust had been abused, but also those whose personal lives were subjected to unwarranted intrusion. Sedley L.J. said the law no longer required the construction of an artificial relationship of confidentiality between intruder and victim. Privacy itself could be acknowledged as a legal principle drawn from the fundamental value of personal autonomy. In the particular case the court discharged the injunction against *Hello!*, on the basis that the judge who had granted the injunction had failed to give his reasons. The case is also important because it establishes that the provision in Art.10(2) permitting restriction of the right of freedom of expression "for the protection of the reputation or rights of others" is to be given as much weight as the substantive right itself in deciding whether to order an injunction limiting freedom of expression. [2001] 2 W.L.R. 992 (CA).

Commentary
The court also considered s.12 of the Human Rights Act, which prohibits prior restraint unless the claimant establishes a strong case that the restraint is justified. The court treated it as a balancing mechanism between existing codes of practice on privacy and freedom of the press. Breach of the Press Complaints Commission code was likely, Brooke L.J. said, to result in the grant of an injunction since the claimant's rights under Art.10(2) would then "trump" the publication's right to freedom of expression. The court extended the existing law on confidentiality to situations where the party that was intruding had no relationship of trust or confidence with the claimant. The court took the view that "a development of the present frontiers of a breach of confidence action could fill the gap in English law which is filled by privacy law in other developed countries". But it stopped short of

creating a new cause of action which would have meant interpreting the Human Rights Act to have horizontal effect. In *A v B and C Plc (No.2)* (*The Times*, November 2, 2001) a footballer, who was married with a family, had sex with two women at one session, and one of the women sold the story to a newspaper. The footballer sought an injunction to prevent publication. The Court held that in order to be confidential, information must have the necessary quality of confidence about it, it must be imparted in circumstances importing an obligation of confidence, and there must have been an unauthorised use of the information. The law ought to protect the confidentiality of facts about sexual relations both within and outside marriage, in appropriate circumstances. On the facts there was no public interest in publication, nor were the details of the sexual intercourse in the public domain since they were not of interest to anyone save the participants. The footballer was likely to be able to show at trial that his right to privacy should prevail over the defendant newspaper's right to freedom of expression in the balancing operation between s.12 of the Human Rights Act 1998 and Art.10 of the European Convention on Human Rights. On that basis an injunction should be granted. This decision, if it survives appeal, could mark the beginning of the end for the "kiss and tell" story as we have known it. It is likely to be fiercely contested. The media will argue that it is a cad's charter and that the proposition that sex is confidential has no precedent in law and no statutory authority. The sexual act can hardly be regarded as an imparting of information, since the facts of the relationship are within the direct experience of the participants. It has been noted that there is now an emergent "right of celebrity" (see *The Times Law*, February 5, 2002) with the courts affording greater protection to public figures than the voluntary Press Complaints Commission. The trial judge in *Douglas v Hello!* ultimately decided the case without considering the actors' claim for a separate right of privacy, preferring to follow *Secretary of State for the Home Department v Wainwright*.

The latest litigation resulting from the wedding is [2005] EWCA Civ 595, in which the Court of Appeal applied the European Court decision in *Von Hannover v Germany* (2005) 40 E.H.R.R. 1, which stressed the need for a high degree of protection against media invasions of privacy. This should be done, the court held, by developing the action for breach of confidence so as to uphold rights under Arts 8 and 10. The court complained nonetheless it was unsatisfactory to "shoe-horn" a claim about publication of an unauthorised picture of a private occasion into an action for

breach of confidence. The House of *Lords in Campbell v MGN Ltd*
[2004] U.K.H.L. 22 attached special significance to photographs,
which were considered particularly intrusive and revealing.

Key Principle: **The law of confidence could, exceptionally, be
extended to cover information as to the identity or whereabouts of individuals where its disclosure would put them at
risk of serious injury or death.**

Venables v News Group Newspapers Ltd

Jon Venables and Robert Thompson, the killers of two-year-old
James Bulger, were sentenced to be detained at Her Majesty's
pleasure. They were aged 11 when they committed the crime,
and when they reached 18 became eligible for parole. The
mother of their victim headed an influential campaign against
the grant of parole, and several newspapers wished to publish
up-to-date photographs of the boys and details of their present
whereabouts. Thompson and Venables sought a continuing
injunction against such publication on the basis that injunctions
were necessary to protect their rights of confidentiality and their
rights to life and freedom from persecution and harassment
under the Convention.

Held: (Family Division) The ECHR did not give rise in private
law proceedings to a free-standing cause of action based on
Convention rights but the court as a public authority was
obliged to act compatibly with Convention rights in adjudicating on common law causes of action, and had by s.12(4) of the
Human Rights Act to give direct effect to the right to freedom of
expression under Art.10. Freedom of the media could be
restricted only if the need for restrictions was such that they
were in accordance with the law, necessary in a democratic
society and proportionate to the legitimate aim pursued. The
law of confidentiality could extend to cover information about
the identity and whereabouts of people in circumstances where
publication could put their lives at risk. The injunctions were
necessary to protect the applicants against the "real and strong
possibility" of physical harm or death. Injunction granted
against the whole world to stop publication of the identity and
whereabouts of the claimants. [2001] 2 W.L.R. 1038.

Commentary

The court was here applying *Douglas v Hello! Ltd*. These cases illustrate that a new right is developing out of existing law. Butler-Sloss P. referred to the rights of the boys under Arts 2 and 3 as well as 8 and stated: "under the umbrella of confidentiality there will be information which may require a special quality of protection. In the present case the reason for advancing that special quality is that, if the information was published, the publication would be likely to lead to grave and possibly fatal consequences. In my judgment, the court does have the jurisdiction, in exceptional cases, to extend the protection of confidentiality even to impose restrictions on the press, where not to do so would be likely to lead to serious physical injury, or to death, of the person seeking that confidentiality and there is no other way to protect the applicant other than by seeking relief from the court." It must be emphasised that this case was a particularly extreme example because the invasion of privacy might lead to threats to the lives of the boys. This is another case in which legal concepts of confidentiality have been stretched to the limit to impose restraint on the media. It demonstrates the judiciary's considerable power and discretion within the new regime brought about by the Human Rights Act. See also *Re A (Children, Conjoined Twins: Surgical Separation)*. [2001] 2 W.L.R. 480.

Key Principle: **An interim injunction may be made to restrain publication in the interests of national security.**

Attorney-General v Guardian Newspapers Ltd

A former MI5 employee, Peter Wright, wrote *Spycatcher*, detailing unlawful activities carried out by the security services. Confidentiality clauses in his contract prevented publication in the United Kingdom but it was published in the United States. The *Observer* and *Guardian* published an outline of his allegations and were restrained by injunction from further publication. The newspapers' appeal against the injunction was dismissed. The *Independent* then published large extracts, and two London evening papers published parts of what had appeared in the *Independent*. The *Guardian* and the *Observer* then sought to vary the injunction against them on the basis that circumstances had changed. The Vice-Chancellor held that the

Independent and the two London evening papers were not in contempt because they were not restrained by any injunction. The *Sunday Times* then published extracts timed to coincide with the United States publication of *Spycatcher*. The Court of Appeal reversed the decision that the *Independent* was not in contempt and the Attorney-General obtained an injunction against the *Sunday Times*. The Court of Appeal allowed the newspapers to publish a general summary of Wright's material. All the parties appealed.

Held: (HL) The injunction should be continued until the hearing of the Attorney-General's action against the *Guardian* and the *Observer* since to allow publication would deprive the Attorney-General of the opportunity of having the matter decided at trial. The court had a duty to prevent harm to the security service and uphold its secrecy and to ensure that court orders were not flouted. [1987] 1 W.L.R. 1248.

Commentary
This majority decision restored the original interlocutory injunctions without the exception permitting inter alia reporting of what had taken place in open court in the Australian proceedings. Government claims of the threat to national security impelled the decision to maintain the injunctions despite the massive publicity the book had received in the United States and elsewhere. In a subsequent decision the House of Lords confirmed that a third party although not named in an injunction restraining another newspaper from publishing confidential information was guilty of contempt if it nullified the purpose of the original proceedings by destroying the confidentiality of the information by publishing it (see *Attorney-General v Times Newspapers Ltd* p.231).

Key Principle: **The government is only permitted to restrain a breach of confidence if it can demonstrate that it is in the public interest to do so. It is entitled to profits from publications in breach of confidence.**

Attorney-General v The Observer Ltd
(On appeal from *Attorney-General v The Guardian Newspapers (No.2)*. The Attorney-General's action against the *Guardian* and *Observer* came before Scott J. who held that Wright had broken

his duty not to disclose information he had obtained while employed by MI5 but that the *Guardian* and *Observer* were not in breach of their duty of confidentiality in publishing the articles they had published. The *Sunday Times* had been in breach of duty in publishing the first extract from the book, but secrecy had been destroyed by publication abroad of *Spycatcher* so the Attorney-General was not entitled to further injunctions, though the *Sunday Times* was liable to account for profits to the Attorney-General. The Court of Appeal dismissed appeals by the Attorney-General and the *Sunday Times*. Both appealed.

Held: (HL) A duty of confidence could arise in contract or in equity. A third party with information known to be confidential was bound by a duty of confidence unless the material became generally known or there was a public interest in publication which outweighed the duty of confidence. The Crown could not show publication would be damaging since the confidential material had been published abroad. The Crown was entitled to profits for publication in breach of the injunction but not for future serialisation by the *Sunday Times*. [1990] 1 A.C. 109.

Commentary
This case marked the end of the long *Spycatcher* saga in the English courts, the trial on whether the injunctions should be permanent. In his speech Lord Goff saw no inconsistency between English law on this subject and Art.10 of the European Convention on Human Rights. He saw it as his obligation when he was free to do so "to interpret the law in accordance with the obligations of the Crown under this Treaty". He continued:

> "The exercise of the right to freedom of expression under article 10 may be subject to restrictions (as are prescribed by law and are necessary in a democratic society) in relation to certain prescribed matters, which include 'the interests of national security' and 'preventing the disclosure of information received in confidence'. It is established in the jurisprudence of the European Court of Human Rights that the word 'necessary' in this context implies the existence of a pressing social need and that interference with the freedom of expression should be no more than is proportionate to the legitimate aim pursued. I have no reason to believe that English law as applied in the courts leads to any different conclusion."

In the event in *Observer and Guardian v United Kingdom, Sunday Times v United Kingdom* [1991] 14 E.H.R.R. 153, 229, the European Court of Human Rights considered that under the Convention the injunctions were necessary before publication of *Spycatcher* in the United States but not afterwards.

Key Principle: **Ss.1 and 4 of the Official Secrets Act 1989 were compatible with Art.10 of the ECHR.**

R v Shayler

A former member of the security services was charged with the unlawful disclosure of documents and information contrary to ss.1 and 4 of the Official Secrets Act 1989 (OSA). He claimed that he acted in the public interest in drawing attention to deficiencies in the security services. Moses J. in a preparatory hearing held that there was no public interest defence under ss.1 and 4 of the OSA. He considered the applicability of defences of duress and necessity.

Held: (CA) The case did not raise issues of duress or necessity. There was no public interest defence in the relevant sections. Ss.1 and 4 were compatible with the Convention since the interferences with freedom of speech were not greater than required to meet the legitimate objective the state sought to achieve. There were procedures available enabling a member of the security services to make lawful disclosure.

Commentary

The House of Lords had approved the use of a preparatory hearing to decide whether there was a public interest defence. Such a procedure is available under the Criminal Procedure and Investigations Act 1996.

Contempt of Court

Contempt of Court Act 1981 (CCA)

Key Principle: **S.2(2): The strict liability rule applies only to a publication which creates a substantial risk that the course of justice in the proceedings in question will be seriously impeded or prejudiced.**

S.5: A publication made as or as part of a discussion in good faith of public affairs or other matters of general public interest is not to be treated as a contempt of court under the

strict liability rule if the risk of impediment or prejudice to particular legal proceedings is merely incidental to the discussion.

Key Principle: The word "substantial" in s.2(2) serves only to exclude remote risks, and "serious impediment or prejudice" refers to the consequences of publication. The burden of proof is on the prosecution to show s.5 did not apply and the test for the application of s.5 is (1) is the publication a discussion? (2) was the risk of prejudice merely an incidental consequence of the publication?

Attorney-General v English

A consultant paediatrician was on trial for the murder of a Downs syndrome baby. The basis of the charge was an allegation that with the parents' approval he had allowed the baby to starve to death. During the trial, the *Daily Mail* published an article in support of a Pro-Life candidate at a by-election. The article said the candidate had been born without arms, but her chances of survival today were slight because she would probably be allowed to starve to death. The Divisional Court upheld an application by the Attorney-General for an order that the newspaper was in contempt of court. The newspaper appealed.

Held: (HL) The article suggested that it was a common practice among pediatricians to do what was charged against the defendant, so the risk of prejudice was not remote and s.2(2) was satisfied. The newspaper was entitled to the protection of s.5 of the Contempt of Court Act 1981 because publication was made as part of a discussion of a matter of general public interest. It was for the Attorney-General to prove that a publication did not fall within s.5 and that the risk of prejudice to a fair trial was not "merely incidental" to the discussion. S.5 was not merely an exception to the strict liability rule in s.2 of the 1981 Act, but stood on an equal footing with it and stated which publications should not amount to a contempt of court despite their tendency to interfere with the course of justice in particular proceedings. [1983] 1 A.C. 116.

Commentary

The court here seemed to be combining a liberal interpretation of s.2(2) with setting rather high standards for the prosecution to discharge under s.5. The interpretation of s.5 leaves the possibility that it cannot be applied to those articles which are aimed at exposing the behaviour of a particular individual because any prejudice will be a direct result of the main theme of the article rather than being an incidental effect of a discussion of matters of general public interest.

Key Principle: **In relation to Contempt of Court Act s.1 and s.2 there had to be a practical, not a theoretical, substantial risk that the course of justice would be seriously impeded or prejudiced.**

Attorney-General v Guardian Newspapers (No.3)

The judge in a fraud trial imposed reporting restrictions until other pending criminal proceedings against the defendants were complete. The newspaper published an article under the heading "In big fraud trials, judges appear to be over-sensitive". On an application from the defence, the judge discharged the jury because the article might have affected the fairness of the trial. The Attorney-General brought committal proceedings against the newspaper for contempt of court.

Held: (DC) The court was not convinced that in the circumstances the article had created a substantial practical risk that the course of justice would be seriously impeded or prejudiced. The publication was made as a discussion in good faith of a matter of general public interest to which the risk of prejudice to the proceedings was merely incidental. [1992] 1 W.L.R. 874.

Commentary

On delay before trial see *Attorney-General v News Group Newspapers* [1987] Q.B. 1.

Key Principle: **S.10 of the CCA: No court may require a person to disclose, nor is any person guilty of contempt of court for refusing to disclose, the source of information contained in a publication for which he is responsible, unless** it be established to the satisfaction of the court that disclosure is necessary in the interests of justice or national security or for the prevention of disorder or crime.

———————

Key Principle: **1. A publisher could rely on s.10 even when an owner made a proprietary claim for the return of property; and 2. the onus of proving the matter fell on the party seeking disclosure.**

Secretary of State for Defence v Guardian Newspapers Ltd

The newspaper obtained a leaked copy of a secret government memorandum on the handling of publicity about the installation of nuclear weapons at an airbase. The Secretary of State sought the return of the leaked document so that it could identify the informant. The newspaper resisted on the basis that it was protected by s.10 of the Contempt of Court Act 1981.

Held: (HL) S.10 applied if the order for disclosure might force the newspaper to reveal a source of information. The publisher was not precluded from relying on s.10 in the face of a proprietary claim by the owner for the delivering up of his property. It was for the party seeking the order to prove on the balance of probabilities that the case fell within one of the four exceptions specified in s.10. The Crown had proved that disclosure was necessary in the interests of national security because whoever leaked it might in future leak other classified documents. [1985] A.C. 339.

X v Morgan Grampian Ltd

Bill Goodwin, a journalist on *The Engineer,* received from a source whose identity he agreed not to disclose a document about the financial affairs of two private companies. The companies obtained an injunction against publication and an order that the journalist disclose the source. He refused to comply with the order. He also refused to comply when the Court of Appeal varied the order to allow him to place the required information in a sealed envelope lodged with the court. He was found guilty of contempt and was refused a hearing at the Court of Appeal because of his refusal to comply with the order. The publishers and the journalist appealed.

Held: (HL) The Court of Appeal had erred in refusing to hear the journalist, since the claimants did not oppose his being heard and his appeal was based on an alleged lack of jurisdiction of the court to make the order. The court had power to order disclosure notwithstanding that the claimant's object in seeking it was to identify the source. The potential damage to the companies' business was great and there was no public interest in publication. [1991] 1 A.C. 1.

Commentary

Lord Bridge here disagreed with Lord Diplock's view in *Secretary of State for Defence v Guardian Newspapers Ltd* (see p.224) in confining the meaning of "justice" in the section to "the technical sense of the administration of justice in the course of legal proceedings in a court of law". He said "It is in my opinion 'in the interests of justice' in the sense in which this phrase is used in s.10 that persons should be enabled to exercise important legal rights and to protect themselves from serious legal wrongs whether or not resort to legal proceedings in a court of law will be necessary to attain these objectives". However, this broad interpretation of the meaning of "interests of justice" in s.10 was limited in the judgment by the nature of the balancing exercise to be carried out. Disclosure will only be necessary in the interests of justice if such an interest is greater than the interest in protecting the source. One factor which weighed heavily here was the manner in which the information was obtained. Illegality in this connection will lessen the importance of protecting the source. In *Goodwin v United Kingdom, The Times*, March 28, 1996, the European Court of Human Rights held that the order to disclose the source was a violation of Art.10.

———————

Key Principle: **The balance between the public importance attached to the protection of sources and the "interests of justice" in securing the loyalty of employees depended on the specific facts in each case.**

Camelot Group Plc v Centaur Communications Ltd

Draft accounts of the company which ran the national lottery were sent by an unknown employee to a journalist, who published details. The company obtained an order for the return of the documents to assist it in identifying the source of the leaked information. The judge held that delivery-up of the documents was necessary in the interests of justice and refused to apply Art.10 of the Convention on Human Rights. The defendant appealed.

Held: (CA) The public interest in the protection of journalistic sources, though important, was not absolute. A relevant factor was the wish of an employer to identify the employee so as to dismiss him. Whether disclosure was justified depended on the facts, though different tribunals might reach different conclusions on the same facts. When considering an application under s.10 of the Contempt of Court Act 1981 the court should give great weight to ECHR judgments. But in the circumstances, the public interest in enabling the plaintiffs to discover a disloyal employee who leaked confidential information was greater than the public interest in enabling him to escape detection. The judge's order would be upheld. [1999] Q.B. 124.

Commentary
This case was heard after the ECHR decision *Goodwin v United Kingdom*. The Court of Appeal claimed to be applying the test set out in that case and the difference in outcome was attributable to the different perceptions of the facts in each case.

Key Principle: **The possibility that a professional judge or an appellate court would be influenced by any publication concerning cases they had to decide is remote.**

Re Lonrho Plc
Lonrho began judicial review proceedings in relation to the decision by the Secretary of State for Trade and Industry not to publish a report on the acquisition of House of Fraser by the Al Fayed brothers. While an appeal was pending in the proceedings, Tiny Rowland, Lonrho's chief executive, published a leaked copy of the report in the *Observer* which he owned. The Secretary of State obtained an injunction too late to prevent widespread distribution, and 3,000 copies were posted to various recipients, including to four of the Law Lords due to hear the appeal. The Secretary of State claimed that this was contempt of the House of Lords.

Held: (HL) Only the House of Lords could decide whether there was a contempt. There was no risk that the course of justice would be impeded by the publication. It would be an extension of the law of contempt to hold that direct action by a litigant to secure the substance of a remedy which he was seeking in judicial proceedings amounted to a contempt of those proceedings. [1990] 2 A.C. 154.

Commentary

The decision makes it unlikely that publication of any material concerning a case before an appellate court or a judge in a civil trial without jury will be treated as contempt on the grounds that it is likely to prejudice the course of justice.

Key Principle: **Contempt of Court Act, s.8: (1) Subject to subs.(2) below, it is a contempt of court to obtain, disclose or solicit any particulars of statements made, opinions expressed, arguments advanced or votes cast by members of a jury in the course of their deliberations in any legal proceedings. (2) This section does not apply to any disclosure of any particulars— (a) in the proceedings in question for the purpose of enabling the jury to arrive at their verdict, or in connection with the delivery of that verdict, or (b) in evidence in any subsequent proceedings for an offence alleged to have been committed in relation to the jury in the first mentioned proceedings, or to the publication of any particulars so disclosed.**

Key Principle: **A party may be liable under this section for disclosing information even where it was actually obtained by a third party.**

Attorney-General v Associated Newspapers Ltd

The *Mail on Sunday* revealed what had happened in the jury room during a criminal trial, with accounts by three of the jurors as to how they had reached their decisions. The Attorney-General brought contempt proceedings against the newspaper under s.8(1) of the Contempt of Court Act 1981, prohibiting disclosure of jury deliberations. The judge found contempt and the newspaper appealed.

Held: (HL) The Act was intended to prevent publication of jury deliberations as well as their disclosure by individual jurors and the newspaper had been in contempt. The word "disclose" in the Act covered publication by a newspaper as well as disclosure by the jurors themselves. [1994] 2 A.C. 238.

Commentary

This section was brought in after the *New Statesman* was acquitted of contempt for publishing an interview with one of the jurors in the *Jeremy Thorpe* trial which revealed how the jury had reacted to certain witnesses. It revealed that the credibility of Peter Bessell, the chief prosecution witness, had been greatly damaged by his arrangement with the *Sunday Telegraph* that the fee for his story would be higher if there was a conviction. Contempt proceedings were not brought against the *Sunday Telegraph*. The new clause was brought in to stem what was thought to be a threat of chequebook journalism. It also has the disadvantageous effect of making research into jury decision-making more difficult.

Key Principle: **The provisions of s.8(1) of the Contempt of Court Act 1981 are compatible with Art.10 of the European Convention on Human Rights.**

Attorney-General v Scotcher

A member of a jury which convicted two brothers wrote to their mother after the trial, saying that in his view they had been "fitted up" by police and that the majority of his colleagues on the jury had only voted to convict because they wanted to get home. He was convicted of contempt by the Divisional Court and sentenced to two months' imprisonment suspended for a year. He appealed to the House of Lords.

Held: (HL) Had the juror written to the Crown Court or to the Court of Appeal, he would not have been in contempt of court in terms of s.8(1). Nor if he had spoken or written to the jury bailiff or to the clerk of the court. Similarly, if he had sent a sealed letter containing his complaint to the defendant's solicitors or counsel or even to a citizens' advice bureau or similar organisation, and had asked them to forward it unopened to the appropriate court authorities, any disclosures in the letter would have been disclosures to the court and so outside the terms of s.8(1). However, he had disclosed the jury's deliberations to a third party. Thus his action created all the risks to the confidentiality of the jurors' deliberations which s.8(1) was designed to prevent. [2005] 1 W.L.R. 1867.

Commentary

The House of Lords had decided in *R. v Mirza* [2004] I A.C. 118 that a trial judge, on being informed about any misconduct during the jury's deliberations but before the verdict, could look into the matter. As a result of this decision, correcting a previous interpretation of s.8(1) which the Divisional Court had applied in *Scotcher*, the arguments put before the House of Lords were different from those heard in the Divisional Court. Lord Woolf C.J. issued *Practice Direction (Crown Court; Guidance to Jurors)* [2004] 1 W.L.R. 665 which stated, "Trial judges should ensure that the jury is alerted to the need to bring any concerns about fellow jurors to the attention of the judge at the time, and not wait until the case is concluded." This advice was not available at the time Scotcher was a juror. However, despite this the House held that although the warnings to the jurors at the time of the trial hearing were wrong, the statute itself was not.

Common Law Contempt

Key Principle: **Contempt of Court Act, s.6: Nothing in the foregoing provisions of this Act: (a) prejudices any defence available at common law to a charge of contempt of court under the strict liability rule; (b) implies that any publication is punishable as contempt of court under that rule which would not be so punishable apart from those provisions; (c) restricts liability for contempt of court in respect of conduct intended to impede or prejudice the administration of justice.**

Key Principle: **Common law contempt of court includes deliberate or accidental interference with the outcome of particular judicial proceedings.**

Attorney-General v Times Newspapers Ltd

Distillers Ltd manufactured the drug Thalidomide which led to the birth of deformed children when taken in pregnancy by their mothers. The company was sued by victims and there were negotiations on a settlement of their claims. The *Sunday Times* published an article drawing attention to the plight of

Thalidomide children. The company complained that the article was a contempt of court because litigation was still pending. The Divisional Court granted an injunction against further publication on the Attorney-General's motion. The matter was then raised in Parliament and there was a national campaign directed to putting pressure for a better deal for the victims. The Court of Appeal discharged the injunction. The Attorney-General appealed.

Held: (HL) It was contempt of court to publish material which prejudged the issue of pending litigation. The article, which charged the company with negligence, was a contempt because negligence was one of the issues in the litigation. But temperate comment might have been permissible on the questions whether the legal remedies available were adequate and whether too much time had been taken up in legal proceedings. [1974] A.C. 273.

Commentary
The case was referred to the European Court of Human Rights and its judgment, holding that there had been a violation of Art.10 of the Convention led to the passing of the Contempt of Court Act 1981.

Key Principle: **Interfering with the administration of justice may constitute common law contempt even though no particular proceedings are at risk.**

R. v The Socialist Worker Printers and Publishers Ltd Ex p. Attorney-General
During a blackmail trial at the Old Bailey the judge directed that the two victims of the alleged blackmail be referred to as Mr Y and Mr Z. Both gave evidence for the prosecution. Before the end of the trial, the *Socialist Worker* published an article by Paul Foot which gave the names and other details of the two men. The Attorney-General brought proceedings for contempt.

Held: (QB) It was unlikely that the minds of the jury would have been influenced by the article, but its publication during the trial was an affront to the authority of the court and the publishers were in contempt. [1975] 1 Q.B. 635.

Commentary
At common law there is a power to order that witnesses be given anonymity in the wider interests of the criminal and civil process, quite apart from the need to do justice to the parties in any particular case. The rationale behind the finding here was that the publication was an affront to the court's authority and likely to inhibit blackmail victims from coming forward in the future.

Key Principle: **Orders as to publication may bind third parties if they know of the order and have the requisite** *mens rea.*

Attorney-General v Times Newspapers Ltd
Following the publication in various newspapers of extracts from Peter Wright's book *Spycatcher* (see *Attorney-General v The Guardian Newspapers Ltd* and *Attorney-General v The Observer Ltd* above) the Attorney-General brought committal proceedings for contempt of court against the *Sunday Times* and *Independent*. Fines of £50,000 were imposed by Morritt J. and upheld on appeal. The *Sunday Times* appealed on the grounds that although the *mens rea* of contempt was present, the newspaper's conduct did not constitute the *actus reus* of contempt.

Held: (HL) The injunction against publication of *Spycatcher* material had been granted pending trial of breach of confidence actions. The newspapers' actions had partly nullified the purpose of that trial and their conduct had impeded or interfered with the administration of justice, which was the *actus reus* of contempt. [1992] 1 A.C. 191.

Commentary
The case marked a controversial inroad into the general principle of justice that a court order should only affect the party to which it is directed so that it can answer the case.

The case also underlines the necessity for *mens rea* in cases of contempt at common law. The parties had here conceded *mens rea*. At an earlier hearing the Court of Appeal had made it clear that the *mens rea* for common law contempt is specific intent and cannot include recklessness. The test is, did the defendant either wish to prejudice proceedings or foresee that such prejudice was a virtually inevitable consequence of publication? Intentional contempt was a possible but not necessary inference if a person knows of an injunction and publishes anyway. Here the editors did not wish to interfere with the administration of justice but that did not preclude contempt. For a full discussion of *mens rea* see *Attorney-General v News Group Newspapers Plc* (see below).

***

Key Principle: Common law contempt may exist alongside statutory contempt.

Attorney-General v Hislop

The Attorney-General sought to commit the editor of *Private Eye* for contempt of court. The proceedings related to articles published in February 1989 concerning the wife of the Yorkshire Ripper, while a previous libel action was pending. The application was dismissed on the grounds that the proceedings were unlikely to be prejudiced. The Attorney-General appealed.

Held: The articles went beyond reasonable criticism. There was an intent to pervent the course of justice by trying to deter the Ripper's wife from pursuing her action and there was both common law and statutory contempt under the 1981 Act. Jurors might have read and been influenced by the articles. Appeal allowed. [1991] 1 Q.B. 514.

Commentary

The *actus reus* of common law contempt is making a publication which creates a real risk of prejudice to the administration of justice (see *Attorney-General v Thompson Newspapers* [1968] 1 W.L.R. 1. In *Attorney-General v Times Newspapers Ltd* (above, p.229) the *actus reus* of contempt lay in one newspaper publishing despite a court order against another. In *Hislop* it lay in the threat to create prejudice in the jury.

***

Key Principle: The *mens rea* of contempt is specific intention. Recklessness is not sufficient at common law.

Attorney-General v News Group Newspapers Plc

The family of an eight-year-old girl alleged that she had been raped by a doctor. Police investigated but it was concluded there was insufficient evidence to justify prosecution. The *Sun* newspaper published details of the case and organised support for a private prosecution, which was brought in the Crown Court by the child's mother. The Attorney-General brought proceedings against the newspaper for contempt at common law.

Held: (DC) The newspaper had shown the necessary intention to prejudice a fair trial by bringing to the attention of potential jurors damaging matters affecting the doctor which would be inadmissible in criminal proceedings. There could be common law contempt even though there were no pending or imminent proceedings. The newspaper's conduct in publishing the articles at the same time as encouraging and supporting a private prosecution was sufficient to constitute a common law contempt. [1989] Q.B. 110.

Key Principle: **Proceedings need not be active for common law contempt.**

Attorney-General v Sport Newspapers Ltd

After the disappearance of a schoolgirl in North Wales a local man with previous convictions for rape suddenly left the area. The police sought public help in tracing him but warned newspapers against publishing details of his previous convictions. The *Sport* newspaper published the details of his convictions. Two days later a warrant was issued for the man's arrest. The Attorney-General brought committal proceedings.

Held: (DC) At the time of publication, there were no "active" proceedings, so the newspaper could only be guilty of contempt at common law. Common law contempt required specific intent to cause a real risk of prejudice to the due administration of justice. No such intent had been shown, so the newspaper had not been guilty of common law contempt. The court was divided over whether there could be contempt of imminent proceedings. [1991] 1 W.L.R. 1194.

Commentary

The law is in some doubt whether it is necessary to establish imminence. In *Attorney-General v News Group Newspapers Plc* (see p.223) proceedings could not have been regarded as imminent but the court held *obiter* that where a publication was intended to interfere with justice and created a real risk of prejudice to proceedings, contempt proceedings could be taken notwithstanding proceedings were neither pending nor imminent. The court was divided on this point in this case. Hodgson J. held contempt could not be committed at common law in relation to proceedings not yet in existence even if they were imminent. Bingham L.J. however held that a publication made with the intention of prejudicing proceedings which although not in existence, are imminent, may be contemptuous. The matter is yet to be decided.

INDEX

LEGAL TAXONOMY
FROM SWEET & MAXWELL

This index has been prepared using Sweet and Maxwell's Legal Taxonomy. Main index entries conform to keywords provided by the Legal Taxonomy except where references to specific documents or non-standard terms (denoted by quotation marks) have been included. These keywords provide a means of identifying similar concepts in other Sweet & Maxwell publications and online services to which keywords from the Legal Taxonomy have been applied. Readers may find some minor differences between terms used in the text and those which appear in the index. Suggestions to *taxonomy@sweetandmaxwell.co.uk*.

(all references are to page number)